T0268437

Government Project

Government Project

Edward C. Banfield

AEI Press

Publisher for the American Enterprise Institute
WASHINGTON, DC

ISBN-13: 978-0-8447-5064-4 (Paperback)

Library of Congress Cataloging in Publication data have been applied for.

© 2023 by Edward C. Banfield. Published with permission by the American Enterprise Institute for Public Policy Research. All rights reserved. No part of this publication may be used or reproduced in any manner whatsoever without permission in writing from the American Enterprise Institute except in the case of brief quotations embodied in news articles, critical articles, or reviews. The views expressed in the publications of the American Enterprise Institute are those of the authors and do not necessarily reflect the views of the staff, advisory panels, officers, or trustees of AEI.

An imprint of AEI Press, publisher for the American Enterprise Institute for Public Policy Research
1789 Massachusetts Avenue, NW, Washington, DC 20036
www.aei.org

Printed in the United States of America

Contents

Foreword to the 2024 Edition

The reader may wonder, "Why would the American Enterprise Institute (AEI) republish a 1951 book about a failed New Deal experiment that has been out of print for decades?"

The short answer is that Edward C. Banfield's *Government Project* is a profound book that holds lessons for our present era, when the political left and right increasingly turn to the government to ameliorate America's problems. The book also is a pleasure to read, despite its sobering conclusion and implications.

Readers familiar with Banfield (1916–99) may remember him as a maverick professor of urban studies who raised questions about the efficacy of various urban renewal and antipoverty programs. This is understandable; Banfield spent the better part of 40 years at Harvard University and wrote nine books on urban politics and policy. His *The Unheavenly City: The Nature and Future of Our Urban Crisis* (1970) was excerpted in the *Wall Street Journal* and widely reviewed. Banfield's research on urban studies got him both appointed to a White House commission advising President Richard Nixon and canceled on campus by radical students who disrupted his classes and protested his off-campus speeches.

Less well-known is that Banfield had a lengthy relationship with AEI. It formally began in 1963, when AEI published Banfield's treatise *American Foreign Aid Doctrines*. The connection for this project may have come through Milton Friedman, who was on AEI's advisory board and whom Banfield had met at the University of Chicago. Regardless, the AEI-Banfield collaborations lasted three decades.

In 1974, AEI published Banfield's lecture "The City and the Revolutionary Tradition" and had him deliver a talk in Philadelphia, Pennsylvania, at the Franklin Institute's Franklin Hall. Banfield subsequently contributed to five books edited by AEI scholar Robert A. Goldwin. The AEI-Banfield collaborations continued through 1991, when AEI Press released a second edition of *Here the People Rule: Selected Essays*, a volume of Banfield's best articles on American governance.

No discussion of the AEI-Banfield connection would be adequate without mentioning Christopher DeMuth and Bruce Kovner. Both were students of Banfield at Harvard and dear friends of him and his wife, Laura. DeMuth was AEI's president from 1986 to 2008; Kovner has been a generous AEI benefactor for decades.

Before Banfield turned his attention to America's cities, he took on one of the federal government's newly initiated efforts to manage the economy and ameliorate poverty. Banfield's famed student James Q. Wilson (1931–2012) rightly points out that *Government Project* addresses questions central to nearly all Banfield's subsequent writings: "How can people be induced to cooperate? And since some degree of cooperation is essential for any society, the larger question is: how can a decent society be sustained?"[1]

* * * *

Government Project's origins lie in Banfield's experience working for the federal government as a public information officer. Fresh from earning an undergraduate degree in English in 1938, Banfield landed a job at the US Department of Agriculture's Northeast Timber Salvage Administration.[2] This job provided Banfield with firsthand experience of government economic planning. He wrote dispatches for media consumption and republication that extolled the agency's work to stabilize lumber prices.

In 1941, Banfield joined the Farm Security Administration (FSA), an agency that replaced the short-lived Resettlement Administration (1935–37). The FSA sought to help destitute migrant farm workers, like those depicted in John Steinbeck's novel *The Grapes of Wrath* (1939). The migrant crisis had been produced by the terrible weather of the Dust Bowl years, the collapse of food prices during the Great Depression, and the replacement of family farms by mechanized mega-farms that paid subsistence wages to droves of seasonal workers.[3] The FSA aimed to solve this rural poverty problem by settling migrants on farms and in government-created communities.

Banfield's job as an FSA public information officer was to answer media questions about the nearly 200 FSA migrant resettlement projects. A committed New Dealer, Banfield touted FSA success stories and tried to rebut conservative criticism that the FSA efforts were boondoggles akin to Soviet collectivism.

Through his work, Banfield became acquainted with the FSA's Casa Grande Valley Farms in Pinal County, Arizona, the subject of *Government Project*.

The FSA established Casa Grande by recruiting four destitute farmers and incorporating a cooperative association in their names. The federal government then loaned the cooperative association the funds to lease 5,000 acres of land and used federal dollars to build roads, homes, and farm buildings on the land. The FSA recruited about 60 families to live on the project.[4]

Between 1937 and 1942, Casa Grande bloomed. The farms produced alfalfa, cattle, chickens, cotton, grain, hogs, and sheep for markets as far away as Los Angeles. In today's dollars, Casa Grande's assets were valued at more than $4 million, and its annual profit reached nearly $500,000. The settlers' equity in the project was about $1 million.

Banfield visited Casa Grande twice in 1943 and later reported in *Government Project* that it offered settlers "freedom, opportunity, and the stabilizing influence of property." Their lives had been transformed and bettered. They had gone from shacks and tents to, in the FSA's words, "completely modern" houses, with "bathrooms, running hot and cold water, electric wiring and fixtures, and a garage attached to the house."

Yet in 1944, Casa Grande Valley Farms entered legal liquidation, and the farms' settlers left the project. Some of them walked away with sufficient funds in their pocket to acquire their own land. Many settlers did not, and they returned to living as migrant farm workers. Charles McCormick, one of the farmers, later groused, "We not only killed the goose that laid the golden egg.... We even threw the goddam egg away!"

What went wrong?

Casa Grande collapsed, *Government Project* explains, because its residents "were unable to cooperate . . . because they were engaged in a ceaseless struggle for power." Despite their immensely improved material conditions, Casa Grande's settlers were dissatisfied. They feuded with the FSA officials and one another over the farms' operations. The settlers could not form a cohesive community with mutual trust.

* * * *

Congress abolished the FSA in 1946, and Banfield subsequently decamped to the University of Chicago. He had been invited to attend graduate school there by Rexford Tugwell, a former member of President Franklin D. Roosevelt's "brain trust" of academics who had headed the Resettlement Administration. Banfield, still a New Dealer at heart, was attracted to the scholarship of progressive political theorists and economists. He met urban planners such as Julius Margolis and Martin Meyerson and became interested in what he called "the sociology of efficiency"—that is, the conditions under which resources are used rationally. He published articles arguing in favor of government economic planning.[5]

But the Casa Grande project's failure gnawed at Banfield. He studied many other federal relief projects and wrote articles that criticized their conceptual and practical errors.[6]

By the time he published *Government Project* in 1951, Banfield was having real doubts about the entire notion of government planning. As Wilson notes, government planning presupposes planners possess an extraordinarily high level of rationality and information; the very act of planning also imagines planners and their efforts exist outside politics and representative government.[7] Moreover, planning assumes the individuals it intends to benefit agree with the planners' designs and are willing and able to embrace them.

Government Project richly details the collisions of planners' presuppositions with reality. If, as Irving Kristol quipped, "a neoconservative is a liberal who got mugged by reality," then Banfield was the earliest neoconservative, and *Government Project* is the first neoconservative book.[8]

* * * *

It is difficult to say why *Government Project* fell into obscurity. It received favorable scholarly attention in publications such as the *Journal of Farm Economics*, the *American Political Science Review*, and the *American Journal of Sociology*. The *New York Times* found it worth mentioning in its June 2, 1951, issue.

Some years ago, Wilson suggested to me that since *Government Project* appeared after the New Deal was over, its readership may have been limited by the misperception that it was a book about farm policy. When I asked Martha Derthick (1933–2015), another of Banfield's renowned students and collaborators, she ventured that *Government Project* was overshadowed by Banfield's *The Moral Basis of a Backward Society* (1958), which was highly acclaimed and also assessed poverty and human cooperation. Possibly, *Government Project* slid into obscurity because it is difficult to categorize. It blends political science, public administration, sociology, and political theory. That makes it an unlikely candidate for professors of any particular discipline to adopt.

Whatever the causes for the book's obscurity, this new edition aims to remedy the situation by introducing new readers to *Government Project*. It is a superbly written book that reads like top-quality journalism rather than scholarship—despite its methodological rigor.

The book carries the reader back to the remarkable New Deal period of American history, which for all its distance will not be unfamiliar to the present-day reader. It was a period of repeated national crises that imbued American politics with an existential dimension. Amid the tumults, government spending and authority grew rapidly, and executive agencies often had nearly carte blanche authority to craft policies to address economic and social problems.

Yet those readers who hope for a cheerful tale of triumph will not find it in these pages. Tugwell writes in his 1951 foreword to the book:

> It is not a nice story. Our simple impulse to better the economic situation of a few almost hopelessly poverty-stricken folk in the Southwest came to grief. . . .
>
> Mr. Banfield finds that we were too exclusively preoccupied with the material circumstances of success—and that we neglected the psychological. But improvement of economic circumstances was all we had set out to do, and, as I still think, all we could do. . . .
>
> At any rate here is the full case history. We can see in it many lessons if we will.

Tugwell is surely correct that the lessons of Casa Grande's failure are many. *Government Project* illustrates the conflictual nature of politics and the misunderstandings between policymakers in the nation's capital and the administrators on the ground tasked with implementing programs.

The book colorfully depicts the inevitable diversity of opinions among individuals—even when they are presented with the same information.

Most certainly, *Government Project* is a cautionary tale. Despite policy-makers' good intentions, Banfield convincingly explains, Casa Grande Valley Farms failed because of a cultural mismatch between the project and the settlers. Government officials presumed that providing poor people with homes and other material benefits would incentivize them to cooperate. They failed to account for the settlers' worldview. The settlers were not credulous people inclined to believe in a federal government project and trust their neighbors. They lived in tight-knit family units and had spent their lives doing whatever they saw fit.

At Casa Grande, the settlers had no shared history nor collectively conceived future to bond them together in pursuing the common good. They were strangers to one another living in a government-invented settlement.

The farmers' ownership of their homes and land depended on obeying the rules set by federal government authorities. Their material wealth had been given to them, not earned, which left them less attached to it than they might otherwise have been. This is why they quarreled instead of cooperated and quit the enterprise the moment the government permitted them.

In recounting the FSA's failure in Pinal County, *Government Project* also tells a deeper story about humanity and governance in modern times that holds true today all the more. Banfield writes:

> The most characteristic feature of modern society, perhaps, is the great and increasing role of formal organizations of all kinds. Primitive societies were (and are) held together chiefly by the non-logical bonds of custom and tradition; in modern society the relations of individuals are to a large extent consciously and deliberately organized by the use of intelligence and the rules of logic. . . .
>
> This attempt to organize society along rational lines is a stupendous experiment. Nothing in history promises that it will succeed. But like Faust we are bound by our bargain, and so the study of formal organization and planning—of the techniques by which control may be exerted deliberately and intelligently—is a matter of profound importance. If it is placed in

the widest possible framework, then, *Government Project* may be regarded as a study of one of mankind's countless recent efforts to take command of its destiny.

For all our cleverness, we humans tend to forget wisdom learned in earlier times. Among other things, Banfield's *Government Project* reminds us of the eternal challenges of fostering human cooperation for mutual benefit.

Kevin R. Kosar, Washington, DC

Kevin R. Kosar is a senior fellow at the American Enterprise Institute, where he studies the US Congress, the administrative state, American politics, election reform, and the US Postal Service.

Notes

1. James Q. Wilson, "A Connecticut Yankee in King Arthur's Court: A Biography," in *Edward C. Banfield: An Appreciation* (Claremont, CA: Henry Salvatori Center, 2002), 49, https://pdfcoffee.com/qdownload/edward-c-banfield-an-appreciation-pdf-free.html.

2. Kevin R. Kosar and Mordecai Lee, "Defending a Controversial Agency: Edward C. Banfield as Farm Security Agency Public Relations Officer, 1941–1946," *Federal History*, no. 5 (January 2013): 123, https://shfg.wildapricot.org/resources/Documents/FH%205%20(2014)%20Kosar-Lee.pdf.

3. Kevin R. Kosar, "A Nearly Forgotten Classic Study in Public Administration: Edward C. Banfield's *Government Project*," *Public Administration Review* (September–October 2009): 993–97, https://onlinelibrary.wiley.com/doi/pdf/10.1111/j.1540-6210.2009.02053.x.

4. Photographs of the Casa Grande farms and other FSA projects are available at US Library of Congress, Farm Security Administration/Office of War Information Black-and-White Negatives: Search Results, https://www.loc.gov/pictures/search/?q=%22casa%20grande%22&co=fsa.

5. See, for example, Edward C. Banfield, "Planning Under the Research and Marketing Act of 1946; A Study in the Sociology of Knowledge," *Journal of Farm Economics* 31, no. 3 (February 1949): 469–86; and Edward C. Banfield, "Congress and the Budget; A Planner's Criticism," *American Political Science Review* 43, no. 6 (December 1949): 1217–28.

6. See, for example, Edward C. Banfield, "Ten Years of the Farm Tenant Purchase Program," *Journal of Farm Economics* 31, no. 3 (August 1949): 469–86.

7. Wilson, "A Connecticut Yankee in King Arthur's Court," 41–53.

8. Irving Kristol, *Neoconservatism: The Autobiography of an Idea* (New York: Free Press, 1995).

Foreword to the 1951 Edition

In the spring of 1935, at what might be called the apogee of the New Deal, President Roosevelt signed an Executive Order establishing the Resettlement Administration. The condition of the low-income folk in the rural areas of America was very much on his mind. It had been on his mind for some time as can be seen from his public statements on the subject when he was Governor of New York State. As Governor he had appointed an Agricultural Advisory Commission and on its advice had done what a Governor could do to mitigate rural poverty and forward a program of conservation. During these years he had, moreover, held steadily to the belief that sub-marginal lands ought to be retired from use and that rural communities ought to be established to which many of the unemployed in the cities might be moved. One of his life-long interests had centered in conservation. He loved well-tended farm lands, forests and parks. He thought our farm lands were misused and that our forests, parks and streams were ill-managed and not so extensive as they ought to be.

As for me, who was named Administrator in the Executive Order, I had my own reasons too. My impulse, like President Roosevelt's, went back to my earliest days. He had been a boy on an estate in Dutchess County of New York and had gone to a private school in New England; but he had seen plenty of eroded farms and hard-scrabble farmers. He had travelled widely and seen the contrasts between high- and low-income folk everywhere in our land and in Europe as well. Also he had followed closely the attempts of Theodore Roosevelt to organize the conservation movement; and he had been a friend of that great pioneer forester, Gifford Pinchot. I had not had those contacts and advantages. I had come, some years later, into some consciousness of the relation between poor land and poor people; but it had been a realistic experience. For the New York County in which I had been born and had lived my early years had been Chautauqua, the most western of the southern tier counties of New York. That region had passed its period of prosperity during my boyhood and, as a consequence of deforestation, erosion and competition from new farming areas in the West, had begun to decline. The prosperous farms I had known as a boy and the great families of my neighborhood were by the time of my adolescence, falling into neglect and poverty.

It was thus natural, although our circumstances had contrasted greatly, that we should agree on trying to do something to better the situation of rural people and to improve the face of the land. Resettlement was the product of this agreement. It was not the first effort; it was merely more intensified than the ones that had been tried before. The Civilian Conservation Corps had been organized at the very beginning of President Roosevelt's Administration, relief was being extended to rural as well as to urban areas and a program for retiring submarginal land from cultivation was under way. These efforts were all brought together in Resettlement with the idea of better coordination and more effective administration; and, also, the Division of Subsistence Homesteads, set up in the Department of the Interior under the authority of the National Recovery Act was transferred to it.

So that when the Executive Order was signed on 1 May, I found myself the Administrator of several organizations already in being with many thousands of employees and a huge task to be accomplished. The effort had not been specifically authorized by the Congress; but the funds for operating it beyond the first year were dependent upon appropriations by that body. We were not very favorably regarded by several powerful interests with considerable legislative influence. The larger farmers were more interested in having the prices of their products raised than in extending assistance to their poorer neighbors; and those who were economy-minded grudged the funds for our work. As a result much of my effort and that of my immediate assistants had to be devoted to simple perpetuation of the organization against objections which grew as recovery occurred. Besides this, the notion of agricultural communities seemed somehow— or was made to seem—a radical departure from American practice.

A nice division of effort had to be made in Washington between merely keeping alive and the work of creating and maintaining an organization devoted to the policies outlined in the Executive Order. The task proved to be too formidable a one. We neither overcame the opposition in the Congress nor conveyed to the furthest reaches of our agency the policies necessary to its success. As it was first conceived, Resettlement only survived two years, although much of the work it undertook went on for a good deal longer.

Casa Grande, as Mr. Banfield tells its story, is the history of a failure—one of many. It was a noble failure, perhaps, but that nobility was small comfort to those who had hoped for its success. As the Administrator, I had hoped that our experiment would find its own sources of strength and gain support as the necessity for this kind of thing was demonstrated. Instead of that, support very rapidly leaked away. The sources of this unfriendliness were very broadly and deeply characteristic of American life; and as I look back now after almost two decades it seems to me that we were doomed to failure from the start. We did all we could. The administration was not inefficient, considering the difficulties; there was always a priceless enthusiasm in the organization; but those who had to do the work were always conscious, necessarily, of moving in an atmosphere of disapproval.

It is one of the penalties of a large organization that its Administrator has always to deal with problems of policy at the center and that he has a constant burden of paper-work whose end result he can never see. It is only now, as I read Mr. Banfield's account of Casa Grande, that I can really visualize the meaning of many Washington conferences and many reports and documents with which I had to deal. But I was always conscious of dissatisfaction.

It is not a nice story. Our simple impulse to better the economic situation of a few almost hopelessly poverty-stricken folk in the Southwest came to grief not because the conception was bad or because the technique was mistaken but because the people there could not rise to the challenge. It was character which failed. And that was not because the human stock was feeble; it was because the environment was hostile to the development of character. Mr. Banfield would have had a different end for his story if Americans had approved what was being tried at Casa Grande; since they did not approve, how could a few families—who were Americans too—wrestle successfully with that impalpable hostility?

This account is as complete as it could well be made. We see these few families being taken from the hovels and ditch-bank squatting places so characteristic of the depression years; we see them settled into decent homes with incomes adequate to their support; we see them approach something like prosperity; and then we see them disintegrate, returning to what they were before. Our troubles in Washington prevented us from knowing enough of what went on in what we called "the field," but there was no other decisive inadequacy in Washington. Funds did not fail; and administrators were available who did what could have been done to check the disintegration. We should not have allocated more funds or had better administrators in any case.

Mr. Banfield finds that we were too exclusively preoccupied with the material circumstances of success—and that we neglected the psychological. But improvement of economic circumstances was all we had set out to do, and, as I still think, all we could do. A rural rehabilitation project—or many of them—could not make any large contribution to general change; and it was a general sickness which was at work here. I was made aware from the very first that there were very powerful forces which opposed helping the unfortunate, especially when the unfortunate were encouraged to organize cooperatively to better themselves. The maleficent and the friendly impulses in all of us are incessantly at war. Sometimes we see startling evidences of irrepressible kindness; sometimes, we see deplorable exhibitions of selfishness; both we recognize as natural, even characteristic. When the unkindness can find a rationale—when for instance it is presented as patriotic, moral, generally the approved thing—we have an added tendency to give way to it. It was given way to during the depression on an almost destructive scale.

We know how constant the struggle was during that time to remind Americans of their neighborly duty to the unemployed and the rural poor. The struggle was a hard one because government, through which neighborliness had to be expressed, is a large concern, and because balancing the budget, or some other excuse, could always be resorted to and could be presented as a superior value. It is difficult for ordinary people to function as they otherwise would in circumstances like these. We are far from being fundamentally accustomed to the projections necessary to finding our duty and doing it in modern society.

The people at Casa Grande were not different from the rest of us except that they were on the receiving end. They were probably instructed by the press and the pulpit that President Roosevelt was wicked when he did not balance the budget, when he was accused of boondoggling, and of pauperizing the unemployed. They shared the hostilities built up in the very careful campaigns of those days to all that was going on. Imagine, if that was so, the conflict which must have been going on within themselves when they considered their own situations. The impulse to resolve the conflict must have been irresistible. Well, it has been resolved now. They are again members of the general public, no better and no worse, and also, no more favored, than we. I sometimes wonder how they look back at the manner of their escape from the intolerable—whether they ever consider that they might have made a success of Casa Grande. But I know well enough the rationalizations they will have made. The other fellow will have been to blame, and circumstances will have made any other reaction than the ones taken impossible.

At any rate here is the full case history. We can see in it many lessons if we will.

Rexford G. Tugwell

Introduction to the 1951 Edition

This is an account of an attempt by one of the biggest, most efficient, and most democratic of governments—that of the United States—to remake the lives of a few of its citizens by establishing a cooperative farm at Casa Grande in the Arizona desert. These few citizens (at no time were there more than 57 families) were among the most desperately poor and disadvantaged in the nation. The government made an elaborate effort to help them, an effort which was sustained for seven years, which involved the investment of more than $1,000,000, and which required the almost constant attention of several officials. Without wishing to prejudice the case (for the author wants the reader to judge for himself) it is fair to say that the government's effort was administered honestly, zealously, and—by the standards of one of the most efficient of governments—efficiently. Nevertheless the cooperative farm was a failure. It collapsed at the very moment when to all outward appearances its chances for prosperity and success were greatest.

This book is intended to describe what happened at Casa Grande in such a way as to give some insight into *why* it happened. There are a number of reasons why it seems worthwhile to make such a study. The story of Casa Grande should have, at the least, a practical value to anyone who may again set out to establish a cooperative farm under similar circumstances; there is a long history of attempts to establish cooperative farms and model communities in the United States and it would be foolish to suppose that Casa Grande will prove to be the last of these. There are other reasons, however, for telling the story. Disadvantaged people like those whom the government tried to help at Casa Grande are still with us. The problem they represent has been obscured by the events of recent years and it is in some ways changed, but it is still awaiting solution. The government, also, although much has been learned about some matters in the last decade, is probably no better prepared to deal directly and intimately with human problems than it was in the 1930's. Perhaps something can be learned from the depression-time experience at Casa Grande that will help to make the government more effective in its next approach to the same and to similar problems.

But of course problems of poverty are only a special category of the problems that government is expected to solve today, and government, although much the largest, is only one of the institutions by which behavior is regulated. The most characteristic feature of modern society, perhaps, is the great and increasing role of formal organizations of all kinds. Primitive societies were (and are) held together chiefly by the non-logical bonds of custom and tradition; in modern society the relations of individuals are to a large extent consciously and deliberately organized by the use of intelligence and the rules of logic; our society is engaged in deliberate, reflective adaption to change, in other words, in planning. As Thomas and Znaniecki observed at the beginning of their great work on *The Polish Peasant in Europe and America*, "One of the most significant features of social evolution is the growing importance which a conscious and rational technique tends to assume in social life. We are less and less ready to let any social process go on without active interference. . . ."

This attempt to organize society along rational lines is a stupendous experiment. Nothing in history promises that it will succeed. But like Faust we are bound by our bargain, and so the study of formal organization and planning—of the techniques by which control may be exerted deliberately and intelligently—is a matter of profound importance. If it is placed in the widest possible framework, then, *Government Project* may be regarded as a study of one of mankind's countless recent efforts to take command of its destiny.

The author is himself very much interested in the wider implications of the story and in the concluding chapter he endeavors to interpret it with reference to them. In telling the story, however, he has thought it best not to press an hypothesis or a particular theory upon the reader; instead the attempt is to understand the Casa Grande people, both the settlers and the officials, not in terms of some doctrine (not in terms of culture, or psychoanalysis, or economic determinism, or behaviorism!), but as sensitive and perceptive people generally try to understand other people, and to tell what happened in a reasonably detached manner. So far as it succeeds in its intention the approach is what Charles H. Cooley called the "life study method":

The aim of a descriptive technique in rural sociology should be, I take it, so to picture the essential functional behavior of rural persons and groups that their life can be understood in as much of its dramatic reality as possible. It seeks to give 'revealing instances' about which the reader may build a lifelike and just conception of what is going on. This involves a judicious selection of those events that *are* essential, that reveal the critical functions, the high spots as it were. There must be nothing lax or superfluous in scientific description, any more than in a play. Only the indispensable must be shown; but that must be shown so deliberately and graphically as to be convincing.

Something needs to be said of the circumstances which caused the government to establish a cooperative farm in the Arizona desert.

* * * *

Motives are always mixed. There were some in the government who had the itch to create a real, live Utopia and there may have been others who supposed that capitalistic agriculture would be overthrown by the mere example of a successful collective. These people were anxious to try their ideas at Casa Grande. But the motives that were really decisive were of a much more practical and prosaic kind: the cooperative farm was invented as an expedient way of helping people who were destitute. Ever since 1933, when the New Deal discovered that there were more than a million poverty-stricken farm families, government officials had wrestled with the problem of finding practical and permissible ways of alleviating suffering and of finding some permanent solution for the chronic rural poverty which stared them in the face on every side. The Casa Grande project was one of a long line of these emergency endeavors.

The earliest ancestors of the cooperative farm were called subsistence homesteads. These homesteads represented the culmination of a drive by certain lovers of country life and country virtues (including Bernarr Macfadden, Henry Ford, Ralph Borsodi, and Governor F. D. Roosevelt) to launch a back-to-the-farm movement for the purpose of relieving urban unemployment and distress. In 1933 an amendment to the National Industrial Recovery Act authorized creation of a revolving fund of $25,000,000 to set up subsistence homesteads for the "redistribution of the over-balance of population in industrial centers." One of the early proponents of this legislation and, as director of the Subsistence Homesteads Division of the Interior Departments, its first administrator was M. L. Wilson, a former Montana wheat farmer and Land Grant College economist. Wilson, as director of the subsistence homesteads program, advocated experiments with farm colonies, but he gave the principal emphasis to subsistence projects for industrial workers, including particularly stranded miners. The homestead movement, he said, was "laying the basis for a new civilization in America."

The legislative authorization for the subsistence homesteads program was allowed to expire in 1935 and the Resettlement Administration was then created by executive order. Financed from the Emergency Relief Act of 1935 and then from later relief acts, the Resettlement Administration had three main functions: to make loans and grants to needy farm people; to carry on erosion, flood control and land retirement projects; and "to administer approved projects involving resettlement of destitute or low income families from rural and urban area, including the establishment, maintenance and operation, in such connection, of communities in rural and suburban areas."

The Resettlement Administration inherited 33 projects which had been initiated by Wilson's Division of Subsistence Homesteads and, in addition, 34 somewhat similar projects which had been set up by the Federal Emergency Relief Administration. By this time the projects had already run into serious trouble. It had become clear that communities would not attract industries, as Wilson had expected and as was necessary if the homesteaders were to have a cash income. One possible solution was to establish government-owned factories in these communities, but this was ruled out by Congress in 1934 on grounds that it would put the government into competition with private enterprise. Rexford G. Tugwell, the head of the Resettlement Administration, did not believe in the philosophy or economics of the back-to-the-land movement. He had the projects on his hands, however. The only hope of making them work, it seemed to him, was to enlarge their land base sufficiently to give the settler families an opportunity to produce farm products for sale as well as for use. For this purpose group operation of the land seemed to him to be a "sheer necessity"; it was for this reason, rather than because of any theoretical or ideological interest in cooperation or the cooperative movement, that the cooperative form of organization was adopted.

The Resettlement Administration, although its leaders did not favor attempts to move city people to the land, was also engaged in making projects. Resettlement projects were intended to provide opportunities in better land areas for farm families who would move from "submarginal" land that was purchased by the government for retirement from depleting uses. These projects were of two types. The "infiltration" type consisted of individual farms scattered through existing farm districts. The other type included group projects in which the farms, although individually operated, were contiguous and in which certain community services such as schools, neighborhoods, canneries and the like were provided as part of the project. At the end of its first year the Resettlement Administration had completed or planned 51 infiltration-type projects and 35 community-type projects. Five of these latter differed from the others; on these five all farming operations were to be carried on not by individual farmers but by cooperative associations. In its second annual report the Resettlement Administration indicated that it did not intend to move far in the direction of this communal farming; "greater emphasis," the report said, "has been laid upon the development of resettlement projects of the infiltration type or individual farm as opposed to rural communities."

In September 1937 the Farm Security Administration was created as the successor to the Resettlement Administration. FSA's main business was making operating and farm purchase loans to low-income farm families. (It loaned nearly a billion dollars to nearly a million families before it was merged into the Farmers Home Administration in 1946). The management of the projects created by its predecessor agencies and the completion of some projects planned by the Resettlement Administration were activities of secondary importance for FSA. By 1938 there was loud opposition to the project idea in the press and in Congress. It became clear, finally, that no new projects would be undertaken. By this time FSA was managing 195 projects, only eight of which it had itself developed. Ninety-seven percent of all the project units (the resources attributable to the support of a single family were counted as a unit) were operated on an individual, family-farm basis. In addition to projects which consisted mainly of individual farms, there were nine cooperatively-operated farms. Only four of the projects were given over solely to cooperative farming. The Casa Grande Valley Farms, Inc. was one of these four.

* * * *

The sources upon which the author drew in the making of this book were mainly three. The chief source was the files of the Farm Security Administration at the project, in San Francisco and in Washington. These files contained the numerous versions of the project proposals and plans, the family selection records, minutes and financial reports of the cooperative farm association and of the community council and a great deal of correspondence between FSA officials at various levels, between officials and members of the association, and between officials and outsiders, including for example, members of Congress.

A second important source of information was notes made by Dr. Bernard Bell, a social scientist who visited the project for the Bureau of Agricultural Economics in 1941. Bell spent a month at Casa Grande. He interviewed thirty of the settlers and a number of project officials and townspeople of Coolidge and Florence, keeping notes which were almost verbatim records of the interviews. Because Bell did his work with skill and insight and because his visit to the project coincided with an acute crisis in the life of the community, these interview records have been drawn upon heavily, especially in Chapters 6, 7, 8, 9 and 10. Many of the quoted statements attributed to the settlers in these and other chapters are taken directly from these interviews. The author's interpretation of the material may have been considerably influenced by the questions Bell asked the settlers, by his understanding of their replies, and by his general impression of the project.

The third important source of information was the author's own direct observation of the project during two visits there in 1943, and numerous interviews he had with FSA officials whose association with the project was long and intimate. Several years experience as an Information Specialist for FSA gave the author the advantage of familiarity with the ways of bureaucracy in general and with FSA projects and FSA administrators in particular. Subsequent experience and analysis, including the writing of this book, have not changed the author's opinion that these administrators, taken as a group, are men of devotion and competence.

The names of the settlers (but not of any others) have been changed. Source materials for each chapter are cited in detail at the end of the book.

In addition to the acknowledgements made above, the author wishes to express appreciation to the following: in the Farm Security Administration (now the Farmers Home Administration), Ralph W. Hollenberg and Robert G. Craig; at the University of Chicago, Professors Herbert Blumer, Morton M. Grodzins, Charles M. Hardin, Julius Margolis, Martin D. Meyerson, Edward A. Shils, and Rexford G. Tugwell; elsewhere the following other friends: Dorothea Lange and Professor Paul S. Taylor of the University of California at Berkeley, Margy Ellin Meyerson, John Collier Jr. and Herbert H. Rosenberg. Finally he wishes to thank his wife and children for making life pleasant while the book was in preparation.

1

Beginnings

The government project at Casa Grande would later be described as "a modern Brook Farm," "a little Soviet that washed the window-panes of life," "a peon camp," an experiment "without parallel in history," "a rather unusual farm," and "an experiment designed to interest private capital in large-scale farming." It would turn out to be in some sense most of these things, but none of them was intended when the Resettlement Administration set about optioning 3,600 acres of land in Pinal County, Arizona. The Resettlement Administration was in fact acting in a hallowed American tradition. Americans had always wanted land, and the government had always given it to them. The Preemption Act, the Homestead Act, the Desert Land Act, and the Reclamation Act were links in a chain that stretched back nearly a hundred years. And now, in the winter of 1935–36, the Resettlement Administration, an independent agency established by executive order and supplied with funds from a relief appropriation in 1935, was adding another link to the traditional land policy.

One might better say that it was repairing an old link. All of the old laws were intended to distribute land ownership widely among working farmers; all contained specific limits on the amount of land any one settler might claim, for Americans have always believed that to distribute the ownership of land widely among independent farmers is to guarantee the preservation of free institutions, and Americans have always hated and feared land monopolies. In Pinal County, as in many other places, the laws favoring the small, independent farmer had failed miserably. The Resettlement Administration, which proposed to buy 3,200 acres in the Casa Grande Valley between the towns of Coolidge and Florence some 65 miles southeast of Phoenix and to divide it into 80 separate farms of 40 acres each for sale to individual settlers, meant to do what the American land policy had been attempting for a century or more.

In the Casa Grande Valley the failure of the traditional land policy had been quick and complete. Most of the land there had been patented under the Homestead Act or purchased from the State (which got it from the Federal domain) only 20 or 30 years before. Both the Homestead Act and the Arizona land law limited the individual purchaser to not more than 160 acres. Moreover, two-thirds of the land taken up under these two laws was irrigated by a $10,500,000 Federal reclamation project from which (if the reclamation laws had been enforced) a single owner could obtain only enough water to irrigate 160 acres. Yet despite these three laws— any one of which should have prevented land monopoly—two-thirds of the Valley was farmed in units of 430 acres or more, and one-twelfth of the farmers owned 41 percent of the cultivated land. The laws had been passed to help the working farmer own his land, but here in the Casa Grande Valley three-fourths of the land was operated by tenants and nearly half of it was owned by people who lived outside the county—in Arizona, and in 19 other states, Hawaii, and Mexico as well. Pinal County offered an extreme example of a tenure pattern which had spread over much of the irrigated West; it was, therefore, a logical place to make a test of reform.

The Resettlement Administration dealt with only nine owners when it optioned a tract of 2,432 acres near the town of Coolidge. Only one of these owners—a widow—lived on her land. Two lived elsewhere in Pinal County, four lived elsewhere in Arizona, and two lived in California. All but one of the owners leased their lands to tenants, and some of the tenants were absentees themselves who operated the land through salaried managers. One of these non-resident tenants rented 13 other farms as well as his Casa Grande holdings.

"At the time the options were taken, in the winter of 1935–36, only seven families were living on the entire 3,600 acres, although all of the land had been in cultivation," Dr. Walter F. Packard, who had been Regional Director and then chief of the Resettlement Division of the Resettlement Administration, later told a Congressional committee. "Four of the farms were wholly unoccupied during the cotton-picking season as many as 35 families lived in temporary camps on a single holding. During the balance of the year these seasonal laborers migrated elsewhere.

"Housing on the project was wretched. The foreman for one of the large tenant operators lived in a shack valued at $300, while the labor on that farm lived under conditions of unbelievable squalor. Eight families occupied a shed, divided by chicken wire into compartments measuring 18 by 24 feet, with dirt floors. Other families lived in sheds made of old box wood and cardboard, tin cans flattened out, and a few boards and sheets of galvanized iron, gathered from various sources. . . . These hovels had no floors and were located next to the stables. One well and one privy were the only facilities of this camp, where over 100 people lived during the peak of the season.

"Five of the farms had no buildings at all. The laborers and sharecroppers either lived in town or in temporary camps. There was one fairly good seven-room house on the property, which 50 years ago was one of the finest houses in Arizona, but in 1935 it was in a dilapidated condition. This was occupied by a hired foreman of one of the larger farms. None of the houses on the project had electric lights. Only one had running water, a bathtub, and inside toilet. None had telephones."

Many causes had conspired to frustrate the American land policy in the Casa Grande Valley. One was Nature herself—it took a very large investment to level and irrigate this land. Machinery—the Diesel tractor especially—was another cause; what was a large farm for a man and two mules under the blazing Arizona sun was only a small patch for the skinless Diesel. A third and very important cause was the abundance of cheap labor which the big farmer could draw upon from day to day as he wished, with no responsibility for its support in the days, weeks, and months between seasonal peaks. The tenure system which seems to be inherent in cotton culture (80 percent of the land in big farms was planted to cotton), the urge to speculate in land values, the American love of bigness, and the reluctance of the Department of Interior and the State of Arizona to enforce the laws were other causes that made for land monopoly and for the disappearance of the small, independent farmer. Of course once the process was well begun it picked up a momentum of its own—more land and more Diesels made it possible to buy still more land and still more Diesels until, finally, there was not a house in sight.

The Resettlement Administration, with its plan for making 80 farms of 40 acres each for ownership in fee simple by working farmers, was setting out to re-create the familiar image of American rural life. Lincoln, who signed the Homestead Act, had once speculated on the feasibility of a steam plow; the Resettlement Administration would have to cope with the reality of the Diesel. This was the essential difference between 1862 and 1936, and it was a difference that made it very doubtful whether the new attempt could succeed where the old had failed so dismally.

As it came to the desk of the Administrator, Dr. Rexford G. Tugwell, for approval on March 11, 1936 the proposal (or as it was then mistakenly called, the final plan) was as follows:

To: Dr. R. G. Tugwell, Administrator
From: Carl C. Taylor, Assistant Administrator, Rural Resettlement Division
Subject: Approval of Final Project Plan, Casa Grande, Pinal County, Arizona

The Casa Grande project is of the infiltration type and involves the establishment of 80 farm units of 40 acres each. This project is located near Florence in Pinal County, Arizona. It is designed to resettle destitute or low-income families from this area.

At the present time we have under option 3,994 acres, and it is proposed to select 3,200 acres of irrigated and cleared land for the use of the project.

It will not be necessary to effect any road improvements, due to the fact that all the units will be erected on existing highways which are maintained by the County of Pinal.

The Arizona Edison Company serves this general area and electricity will be available for all units. The only expense to be incurred will be that for house connections.

The water supply will consist of individual driven wells estimated at 60 feet depth, equipped with electric pumps, pressure tanks, and pump houses.

Septic tanks of redwood, with a capacity of 375 gallons, and tile drain fields will be installed for the disposal of sewage.

The water supply for the irrigation of the farmsteads will come principally from the canals of the U.S. Indian Irrigation Service, San Carlos Project. A "Government" canal runs through the area and headgates are provided for taking the water into local ditches for field irrigation.

Furthermore, there are two wells located on the property equipped with electric motors and deep well turbines that provide an additional water supply which can be routed to any part of the project by means of the existing irrigation ditches.

The houses proposed for the Casa Grande project will be of adobe construction, with cement floors and insulated roofs. This is the type of construction generally found in the neighborhood and considered to be the most satisfactory in this climate. They are completely modern, having bathrooms, running hot and cold water, electric wiring and fixtures, and a garage attached to the house. An inside patio is provided and these houses are of unique and pleasing design and should be instrumental in creating a finer type of home in this community.

The houses are designed in four types with one, two, three, and four bedrooms. $200 is provided for household equipment and furniture.

The outbuildings will consist of a poultry house and a milk house. Due to mild weather conditions, no housing is required for the animals on the farmstead.

The Farm management plan involves the production of approximately 18 acres of alfalfa, 10 acres of cotton, 10 acres of wheat and grain sorghum (double crop) with two acres in the farmstead and garden. Each unit is expected to have two head of work stock, 10 milk cows, two brood sows, and 200 chickens.

From this unit the following returns are anticipated:

Receipt from farm		$1,767
Living from farm		$353
	Total	$2,120
Expense for farm		$692
Living from farm		$353
Cash living expense		$540
	Total	$1,585
	Net Income	$535

A rehabilitation loan of $2,200 is suggested for each unit.

The net income from the farm will not pay $2,200 rehabilitation loan and the interest and amortization on the capital investment, but will pay interest and amortization on a capital investment of $12,000 when the rehabilitation loan is included with the capital investment for the project.

Information contained in the project book, and reports from the Project Manager indicate that school, recreational and social facilities are available in the area.

No cooperative features have been planned for the project, although it is expected that cooperative organizations will be established as the need arises. The existing marketing agencies are adequate for present.

Total estimated cost to complete	$699,000
Rehabilitation loan estimate	$176,000
Total cost	$875,000

Unit cost $10,937 which is within the economic limit.

The Regional Attorney reports there are no hindrances to a clear land title. The Acting General Counsel has examined the project plan and approves of same.

We recommend:

Your approval of the project in accordance with the final plan in the amount of $875,000.

Your approval of the attached allotment request for $8,000 to cover project administration.

Tugwell approved the plan with one minor change—he raised the allowance for household equipment and furniture from $200 to $400 a unit, an increase which brought the total authorization to $891,000. But although he put his name to the proposal and ordered that construction be started at once, Tugwell could have felt no enthusiasm for this venture.

The trouble with it was that it promised too little. A settler on one of these 40-acre, two mule farms might graduate from destitution to poverty, but he could hardly do better. Virtually all of the $535 shown as net income would have to go for debt repayment, and only by putting the

$2,200 rehabilitation loan (an operating loan, for feed, seed, fertilizer and so on) on the 40-year repayment schedule with the real estate had it been possible to get the debt repayment charge low enough so that the settler could repay it from net income. That left the settler family with only $450 for cash living expenses. To be sure, this would be supplemented with $353 worth of milk, eggs, meat and vegetables produced on the farm for home consumption, but even so, the 40-acre farm offered a low standard of living in a "typical" year and Tugwell and his colleagues must have asked themselves whether this plan would end poverty or merely perpetuate it.

Ninety days after Tugwell gave his approval WPA crews were making adobes and leveling land at Casa Grande. But meanwhile the project plan was being restudied. Farm management specialists, engineers, and administrators tested a dozen different ideas for wringing a little more income out of the reluctant desert. The end product of their experimentation was the largest cooperative farm ever established in the United States, but that was nearly a year later, after a file cabinet had been filled with farm plans and sample family budgets. The process by which the 80 forty-acre farms became a 5,000-acre cooperative was gradual and, as it seems in retrospect, ineluctable.

At first it was decided to divide the project land in two and to treat the parts separately. The original plan would be retained on a 1,093-acre tract near the town of Florence, while on the 2,432 acres near Coolidge the farm dwellings would be brought together on two-acre tracts to form a community. Although he would live in the community settlement, each farmer would operate his own, individual outlying 40-acre farm. This plan looked good to the engineers because it offered many opportunities to save on the cost of utilities, the water system particularly. The adobe bricks which the WPA crews had made were hastily moved to a central location on the Coolidge tract and construction of 60 houses began there.

The farm management specialist was not altogether satisfied with this new arrangement which the engineers endorsed; as the farm management man saw it, the advantages of the community-grouping plan were cancelled out by its disadvantages so that there was no net gain in the settlers' probable income. "Numerous plans have been drawn up for operating on a 40-acre, individual basis," he wrote. "None of them promises a satisfactory income; those based entirely upon the sale of crops show a deficit after amortization and non-cash expense have been included. The plans including livestock made a better showing. If a client is set up on his 40-acre farm the investment is built up by the need for a water system, individual barns, pens, etc. If he is considered as living on the two-acre home plot provided in the community plan, the livestock should also be there. However, such savings as are effected by the community facilities, including the water supply, are offset by the losses in time and cost of travel to the farm land and the expense of hauling feed to the livestock."

The advantages of community grouping could be had without the disadvantages if the farm land were operated collectively, and this was the next step the planners took on the Coolidge tract. In September, 1936 the farm management specialist submitted to Tugwell a detailed plan for "corporate" operation of the tract. In it he drew this comparison between the plans for group and for individual operation:

"The cooperative enterprise yields an income of approximately 15 percent on the investment after deducting operating, amortization, and non-cash expenses. This is a net return of approximately $19 per acre, which is comparable to cash rental rates for land in this area. The wages plus the dividend give the client the equivalent of nearly 50¢ per hour of labor.

"The individual 40-acre unit when operated on a straight cropping basis does not yield an income large enough for the family to amortize all costs of the development and maintain the standard of living set by home economists. When livestock, such as dairy cattle and hogs, utilize the crops the enterprise yields 4.5 percent on the investment, which is $14 per acre. The labor income drops to 20¢ an hour.

"The reason for the superior showing of the corporate farm lies in the fact that the investment per acre is lower and the return per acre is higher."

By the end of 1936, when Tugwell and his advisers had definitely decided upon the cooperative plan for the Coolidge tract, sixty houses each on a two-acre plot, were nearly completed. It was unfortunate that the builders had outstripped the planners, for the two-acre plots, which had been provided so that each farmer might keep his livestock on his farmstead, were now unnecessarily large; together with roads, ditches, and wasteland the home plots took up 232 acres, leaving only 2,200 acres of cropland. At the same time the presence of the houses made it impossible to provide the cooperative with sufficient land to support 60 families, and during the first two or three years some extra land would be desirable as a safeguard. Accordingly the plan to create scattered farms on the Florence tract was dropped and, instead, it was decided to lease that land to the cooperative with the understanding that it might later be withdrawn from the cooperative for sub-division into individual farms or, possibly, as the site for another cooperative farm. To the 3,200 acres in the Coolidge and Florence tracts additional land (much of it fit only for sparse pasture) was soon joined, so that by the summer of 1937 the 80 forty-acre farms had become one farm of 4,172 acres of which 3,380 were irrigable. Later another 828 acres, all of it permanent pasture, would be added, bringing the farm's total to an even 5,000.

The old residents of Pinal County watched the Resettlement Administration's preparations at Casa Grande with growing misgivings.

They approved the idea of giving farm laborers a chance to own their own farms. Some of them had been raised in farm communities in states like Vermont and Iowa, and they felt that something valuable had been lost with the coming of machine agriculture and the hordes of seasonal workers who were so different from the hired men who used to eat with the family at the kitchen table. Moreover, they knew that the government's investment would bring relief and a measure of prosperity to the county; the money spent for the project would "prime the pump" for the local businessmen. It was partly in response to pleas for assistance from local leaders that the Resettlement Administration located the project there, and when a rumor spread that the size of the project was to be reduced from the original plan Tugwell himself had to write a letter of reassurance to the Florence Chamber of Commerce.

But when WPA workers began moulding bricks for houses that were to cost $2,000 each and when the Resettlement Administration announced that other WPA crews would soon begin to level land, build fences, and make other improvements Pinal County opinion became sharply critical. This was not the traditional way of making a farm in the West. To be sure, they had asked for the project because it would relieve unemployment. Still, it seemed wrong to make a farm with WPA labor—it was almost immoral.

Traditionally Western homesteads were developed in slow stages by the farmer's own efforts and the efforts of his wife and children—first a well dug and irrigated ditches laid out, a few acres of land cleared by hand, then later more land cleared, fences and outbuildings put up by the settler himself, stock acquired slowly by natural increase until—if all went well— toward the close of the settler's life, or after his death, the farm would be developed for capacity production and a modest dwelling could at last be erected over the cellar hole in which the pioneer family had lived all this time. This traditional way of doing things was based on the absence of credit and on the existence of a subsistence and handicraft economy at the frontier, and of course it involved a tragic waste of effort. But without physical and moral stamina no one acquired a farm in this way.

The trouble with the Resettlement Administration's plan, as the traditionalists saw it, was that ready-made farms would put the settlers in debt for more than they could ever repay and, besides, a farmer would not feel the same loyalty to a farm he had not struggled to create. Arizona's leading farm journal, the *Producer*, urged:

"A chance for the homesteader to owe less money; a chance to work like the very devil and build a home for himself, much as the real homesteaders did; a chance to pay out and get a free, clear deed some time this side of the millennium.

"Now let the Resettlement Administration arrange to guarantee purchase of such lands, in blocks of 40 or 80 acres, by clients carefully selected for ability, industry and tenacity. That is, the Government would guarantee the seller that payments specified in the contract would be met promptly, ending all his worries on that score and persuading him to accept a lower price than he would be willing to take in a deal without Uncle Sam's backing.

"To the settler would be granted a loan of enough for him and his family to subsist on the first year, to buy lumber for a modest house which could be added to as crop sales made it possible, to acquire indispensable equipment and farm animals. A program would be laid out for him to follow, say for five years. It would be a program to fit the farm itself and the family on it. The farmer wouldn't have some theoretical 'expert' coming around every morning to see that he fed the pigs a prescribed ration and that he chopped his cotton on time, but friendly guidance by a man familiar with the climate, the soil and the markets. The adviser would not order the farmer to do anything, never interfere so long as he did not stray so far from the general plan as to jeopardize his ability to make his payments.

"That farmer would clear his own land, make his own ditches, stretch his own fences, plant his own crops, be his own master, and eventually own his own farm. He'd have so much of himself built into the place that he would be very reluctant to leave, regardless of hardships, seasons of low returns, and other vicissitudes. He'd stick."

The Resettlement Administration took no stock in the theory that hardship was the adhesive which would keep a settler on his land. On the contrary, it seemed obvious to Tugwell that a settler would be more likely to succeed if he were furnished a friendly atmosphere at the outset. Moreover, the Resettlement Administration by the terms of its commission could not tolerate the cellar-hole standard of living which the old way of doing things would have necessitated; the difference between pioneer cellar-holes and rural slums would be hard to define. Besides, purely as a matter of economics it made more sense for a settler to use long-term low-interest credit to develop his farm for capacity production at once. Delay in bringing the farm into full production was a waste of resources and labor.

As to the use of WPA labor, the Resettlement Administration had no choice. It was using funds appropriated for relief and it was obliged to use an agreed-upon amount of relief labor. The 150,000 adobe bricks which were needed for the dwelling could have been made by machine at a saving, but hand methods would provide more work, so the bricks were made by hand. There was the same necessary waste in other parts of the job, and in total—according to later estimate—it amounted to about $100,000 or roughly 15 percent of the final cost of the project. It was true that the settlers would have to pay this extra cost; the law made no provision for calling it waste and charging it off.

When Pinal County learned that the houses were to be built in a community settlement rather than on the individual farms the distrust of the old residents deepened. Ignoring the example of the Mormon communities—of which there were at least a score in Arizona, arranged in exactly the manner proposed by the Resettlement Administration—the *Producer* called the idea a ghastly mistake and said it must have "been handed down from some poetic visionary in love with the charm and simplicity of French peasant village life." The Florence Chamber of Commerce through its secretary, Mr. Thum, protested against the community grouping plan in a letter to Tugwell. The Resettlement Administration's reply gave the first intimation that the land would be farmed cooperatively. "In the area (the Coolidge tract) where grouping is planned it is difficult to secure an adequate domestic water supply. The drilling of individual wells would be costly . . . grouping of the houses saves an appreciable amount of money in the cost of electricity, and (the community plan) makes possible the efficient operation of lands now in large holdings."

This reply was unsatisfactory and the secretary of the Chamber of Commerce wrote again. "We feel that your community grouping plan among other things would do the following, viz., create a community trading center, a social and political organization, which eventually will be dominated by one or two individuals, a community of this kind would be in contravention of our democratic form of government. We also feel that a unit plan will insure success of the project, as it will create a pride in ownership . . . something set aside as his own and to build and improve for his descendants." James Waldron, the Resettlement official in charge of Arizona projects, assured the Chamber official that there would be no trading center in connection with the project and he showed him the farm management studies which compared the probable returns from individual and from group operation. "While Mr. Thum is not ready to fully endorse the cooperative idea," Waldron reported to Washington, "still he feels in the light of the information we were able to give him . . . that the government is justified in going forward with the plan." Thum's attitude was probably representative of Pinal County opinion generally: the old way of making farms hadn't worked (for the homesteaders were the first victims of the Diesels) and apparently it couldn't be made to work now. But, unlike the Resettlement Administration, the opinion of Pinal County took into account the reality and the force of the pioneer ideals, attitudes, and prejudices which survived as contemporaries of the Diesel and so it believed the new way to be impractical and visionary.

By the late summer of 1937 the model community had taken form. The houses, set well apart on the two-acre lots, were arranged around a Y-shaped esplanade which was bordered with roads leading (at the top of the Y) into the Coolidge-Florence highway. Although they were all of the same basic plan, the houses had a look of individuality—they were set in varying depths on the lots and at varying angles toward the roads, the arrangement of the rooms was not the same in all houses, and the detached combination garage and storeroom was not placed in the same relation to every house. The differences created by these devices were accentuated by the landscaping of the lots so that the project had none of the monotonous uniformity so often associated with low-cost housing.

The houses were small. They had one, two, and three bedrooms (720, 800, and 1,050 square feet of floor space) and a screened porch which could be used as a sleeping place. They were built on cement blocks, a cheap flooring which was entirely satisfactory in the climate of the Southwest, and they had plenty of windows. The exteriors were stuccoed and painted in pastels which softened the glare of the desert sun; the shed-type roofs were covered with galvanized iron which was painted in bright reflecting colors. Each house had a 10 by 14 foot living room, a kitchen with shelves on either side of the sink and a ventilated food-storage closet built into a corner, a corner shower stall, water closet and lavatory, and bedrooms (each one with a closet) eight feet four inches by seven feet. Hot and cold running water, showers, and flush toilets would have been enough to distinguish these houses among the generality of Arizona farm homes, but they were also equipped with refrigerators, gas ranges, washing machines, and the necessary minimum of furniture. The average cost of the houses, including garages and septic tanks, was $3,873.

In the fork of the Y was a community hall built of adobe in the same style as the dwellings at a cost of $15,650. The community building contained an auditorium, a fully equipped kitchen, and rooms for sewing and other handicrafts. No other community facilities were provided, for the town of Florence was up the highway four miles to the northeast and Coolidge was about the same distance in the other direction and the settlers could use schools, churches, and stores in those places.

In the fields beyond the community settlement, placed with due regard for prevailing winds, were the farm buildings—a hay barn, granary, corral, dairy barn, milk shed, silo, poultry house, and hog pen.

The total cost of the project was $767,490 or $12,791 per family, itemized as follows:

Land (4,172 acres)	$321,092
Dwellings (including garages and septic tanks)	$232,384
Community building	$15,651
Roads, landscaping, and utility systems	$95,460
Farm buildings and fences	$72,850
Land leveling	$19,229
Other—cooperative developments	$10,824
	$767,490

This was somewhat less than the estimated total cost of the 80 individual farms and it included a good deal more land. The cost per family, however, was $1,651 greater than on the individual farm basis. Somehow the savings that had been anticipated by the provision of utilities for a community had failed to materialize. Unless the earning power of the cooperative farm would be greater than that of the individual farms per dollar invested, it looked as if the Resettlement Administration had not succeeded in making its money go further.

The existence of the 60 houses—which had been built on the assumption that the land was to be divided into 40-acre, two-mule farms—dictated the farm management plan for the 4,000-acre, industrialized cooperative, for since there were to be 60 laborers the enterprise had to be organized in such a way as to provide them steady work and steady income. But if the number 60 was something of an accident, it made no great difference; the Resettlement Administration was trying to get as many adequate livings from the land as possible, not to demonstrate the greatest possible economy of operation. If its purpose had been sheer "efficiency", 20 year-around workers would probably have been plenty.

The soil and climate of the Casa Grande Valley are best adapted to relatively low-value crops (like grain, alfalfa, and cotton) which require little labor. To convert these low-value crops into higher value products and to increase and regularize the farm's labor requirements, the farm management plan gave prominence to livestock. Cattle, sheep, hogs, and poultry would convert the crops to meat, milk, and eggs which would yield more profit, provide more work, and build up the fertility of the soil. It seemed sensible to produce as much as possible of the food the settler families would require for a well-balanced diet, and this was another reason for diversification.

The crop rotation plan was based on a cycle of eight years—five years of alfalfa, then one of barley and hegari (double-cropped), and then two years of cotton. At any one time there would be 1,240 acres of alfalfa, 640 acres of cotton, and 320 acres of grain. (Since the Florence tract was regarded as being on loan to the cooperative only until the rest of the land could be fully developed, the plan for the "typical" year was based on the 2,200 cultivable acres in the Coolidge tract. This was approximately the acreage available for irrigation in both tracts during the first year, while land leveling was still in progress.) If 540 acres of alfalfa were pastured to livestock (mainly sheep) there would remain 800 tons to be sold each year. The cotton was to be a short staple variety which would yield 426 pounds of lint and 792 pounds of seed to the acre; the lint would be sold for cash, but most of the seed would be fed to livestock. All of the grain (1,500 pounds of barley and 2,500 pounds of hegari to the acre) would be fed to the stock.

The dairy herd would consist of 120 cows, two bulls, and 40 calves. The milk of 35 of the cows would be required by the settler families (who would pay "roadside" prices for it); the rest would be sold as butterfat and fed to the livestock. The profit on the dairy would be $1,579 a year. The settlers would also need eggs—all that 1,000 hens would lay in a year, but the farm would have 2,000 hens because that was the minimum for economic operation of a poultry enterprise. The yearly profit on the poultry would be $1,357. The hog enterprise would consist of 40 sows. With five pigs raised from each of two litters per sow per year the farm could supply the settlers' requirements for pork (24,000 pounds) and have some to sell. Here the profit would be $476 a year. Arizona is well suited to the production of early milk-fed lambs, and so it was planned to pasture 2,500 ewes on 500 acres of alfalfa and 320 acres of grain stubble. With 2,770 lambs and 650 ewes for sale annually the profit on the sheep enterprise was set at $8,380. By fattening range cattle for four months on the farm's grain, alfalfa, and cottonseed the largest single item of profit could be made— $14,719 on 500 steers.

Unfortunately, even with this diversification only about one-third of the settlers could be kept busy all the year around, although all would have to be paid regularly of course. The dairy would require a crew of seven men, the sheep would require two men, and the hogs and poultry would require one man each. Another nine men—possibly 10—would be needed most of the time for the crops. But with these exceptions the farm work was bound to be seasonal. The steers, for example, would need the full-time attention of three men, but for four months only. There would be a big peak in the labor requirement at cotton-picking time; a little more than one-third of the farm's total labor requirement was for cotton-picking, and even if the settlers' wives and older children picked, some outside labor would have to be hired during the peak. Diversification, it seemed, was not enough to solve the problem of seasonality of employment on the big farm, and it was evident that mechanization and other forms of technical efficiency were to a large degree inconsistent with the Resettlement Administration's objective of providing steady work for 60 families.

The farm's gross income from livestock would be $105,515 and from crops $114,692—a total of $220,207. Against this there would be annual expenses of $139,300. The chief items of expenses would be wages ($37,980), rent ($28,167), feeder steers ($20,000), and auto, truck, and tractor operation and maintenance ($13,100). The cost of management would be a small item—$3,600 for a manager and $1,620 for a bookkeeper. From the gross surplus—$80,907—repayments would be made on an operating loan from the Resettlement Administration. The loan would be $173,288 repayable over five years at three percent interest, making the yearly payment $39,855 and leaving the cooperative a net balance of $41,052. With 10 percent of this set aside as a reserve for contingencies, there would be $36,947 for distribution to the settler families in dividends. This would amount to $615 a family.

The farm would pay wages to the settlers at prevailing rates—$2 for a 10 hour day, or $600 a year. Each family would have a kitchen garden on its home plot and the value of the vegetables was estimated at $60 a year. Together with the dividends which could be expected at the end of the year, this brought the settler's gross annual income to $1,275.

This was the plan as it stood in August, 1937. Fearing that they had made the debt repayment provisions too rigid, the planners proceeded to revise it in several important details.

They had decided to lease the project to the settlers, rather than sell it to them outright, when the cooperative plan was first adopted. Leasing would give the Resettlement Administration a greater measure of control over the project and it would allow more discretion in fixing payment charges. The rental charge, as it was tentatively established, would include the cost of irrigation water, payments the government would make in lieu of local taxes, depreciation on buildings and equipment, and three percent of the capital investment in the project—a total of $28,167. The value of the settlers' homes, the utilities, and the community building was not to be included in the calculation on which the rent was based; these would be leased at a nominal rent to a "homestead association", the sole function of which would be to lease and sub-lease the non-farm property. This plan was dropped in favor of a more flexible arrangement under which the entire property would be leased to one association on a sharecrop basis, the cooperative paying one-fourth the market value of the farm products but in no case less than $8,324 (which covered depreciation and payment in lieu of taxes) or more than $22,847 (which was the minimum, plus three percent of the value of the entire property). On this basis the cooperative farm was to carry its members' house rent (valued at from $10 to $12.65 a month depending on the size of the house) on its books as "house rent credits" to be paid out of earnings. Thus the settler would get his rent free and of course receive a smaller amount in dividends. To reduce the debt charge even further, repayments on the operating loan were extended from five years to ten years.

These and other changes (including provision of a community vegetable garden from which the settler's wife and children could take free vegetables and inclusion of $130 which a settler's wife and children could earn by cotton-picking) raised the anticipated family income somewhat. No "typical" family budget incorporating all these minor changes was drawn up, for the farm was actually in operation before the planning was complete, but the settler's probable income was now somewhat in excess of $1,500.

Tugwell had left the Resettlement Administration by June, 1937, when Dr. Jonathan Garst, a geographer and agriculturalist who had been director of the Resettlement Administration's western region during most of the planning and who would direct its development for the next two years, submitted the cooperative's formal application for an operating loan to Washington. For the new administrator, Dr. Will Alexander, Garst explained Casa Grande's significance:

"We consider this to be a very valuable experiment," he wrote. "I think it might even be termed a yardstick experiment. Large-scale, industrialized farming is becoming more and more prevalent in this part of the country. So far the workers on such large farms have been paid daily or even hourly wages and normally have not been provided with any housing facilities whatsoever and have been called to work or discharged only as actually needed. Their annual income has been very small. The possibilities of continuous employment have been exceedingly hazardous and the social conditions involved in this type of farming are one of the major problems the Resettlement Administration is called upon to help solve.

"On the Casa Grande farms we will organize the farming operations on an efficient basis, paying ordinary wages. It is admitted that the ordinary wages are very much below a satisfactory income. The industrial farmer, however, contends that the wages are all he can pay. The Casa Grande farm will determine whether a farm organized for the benefit of the workers, where the peak-loads of labor have been consciously flattened and where all surplus income, after paying legitimate management and capital costs, is divided among the workers, will not be better for the farm workers than their present position on industrial farms.

"The whole state, and the University of Arizona in particular, is conscious of our experiment in cooperative farming at Casa Grande and is aware of its significance. We think it has an excellent chance of success. . . ."

Sixteen months had passed since Tugwell signed his name to the first project proposal. The contest which the Resettlement technicians had staged between mules and Diesels was over. The Diesels had won and the 80 forty-acre farms were now one of the big industrial farms of the West. The independent farmers—"homesteaders" they had been called in the official correspondence at first—were now farm laborers; in sixteen months the inevitable failure of a generation of pioneers had been reenacted, but since it was reenacted on paper there were no abandoned cellar-holes and wasted lives to mark the outcome.

The Diesels had won again, but this time the farm laborers would share in the fruits of victory. To be sure, they would not be the independent farmers that American land policy had endeavored for a century to foster. But a man who shares in the use-right of a 5,000-acre farm may have more of a property-interest than the owner of 40 acres and two mules; a family with an income of $1,500 may have more opportunity than a family with $893, more than a third of which is in farm produce, and the farmer who works 60 hours a week may have more freedom than the farmer who must follow his mules from sun-up until sun-down. If it was freedom, opportunity, and the stabilizing influence of property that the American land policy had been endeavoring to distribute all these years, was not the cooperative as fit an instrument as the individual farm?

Perhaps not. The member of the cooperative would not own his property as lord of the manor; he could use it only in common with 59 others. So long as he remained a member, his opportunity would not include the opportunity to dispossess his neighbor and put him to work at wages. And his freedom would be limited, one might argue, by the rights of others. Certainly in this context the old words had new meanings, and it might be that many Americans would feel that the new meanings were not as good as the old. But in Pinal County the traditional land policy had failed dismally, and so if the old words were to be used there at all, except in hypocrisy, they would have to be given the new meanings. The Diesel had changed the scene forever, and it was therefore futile to compare the independent farmer and the cooperator. The real choice lay now between the cooperative and other industrial farms—and no one had ever claimed that there was freedom or opportunity or stability in the wretched shacks and shanties which had been swept away to create the cooperative farm which now stood ready, like a great new machine soon to be set in motion.

2

Organizing the Cooperative

Before it could receive an operating loan or even apply for one, the cooperative had to have a legal existence. So in June, 1937, when the preliminary farm plan was complete and ready to be sent to Washington, four farm laborers were hastily recruited and, with a Resettlement official to serve temporarily as secretary-treasurer, Casa Grande Valley Farms was incorporated under the laws of Arizona. The incorporators then passed a motion accepting a set of by-laws, elected themselves directors of the Association, brought their applications for membership before themselves as directors and, as directors, voted to accept themselves as members, then empowered their treasurer to obtain a Resettlement loan of $173,288. By this legal play-acting the cooperative was brought into existence and enabled to engage in the production and marketing of agricultural products with all the rights, powers, privileges and immunities which might be necessary, useful, or incidental to the accomplishment of its purposes.

According to the orthodoxy of the cooperative movement, organization should be the end product of a process of education—the cooperative should arise out of the understanding and conviction of its members. The Resettlement Administration, which had no interest in the orthodoxy of cooperation and which put its faith altogether in the unifying influence of a common need and not at all in that of a common ideal, violated this cardinal principle because to do otherwise would have interfered with the practical business of getting the cooperative farm underway. If the farm laborers had first to be educated to understand their need for a cooperative and to assume the initiative in organizing it, the loan application, urgently needed if the farm was to be ready for spring planting, would be delayed—delayed indefinitely, perhaps. And even if it had seemed important to the Resettlement officials, there would have been insuperable obstacles in the way of applying the traditional educational approach to the organization of low-income, migratory farmers and farm laborers.

Arizona had no law providing specifically for the organization of cooperatives, but incorporation served the purpose well enough. Under its charter the Association could issue no capital stock (certificates of membership were provided instead), each member was to have one vote, and there was to be no voting by proxy except in the election of directors. Membership would consist of one member of each family approved by the government for residence at Casa Grande and the members would elect a board of five directors who would conduct the affairs of the Association. The indebtedness of the cooperative was limited by the articles of incorporation to $250,000. Earnings were to be distributed in the manner provided by the by-laws.

The by-laws vested control of the association in the membership. Regular meetings were to be held quarterly, and special meetings might be called at any time by the Board of Directors or by the petition of at least 10 percent of the members. The business of the association was to be managed by a board of five directors serving staggered terms of three years. Election was to be by ballot and the nominees receiving the highest number of votes to fill the vacancies. The directors would elect a president, vice-president, secretary, treasurer (or secretary-treasurer) and if they wished, employ a general manager. A director could be removed for cause at any time by a majority vote of the membership.

The president was to preside at all meetings and "see to it that all orders and regulations of the Board are carried out." The treasurer was to have custody of the funds and to make disbursements upon order of the board. If the board employed a general manager, he would have direct charge of the association's business in accordance with the instructions of the board and under its supervision.

A member might be expelled for failure to cooperate in the purpose and objects of the association, but he could be expelled only upon recommendation of the board and only if the membership, after giving him an opportunity to appear before it in his own defense, concurred by majority vote with the board.

At the end of each fiscal year, and at intervals as necessary, the board was to fix the equity of the individual member by dividing the net worth of the association by 60. If a member withdrew or died, the board was required to buy his equity and it was to have an option for this purpose. The equity might be re-sold to a new member at the purchase price or $500, which-ever was less. The net earnings of the association were to be distributed among the members in proportion to the hours each had worked.

In their fundamentals these by-laws followed closely the established practices of the cooperative movement which of course places great emphasis on the democratic conduct of affairs. Whether a large indus-trialized farm could be successfully operated on principles as democratic as those of a consumers' cooperative (the form of cooperation out of which the working principles of the movement largely grew) was a some-what doubtful question, the more so in the case of Casa Grande because the cooperators were to be inexperienced farm laborers and because the Resettlement Administration, having invested a large sum of public funds in the project, had certain obvious responsibilities to the taxpayer which it could not properly delegate to its borrowers, the cooperators. Garst, the regional director, believed that the primary function of the cooperative farm was to raise its members' standard of living, not to afford them the moral advantages of "economic democracy," and he maintained that in a producer's cooperative the members should give up their right of management. The by-laws adopted for Casa Grande, which had been supplied hastily from the Resettlement Administration's legal division in Washington so that the loan application could be per-fected, gave the government no authority in the affairs of the associa-tion and provided a kind of town-meeting management for the farm. Garst quickly decided that on this and other points the by-laws needed amendments.

In a letter to Washington, Garst objected to the provision of the by-laws which gave the board of directors discretion to employ or not employ a manager. "I believe it should be mandatory for the association to employ a general manager," he wrote. "The idea of compelling the association to do this is based upon the fact that in our lease of the farm lands to the association we are going to provide that the general manager shall be a per-son approved by the government. Through this device we want to retain a strong hold on management, at least for the first few years. Our experience at Atascadero has convinced us that a cooperative cannot function this side of bankruptcy without strong management, and we are going to insist upon it in the case of Casa Grande from the very start."

Garst's point was accepted in Washington and in their final form the by-laws required the employment of a manager and defined his duties as follows: "(a) to have charge of the direct management of the association's business in accordance with the instructions of the Board of Directors and under the supervision of the Board; (b) to engage, discharge and fix the wages and duties of the employees of the association in accordance with the authority given by the Board of Directors; (c) to cause accurate books to be kept of the business of the association and to submit the same with all files, records, inventories and other information pertaining thereto for inspection at any time by the Board of Directors or by auditors appointed by the Board; (d) to disburse funds of the association in payment of its debts in accordance with the authority given by the Board of Directors, taking proper vouchers for such disbursements; (e) to furnish to the Board once a month a statement in writing of the condition of the association's business and submit a report of the management at the regular meetings of the members; (f) to attend to such other duties and offices as the Board of Directors may require, including such duties as might ordinarily, in the absence of such requirement, be performed by the Treasurer or by some other officer of the association."

The by-laws gave the manager wide powers, but powers that could be exercised only under the supervision of the Board of Directors. Garst might influence the manager and even the members of the Board, but he could not control them legally. Other instruments than the by-laws would be needed to secure the government's control over the association. These, it will be seen, were soon amply forthcoming.

Another provision of the by-laws which the Regional Director changed was that governing the distribution of the association's earnings; in his view non-member, as well as member, employees should share in the earnings. He explained, "We do not want the association ever to exploit labor even though the surrounding farming community does. If you merely provide that the non-member employees will receive wages as full remuneration for their work, it would be the tendency of the association to pay them the prevailing wage in order that the profits of the association—and hence the income of each member—might be as high as possible. To forestall this profit-grabbing tendency we prefer that even non-members shall be entitled to share in the disposition of the earnings of the cooperative. In this way we seek to broaden slightly the effective benefits of this association and extend them to farm laborers."

Neither the Washington nor the Regional office was entirely satisfied with the provision regarding payment of equities to withdrawing members. "There is one big objection to forcing the association to buy anyone's property interest, whether they withdraw, are expelled, become insane, or die," the Regional Director wrote, "for if a number of members should simultaneously put the association in a position of having to buy their memberships at the same time, the association might well be put on the spot financially and might be virtually wrecked overnight." There seemed to be no answer to this argument, so another amendment was drafted which gave the Board the option to purchase a withdrawing member's equity at the value it (the Board) placed upon it. If the Board did not exercise its option within 30 days, the member was at liberty to sell his equity to any person eligible for membership. If the Board did not purchase the equity and the member did not sell it, the equity would terminate 90 days from the date of the member's withdrawal. This change eliminated the danger of a "run on the bank," but it left the settler in doubt that he would get his equity in case of withdrawal or death. The $500 limitation on the selling price of equity was removed.

Several other amendments were prepared at this time. One required the association to maintain standards of hours, wages, and employment, both for member and non-member employees, at least equivalent to those maintained by the private enterprises with which it was in direct competition, and to respect the rights of employees to organize and bargain collectively. Another amendment, suggested from Washington, obligated the Board to set up a reserve and educational fund at the end of each fiscal year. In addition to the usual purposes of a reserve, the association's reserve fund could be used to purchase the equities of withdrawing members or to extend its members any program of social welfare insurance. The educational fund was to be used for the dissemination of information about cooperative organization and cooperative activities. Any surplus remaining after the reserves were established was to be divided among the association's employees, whether members or non-members, in proportion to the hours of labor performed by each. If any employee owed the association any debts, these were to be deducted from his dividend or "labor bonus."

The by-laws could be amended at any time by a majority vote of the membership. To safeguard the provisions it considered essential against later change by the membership, the Resettlement Administration prepared a final amendment which provided that no amendment to those sections dealing with membership, the powers of the board of directors, or the distribution of earnings would be valid if inconsistent with the terms of any agreement entered into by the association. Since the association would have to enter into several agreements with the Resettlement Administration, there was no danger on this score.

When amendments had been drafted to cover all the points raised by the regional staff in San Francisco and the national staff in Washington, only one amendment was needed—to strike out all except the title of the old by-laws and insert the new. This was done at the first annual meeting of the cooperative in February, 1938.

If cotton-planting was to begin as soon as the operating loan was approved, the association needed a manager at once. However, it would have no money to pay his salary until the loan funds were received and, moreover, the membership would not be fully constituted and in a position to elect a Board of Directors authorized to employ a manager until February or later. Since the need for a manager was urgent, and since the government intended to reserve the right to pass on the Board's choice, it seemed logical for the government to detail one of its own employees to the position for the time being. Later he could be switched to the association's payroll.

Garst, the regional director, had insisted that the association be required to employ a manager because he believed that a cooperative could function "this side of bankruptcy" only if it had strong management. Robert A. Faul, whom he assigned to the project in September, 1937, was a man who could be depended upon to provide strong management and he had other qualifications as well.

Faul was in his middle fifties—a "stout, raw-boned, farmer type," a personnel officer noted. He had emigrated from England to Western Canada in his youth and had homesteaded there, living in a sod house on the frontier. He sold his land after perfecting the title and came to the United States as a carpenter. Within a few years he was in charge of construction crews on a number of the largest building projects in the Mid-west.

"He handled crews of 200 to 300 men and got a lot of cooperation from them," one of the construction companies wrote in a letter of recommendation. While the building industry stagnated during the Depression, Faul moved to Arizona and took up 160 acres of raw desert land near Coolidge. By March, 1937, when the Resettlement Administration first hired him, at a salary of $1,800, he had succeeded in making a farm from the desert and he had successfully organized and managed the Arizona Turkey Growers' Association, then in its fifth year of operation. At that time the Resettlement Administration needed a man to organize a feed-buying cooperative in Pinal County and Faul's experience made him a natural choice.

Six months later, when a manager was needed for the Casa Grande project, Faul was again a natural choice. For one thing, he was by now a local man and so would be of decided public relations value to an undertaking which was likely to prove controversial. His experience in construction work and his success in making a farm from the desert near the project were also of special value, for the construction phases of the project, land leveling, particularly, were not entirely completed—it would take at least a year or two of operation to bring the farm through the development stage. To be sure, Faul had practically no formal education and no theoretical knowledge of cooperatives. But he had practical experience, and something else which weighed heavily in his favor—he was known to be tough. "Very practical type; used to giving orders and not asking too many questions," the personnel officer wrote. Regional Director Garst, who was determined to establish the authority of management at the outset and who believed that the cooperative would be a success if it raised its members' standard of living, was well satisfied with Faul and confident that he would teach the settlers a hard but valuable lesson.

As project manager, Faul was paid $3,000. This was an unusual figure; the government salary scale provided for positions at $2,900 and $3,200. When the point was called to his attention from Washington, Garst explained that the manager's salary would soon be assumed by the association and had been set at $3,000 with that in mind. Whether this arrangement would be entirely satisfactory to the settlers was not discussed.

Had the Resettlement officials wished to do so, it would have been difficult or impossible for them to take the settlers into account in making the legal and organizational arrangements that were necessary. As public officials they were not at liberty to pass out funds without adequate safe-guards and without retaining a large measure of control. Moreover the pre-paratory work had to be done before the settlers could be selected. Only the necessary four had been selected when the association was incorpo-rated; by February the number had increased to 13, the minimum, the law-yers said, to make the cooperative a bona-fide applicant for a loan. These few settlers, selected in advance of the others for the convenience of the lawyers, could not well be consulted by the administrators; they were low-income farmers and farm laborers and, even if they could have under-stood the legal and other more-or-less technical points at issue, it would have been impracticable to have them available in San Francisco and Washington where the decisions were constantly and rapidly being made. If they had been devoted to the doctrines of the cooperative movement, the Resettlement officials would have been disturbed that the cooperators could not participate in the organizational preliminaries; as it was, they felt there would be plenty of time to explain matters to the settlers later—the essential thing was to get the first year's cotton crop planted on time.

As it was later described by one of the project officials, the organiza-tional process included little or none of the education which is traditional in the cooperative movement. "With all this material (legal documents) on hand, the Resettlement representatives contacted a few of the most likely applicants and explained that it was going to be necessary to establish a cooperative and requested that they assist to this end—it being explained to these individuals that various steps were going to be required. In most instances I feel that the preliminary organizers of the cooperative had very little idea of the actual situation and of the mechanics necessary. All of the work of setting up the cooperative was done entirely by the represen-tatives of the Resettlement Administration and approved by the Board of Directors. My observation was that whenever legal papers were to be given consideration there was a tendency on the part of the members to want to skim over them and, if they met with the approval of the Administration, to sign them without even knowing the contents."

When the 13 members were assembled for the first annual meeting in February, 1938 they accepted the government's amendments to their by-laws without change—but not without argument. Several of the settlers had already taken up residence on the project and these, it now appeared, had not only read the papers they signed but had agreed among themselves that the by-laws were well enough as they stood, without the changes the government was proposing. Moreover they had met in the dairy barn one day when it was too rainy to work outside and had elected Tom Fortas, one of the incorporators, as manager of the association, informing James Waldron, the Administration's Arizona supervisor, that Faul would no longer be needed. When Waldron pointed out that they were jeopardizing their loan application, the members rescinded their action and voted to accept the required changes in the by-laws. Nevertheless Waldron was alarmed, and he wrote Regional Director Garst urging that steps be taken to give the manager and the Administration more authority over the affairs of the cooperative:

"There are a few inexperienced, rather ignorant, strongheaded individuals (Waldron wrote) who are attempting to so organize the group that when the cooperative loan comes through and the cooperative begins to function that they can obtain control. It is rather doubtful if they will want to keep Faul. Probably they will wish to cut loose from the Government almost entirely.

"At the recent meeting when the amendments to the by-laws were adopted, we took pains at the opening to point out that because of the large investment of the Government and the desire to protect the homesteaders, it would be necessary for the Government to maintain almost complete supervision for probably the first five to ten years. We assured them that as soon as the Government felt that the cooperators could safely take charge, they would gradually be given authority.

"My object in writing at this time is to inform you of this situation and to point out that in the Management Contract or Loan Agreement, which accompanies the check, there must be very definite authority placed in the Government and through the Government to the project manager. The way the by-laws and articles read at the present time, complete control is placed in the Board of Directors. It is our opinion that unless this can be offset by a definite Management Contract there is very little hope of the cooperative's succeeding.

"Mr. Faul was in the office yesterday and was very discouraged, realizing what he is facing; and while I assured him I was confident this matter would be properly adjusted and that he had little to fear in this regard, yet I fully sympathized with him. I cannot too strongly urge, therefore, that you and Mr. Weller (the regional attorney) go over this matter thoroughly so that we may have *full authority* and can *definitely* point out to these people at the very beginning that control of management is in the hands of the Administration and that the project manager has full responsibility and full authority on the job.

"It is my honest opinion that it will do very little good to state this in mere words because these people are reading the by-laws assiduously, and unless the matter is in cold print there will be very little chance of carrying out a successful Farm Management Plan."

Garst heeded Waldron's warning. "Full authority" for the government was contained in the lease, in the agreement which the association's officers signed as a condition to obtaining the loan, and in "Work and Occupancy" agreements between the individual settlers and the association.

The lease not only gave the Administration authority to approve the Board of Director's choice of a manager, but it went much further, requiring that the manager be "such person and at such salary as may, from time to time, be designated in writing by the Government and (the Association) will not discharge such manager without the written consent of the Government." The loan agreement gave the government the right to appoint a creditor's representative, called a Supervisor, whose salary would be paid by the association if the government so requested and whose function was to see that the terms of the loan agreement were carried out. For this purpose the Supervisor had authority "to conduct the business of the borrower in all its branches." The loan agreement prohibited the association from distributing labor bonuses without the consent of the Government, and both the lease and the loan agreement prohibited changes in certain specified sections of the by-laws without approval by the government. All of the association's chattels were mortgaged to the government before the loan was closed, so it could not buy, sell or contract a debt without permission from its creditor.

The Work and Occupancy agreement was a contract between the association and its individual members. The member agreed to accept employment from the association and to devote his full time to it under the direction of the manager. The association did not guarantee to employ the member for any particular time, but it did promise to distribute the available work as equitably as possible among the members and to pay the member not less than $1.50 a day when he worked. The member was entitled by the agreement to occupy a homestead and to receive a dividend if one were declared. If he violated the agreement, it was terminated at once and without notice. The agreement was signed by the member and by the president and the manager of the association. It was also countersigned by the Assistant Regional Director on behalf of the Secretary of Agriculture. Thus there was no doubt that the government had authority to expel a settler who failed to work "under the direction of the manager."

There was now no phase of the cooperative's affairs which was not wholly subject to the government's control. If they were still reading them assiduously, the settlers could find that the revised by-laws, like the original by-laws, said in so many words that "control of the association is vested in the membership." But they knew that, whatever the by-laws said, there was sure to be some other document to the contrary and, although they may not have been entirely reconciled to the situation, they accepted it without a show of resistance. As a regional official would explain three years later in a letter to the Administrator, "At the time these agreements were executed the members had but recently been removed from make-shift shelters to what no doubt appeared to them as quite luxurious homes. It is quite probable that they would have signed almost any kind of an agreement to retain their status as members."

3

Selecting the Settlers

In Mrs. Theone Hauge, an experienced home economist and social worker, the Farm Security Administration[1] had a "family selection specialist" for its Arizona projects. From among the thousands of low-income farm people in the State she would select 60 families for membership in the Casa Grande Valley Farms.

Mrs. Hauge's job was a difficult one. She could not work out a trial balance on paper in the fashion of her colleague, the farm management specialist. There was no way of knowing for sure what combinations of human material would bring about a desirable result; everyone was entitled to draw his own picture of the ideal settler and inevitably every picture would be different. Even if Mrs. Hauge had known for sure what qualities to look for, she had no yardstick by which to measure them in an applicant. None of the common psychological tests would have been of much use to her, and, even if they had been, she would not have been able to use them, for the Farm Security Administration was bound to take its poverty-stricken people pretty much as they came; public opinion would not have permitted the government to supplement the means test with the Binet-Sanford test. Regional Director Garst and his subordinates regarded Casa Grande as a practical problem in farm management, and so they were inclined to give more attention to the selection of tractors than people. To them it seemed obvious that if the cooperative farm were properly organized and managed it would succeed with the same kind of labor force used on other industrial farms. Indeed, it would have to in order to demonstrate a useful advantage over the privately-owned, large-scale farm.

So Mrs. Hauge had only her own womanly intuition to go on, and some common-sense criteria which FSA used nationally in selecting families for projects. These criteria were few and simple. The settlers should be in

1 The Resettlement Administration was transferred into the Department of Agriculture early in 1937 and re-named the Farm Security Administration.

38

reasonably good health and should have agricultural experience. Families were preferable to single men, although very large families could not be accepted because the houses were small. Age was another factor to be taken into account; the head of the family should be between 21 and 50. Above all, the families had to be poor—eligible for relief or nearly so, for the whole purpose of the project was to provide relief and rehabilitation.

Since early in 1936 the Resettlement Administration had accumulated applications for the Casa Grande project, and by the summer of 1937 there were several hundred in the files. All of these applications were from people who wanted individual, 40-acre farms (the cooperative nature of the project was not widely advertised until the beginning of 1938), and this impaired the value of the file somewhat, although few applicants were likely to turn down the cooperative if there was no alternative. There was something else which rendered the file of very little use to Mrs. Hauge— people who had been in urgent need of assistance had not been able to wait six months, a year, or more until the project could be readied for them. So when Mrs. Hauge at last turned to the bulging file, she found only a small number of applications that were active.

But if the selection process could not proceed ahead of project development, neither could it lag behind. On June 2, 1937 Waldron wired Mrs. Hauge from the regional office in San Francisco, "Kindly arrange to interview and prepare applications immediately on five applicants for Casa Grande Project. These should be located near Project if possible. These needed to form cooperative as soon as I return." Two weeks later the cooperative was hastily incorporated so that it could apply early for an operating loan. In July the government's lawyers ruled that the loan application could not be considered bona-fide until the association had enrolled at least 25 percent of its anticipated membership. A few days after this ruling was issued, the Regional Director replied that 20 members had already been selected and 72 applications were under consideration. But in December, when the Solicitor of the Department of Agriculture raised the question again, there were only six members. Seven more were recruited in two days and the news telegraphed to Washington so that the loan application, which was soon to be placed before the Secretary, Henry A. Wallace, could be acted upon promptly. Thirteen members was two short of the required one-fourth (a fact which suggests that Mrs. Hauge may have reached the end of her file of applications) but by the middle of February four more had been added and the loan was at last approved.

Although in some cases it was cut short in order to meet deadlines set in San Francisco and Washington, the selection process was usually thorough. Mrs. Hauge visited an applicant family at home, answered questions about the project in great detail, and collected information about the family's history, composition, living conditions, health, education, and financial status. This information she entered upon a schedule and summarized in a brief narrative appraisal. Each family was asked for references, and the persons whose names they gave—a former landlord or a storekeeper in most cases—were queried by mail. After Mrs. Hauge had made her initial visit, an eligible family was asked to come to the project for an interview with Waldron and Faul ("Are you interested in irrigated agriculture?" Faul always asked) who, along with Mrs. Hauge, comprised an informal committee to make the final selections. Usually the committee had two interviews with a family before reaching its decision.

The 17 families who had been selected by the middle of February took up residence at Casa Grande, a family or two at a time, beginning in November. There was work enough to keep several men busy preparing for the farming operation which would soon begin, but the full quota of labor would not be needed until cotton-chopping time late in May. Meanwhile the selection of the additional families could proceed at a leisurely pace. In the interim until the cooperative could meet its first payroll from loan funds, FSA employed the first arrivals at 35 cents an hour.

They were a diverse group. Only three or four were natives of Arizona; the others had come there at different times, from different places, and under different circumstances. All had been farmers or farm laborers at some time, but most of them had done other work as well, a few having held semi-skilled industrial jobs before the Depression. One man had worked several years in a copper mine. Another had been a ditch-rider for an irrigation company. A third, a former school-teacher, was one of the surveying crew which laid out the project. Three of the men had been on WPA until just before they came to Casa Grande. Several, including a former policeman and a shoe-repairman, left Oklahoma, Arkansas, and Texas farms a year or two in advance of the main body of Dust-Bowl refugees and now considered themselves Arizona residents of long standing. Most of this group of settlers were strays who had come to Arizona not as part of a definable wave of migration but for various reasons such as health. Generally speaking, they had been urbanized, either at home, along the way, or in Arizona. All but a few, in fact, had lived in a good-sized town or city at some time.

Few or none of this first contingent of settlers were drawn from among the thousands of migratory cotton-pickers who were currently streaming into Arizona from the Dust-Bowl states. This resulted partly from the fact that Mrs. Hauge turned first to the file of applications which had been accumulating for two years (and which was exhausted by February) but it resulted also from the deliberate policy of the Farm Security Administration, which, in deference to Arizona opinion which held that the home folks should be served first, had made a systematic effort to secure applications from Arizona residents in all counties of the State.

By the end of February, when approval of the cooperative's loan application made it possible to go ahead with the selection of the remaining settlers, it was evident that the membership quota would have to be reduced. Drought had lowered the Coolidge Reservoir; and the San Carlos Irrigation District, on which the project land was entirely dependent for water, announced that irrigators could not expect their normal supply in the coming year. Instead of the three acre-feet of water it needed, the project would be lucky to get two. This meant that the cooperators could plant only about half as much cropland as had been planned for the first year. With this prospect, the association's membership quota was cut to 56, so that, at the end of February, there remained 39 families yet to be selected.

Now a decided change occurred in the character of the selections. The remaining settlers—most of them—were not chosen from among the established residents of Arizona, as the first lot had been. Instead they came chiefly from among the migratory cotton-pickers who had arrived in Arizona only a few months before (most of them in September, when the picking season started), fresh from the small, impoverished cotton farms of Oklahoma, Texas, and Arkansas, where they had been tenants and laborers until economic pressures at home—boll weevil, drought, and tractors—and the solicitations of Western growers anxious for an abundant supply of cheap labor had lured them to Arizona and on to California.

The 1937 cotton crop was a big one in Arizona and so the year was an extraordinarily good one for the migrants. But, even so, their incomes were low—only one family in five earned as much as $700 during the year and the average family earned only about $400. Considering that most of them had not left home until September and that two-thirds of them had earned less than $300 before leaving, it was evident that if they were badly off in Arizona they had been worse off at home.

By the middle of February, most of the several thousand cotton-pickers who remained in Arizona were destitute or nearly so. There was no use going on to California, as most of them had planned, because fogs and floods there had already created serious unemployment in the pea fields. Stranded in the cotton-picking camps, hungry and diseased, the migrants could get neither WPA nor State relief, beyond emergency care, because they lacked the three years' residence required by Arizona law. In March the county relief board at Phoenix announced that no assistance would be available "even if someone were dying" in the camps.

After 200 desperate migrants congregated on the Statehouse lawn to demand relief, the Governor of Arizona appealed to the Farm Security Administration for a special grant of $50,000. Within a few weeks FSA was giving emergency aid to 12,000 persons in the Salt River Valley. For the most part the FSA assistance was in the form of cash grants for subsistence, but there was room for a few of the cotton-picker families in the Arizona resettlement projects, and Casa Grande, the largest of the projects, filled out most of its remaining membership quota from among the distressed families who applied for grants in Pinal County.

Compared to the first 17 families selected, the newcomers—"Okies," they and their likes were derisively called by people who had come to Arizona in other, earlier waves of migration—were a relatively homogeneous group and a relatively disadvantaged group. Coming from a region of chronic poverty, of land worn thin almost before it was settled—a region which derived its culture from the cotton-tenant system of the Old South—these recent migrants were among the most handicapped of all farm people in the United States. With few exceptions, they had no experience in urban life or in occupations other than agriculture, and, unlike the former migrants who were among the first contingent of settlers, they had had no opportunity as yet to absorb the different standards which prevailed in Arizona—standards of health, education, and material living which, except for cotton-pickers like themselves, were vastly higher than they had been accustomed to as sharecroppers and laborers on the depleted farms of the Indian Territory.

With some few exceptions, this was the background of the 39 settlers who were selected to fill out the cooperative's membership rolls before cotton-chopping time. Between June and December, 1938, eleven families—most of whom were among the first group of settlers, the Arizona residents—dropped out of the association. Their places were taken chiefly by "Okies," so that at the end of the first year the membership, which was then relatively stable, consisted in the main of Dust-Bowl refugees, along with some few strays who had come to Arizona some years earlier by quite different roads.

It is not possible to draw a complete statistical picture of the entire membership as it was first constituted, but 48 of the family information schedules taken by Mrs. Hauge have been preserved and these are probably fairly typical of the others.

All but 10 of this representative group of settlers were natives of Oklahoma, Texas and Arkansas. Two were natives of Arizona. The others came from Illinois, Alabama, Kansas, New Mexico, and South Dakota.

At the time Mrs. Hauge interviewed them, the average age of the men was 36.8. Ten were under 30, and only three were 50 or older. Their wives were somewhat younger—33.2 on the average. Eighteen of the women were under 30 and only one had reached 50.

Two of the men had never attended school and 12 had not reached the sixth grade, while one had finished three years of college. On the average, the men had 7.3 years of schooling. The women had more—8.6 on the average, with only two having as little as six years.

In income status, the settler families were better off than most migrants. In 1937 only about one-fifth of the migratory cotton-picker families in Arizona had earned as much as $700, but this was the average income of the settlers. Twenty-five families had less than this average (13 having $500 or less), and only five families had more than $1,000. The highest income—$1,375—represented the earnings of a father, a wife who did part-time nursing, and their fully-grown son.

A number of the families had lived in Arizona long enough to be eligible for relief and a number had been so situated that they could grow some food for family use. Relief payments (direct relief, WPA, CCC, and FSA grants) swelled the incomes of 13 families by an average of $223 (if it had not been for relief payments, six families, rather than one, would have had incomes of less than $300), and the value of home-produced foods accounted for $69 in the incomes of 17 families. If cash earnings alone are included, the average income of the settler families was only $639 in 1937.

The assets of the average family were valued at $207 by Mrs. Hauge. Liabilities were $64 on the average, making the net worth of the average family $143. The net worth of 23 families was less than $100 and only six had a net worth of more than $400, the highest being $500.

Only four of the families got the major portion of their incomes from WPA or other forms of relief, and only five got most of it from farm production. Thirty depended chiefly on cotton-picking and other farm labor, and nine on non-agricultural employment. All but a few families got some share of their incomes from more than one of these sources.

Most indicative of the settlers' living standards, perhaps, was the fact that only 19 families had water (either running water or a well) on the premises where they lived and only 14 had electricity in their homes. Thirteen of the 48 families had both water and electricity.

To the editor of the Casa Grande *Dispatch*, who asked editorially, "Are these people Americans or do some of their names end in '-vitch' or '-insky'?", it could be answered that they were as real, as American, and as wretched as the Dust-Bowl itself.

In May, when Mrs. Hauge had almost finished her work at Casa Grande, two new criteria of selection came from Washington via San Francisco:

1. All families should have, if not practical experience in cooperative endeavor, at least a general knowledge of the aim of cooperation and willingness to commit themselves to cooperative experimentation.

2. Preference will be given to vigorous, alert, resourceful people, who can reasonably be expected to profit from a cooperative agricultural venture.

The new criteria had been designed especially for the Casa Grande project, but (aside from the fact that they came six months too late) they were a futile gesture. By the necessities of the situation the settlers had been drawn from two groups of farm laborers—those who wanted individual farms and those who wanted subsistence grants. Having been referred to the cooperative farm and finding that they could take it or leave it—it was this or nothing, they soon developed a willingness to commit themselves to cooperative experimentation rather than to starvation, or near-starvation. But as for any special adaptability to cooperation or interest in its aims, that would have to be provided *ex post facto*, if at all, for these people were preoccupied by the very practical question of how to survive.

Without exception, they came to Casa Grande because they were poor. The project offered steady wages when any wages were hard to find. It offered food, or at least a chance to grow food. And it offered housing—clean, new homes with inside toilets, hot and cold running water, refrigerators, stoves, and washing machines. These were reasons enough for people who were often hungry, who lived in tents and shacks, and who sometimes were stranded in the ditchbanks because they couldn't buy gasoline to move their jalopies down the road to the next cotton field and the next ditchbank.

There were also alluring promises from Faul (Mrs. Hauge was painstakingly conservative in her advice) that wages would be $70 a month, that the older boys would be hired at the same rates as the men, and that within five years the settlers could easily save enough money to buy farms of their own. Three years later a careful student would conclude that at least a third of the families had actually been promised more than the farm could possibly provide.

There were a few of the settlers, of course, who figured that this was another government project, something like WPA, where a man was entitled to get something for nothing. But there were very few who came to loaf. Mrs. Hauge knew a bum when she saw one, and so did Waldron and Faul.

There were another few—four or five, perhaps—who came because they were poor but for other reasons as well—because they saw, or sensed, that here was an opportunity to build something and to be a part of something—a great, mechanized ranch or a well-ordered community, which would give a man a status and a function in life. Only one of these, a former miner, defined his vision as producer cooperation. Two others called theirs Technocracy. Probably there were others in whom Casa Grande stirred visions that they could not name.

John Hinton, a Texan who came to Arizona as a cotton-picker in 1936 and whose income was $720 in 1937, was one of those who had applied early, hoping to get a 40-acre farm. When the plan was changed he was disappointed, but he did not withdraw his application because, as he explained later, "I couldn't get started by myself."

William Hall, also a Texan, had assets—an old car and some camping equipment—worth $93 when he applied for an individual farm. He stayed on to join the cooperative because he thought he might eventually save enough money to buy a farm of his own.

"When we came, we needed a job," Jake Lewis once said. "We came down here because it was the best thing we could get. I was fired at Tovrrea's (a large livestock-feeding company near Phoenix) for attending a union meeting."

Ernie Bates had been a renter on a 10-cow farm in Oklahoma. He was just about making a living, he said later, and he wouldn't have moved if his wife hadn't insisted on account of her health. They went first to Texas, then to New Mexico, and finally to Arizona where Bates had a sister living near Casa Grande. Bates set up a tent in a near-by cotton field and he and his wife and their four children lived there while he looked for a job. Mrs. Bates learned of the project but when she told Ernie about it he said it was probably a relief project of some kind. The Bates weren't eligible for relief.

But Mrs. Bates persisted, and one Sunday Ernie walked out for a talk with Faul. Faul said wages would be $74 a month with $14 deducted for rent of a three-bedroom house, and that Ernie's oldest boy would be paid $60 a month.

"Sign up," Faul said.

Bates said no, he would bring his family out the next Sunday to look the place over. If they liked it, why, "okie-dokie."

Mrs. Bates liked the house real well and that settled it.

Harry Coker, a native of Illinois, had farmed 2,000 acres of wheat in Montana until drought, grasshoppers, and Depression broke him. He and his wife were farm laborers in Arizona when they applied for an individual farm. Coker was not seriously disappointed when the project became a cooperative. It would be all right if it worked, he figured, and maybe it would.

By the time George Cole was 16 years old he had finished the fourth grade of school. It wasn't that he was a backward boy; his schooling was intermittent because his father, who owned a 50-acre Arkansas farm, often needed him at home. In 1908, after his marriage, Cole became a sharecropper, and that was his life until he came to Arizona in 1937 to pick cotton. Mrs. Hauge found the Coles living in a one-room shack without doors on the edge of a cotton field. "They wish to remain permanently here (in Arizona)," she wrote, "but they see no chance of bettering their condition at present. They are beaten and have very little hope for the future." Noting that the floor of the shack was swept clean and that the table was covered with a cloth, Mrs. Hauge decided that the Coles "show promise of developing into substantial citizens."

Raymond Bowles came back to Oklahoma from France in 1919, married, got a sharecrop farm, and started a small butcher business on the side. In 1936 he and his wife and their three teen-age children set out for Arizona, where Mrs. Hauge found them a year later living in a two-room shack on a canal bank. Bowles worked part-time in a nearby dairy, his wife picked cotton nearly every possible day, and the children earned enough at cotton-picking to pay for their books and school clothes. The family had no assets and no liabilities. Bowles, Mrs. Hauge found, "was a little bit bitter because he could not give his family the advantages he thought they should have."

Charles McCormick was born in South Dakota but he grew up on his father's wheat and dairy ranch in California. When his step-mother asked him to leave, McCormick came to Arizona. Since 1924 he had done farm labor in the vicinity of Mesa. By 1938 he had a family of five and assets worth $200.

Harry Thomas ranched in Texas until 1919, when his first wife fell ill and they moved to Arizona for her health. After her death and his re-marriage, Thomas lived in the outskirts of Phoenix in a three-room house which Mrs. Hauge found scrupulously clean. Somehow Thomas had never managed to do anything except farm labor. In 1937 he was on WPA. When the relief rolls were reduced at the insistence of cotton growers who feared a shortage of picking labor, Thomas applied for a place at Casa Grande.

Wilbur Allen and his wife, both aged 50 and without children, had farmed all their lives in Illinois. A series of floods and droughts ruined them, and in 1937 they came to Arizona because they had heard that farming was good there. Unfortunately the Allens had no money to buy or rent an Arizona farm, so they were glad to join the cooperative—"asking," Mrs. Hauge wrote, "only a place to work and live in security."

Harry Olivier's father, a Phoenix physician, died when Olivier was a youth, leaving him an interest in a small citrus ranch. Olivier worked the ranch until his late twenties, then got a job with a copper roofing company which paid $1,800 in nine months. He was collecting unemployment insurance after this job when he joined the cooperative, which attracted him because "it looked like an opportunity to learn farming on a large scale using modern technology and to have a permanent home and a good way to live." He understood that the cash wages were to be $60 a month and he thought he could live on that temporarily. Mrs. Hauge said not to come if he was thinking of the $60 primarily.

Warren Nelson was 20 years old and his bride was 17 when they moved to Casa Grande and set up housekeeping. Nelson, the son of an Arkansas sharecropper and part Cherokee Indian, believed that the big mechanized farm was an ideal place for a young man like himself, just starting out, to learn something about farming.

Martin King saw a handbill which advertised $1 per hundredweight for cotton-picking. That brought him and his family from Texas to the vicinity of Casa Grande. Across the road from the cotton field where he found work (at 85¢ a hundredweight) was a stretch of desert that looked just as hard as concrete.

"I thought that would be a swell place for a tent," King recalled later. "We had never lived in a tent and we thought it would be swell. Well, after two days of tromping around, that sand was soft for about a foot deep. We thought maybe if we got us a rug it would be O.K. I got an old Axminister for three dollars and we put it on the floor. It took just two days for the sand to work up through, and then you couldn't tell we had a rug."

Mrs. King had been very much dissatisfied with the tent. "I said I was going to quit if I had to stay in a tent," she said later. "I told him he had better get out and rustle me a house."

The house at the project was swell, so Mrs. King decided not to quit.

Ernest S. Perry sharecropped 40 acres in Arkansas until he caught malaria. Then, in 1924, he came to Arizona and got a job in a copper mine at $5.25 a day. Later he and his wife came to Casa Grande because they wanted to join a producers' cooperative.

"We were living on a small farm at Bisbee and my husband worked in the Phelps-Dodge copper mine," Mrs. Perry explained later. "We tried to organize a collective bargaining unit, had a strike, and were fired. Phelps-Dodge is a labor-baiting company that doesn't stop at murder.

"A bunch of us proposed to the Resettlement Administration that they lend us enough money to settle up in Washington—just a loan to help acquire the land and finance us through the first year. We wanted to build our own houses, to have individual houses and perhaps individual farms, but to own our machinery cooperatively and to do the purchasing and marketing cooperatively. Nothing ever came of it.

"We were on relief when we applied. Mrs. Hauge came to see us and we looked the place over. We understood what it was to be, and we decided it would be a good place to settle. We came to stay. My husband and I wanted a co-op farm, not an individual one. From experience in labor unions we know what cooperation means. We like it."

Whether Hinton, who wanted an individual farm, Hall, who hoped to earn enough to buy one, Lewis, who needed a job, Bates, who wasn't eligible for relief and whose wife liked the Casa Grande houses real well, Coker, who thought it would be all right if it worked—whether these and the others (among whom Mr. and Mrs. Perry, who knew and liked cooperation, were solitary exceptions) could make a success of the cooperative farm was anybody's guess in the Spring of 1938. According to the doctrines of the cooperative movement, they would probably fail, for they held to no common core of understanding, faith, or idealism which would unite them in a common struggle. But to the administrators and technicians of the Farm Security Administration the chance of success at Casa Grande seemed good. According to Tugwell's theory, which his successors in FSA shared, it was not a common ideal, but rather a common need, which would hold a group of this kind together and spur its endeavor, and it was not adversity, but help and encouragement, which would provide incentive for success. There was no good reason why cooperation should be more difficult than individualism, and, besides, the most trying responsibility of cooperation, management, would be almost completely in the hands of FSA during the first five or ten years. During that period at least, the only thing required of the settlers would be conscientious and loyal work in their familiar role of farm laborers. Surely that could be expected of Hinton, Hall, Lewis and the others who had suffered so much, and who had so much to gain so easily.

Still, what would happen at Casa Grande was anybody's guess. "Looking into a future that he admits is anything but clear," Waldron, in an interview with the Arizona *Producer* even before the settlers were all selected, expressed some regrets about what had already happened and implied some misgivings of the future. "Waldron believes that other projects will be set up differently, although operated on the same basic principles," the *Producer* said. "He thinks that the group should be organized first instead of selected from among applicants after a project gets underway. Families who know each other, who are friends, and who believe they can get along as partners, should go to the FSA with a definite proposition to buy or rent a certain piece of land. After approval, and arrangement of credit, the homesteaders should themselves perform as much of the construction and other preparatory work as possible. That way they would keep down costs and would probably take more personal interest in something that they had built from the ground up."

4

The First Year

"This beats anything you could find on an individually-owned farm," Harold Bowles, president pro-tem of the association, told a woman reporter for the Tucson *Star* in the Summer of 1938. "Living and working conditions are far better and the $60 a month is better pay than on the average farm. Besides, we've modern houses instead of tents or shacks.

"Dissentions in our group? Well, mostly we don't have time for them and usually they're over minor things and we don't pay any attention."

The reporter asked George Cole if he thought Uncle Sam had put a protective arm around his particular shoulder. "We're earning what we get here," Cole told her. "The government did a good thing in getting up this proposition, but it's up to us to make it pay. If we get a bunch of men in here who'll put their souls in their work, stick together, we'll make it pay us money and pay off our debts."

"I wouldn't be here if I didn't think it was all right," said Raymond Bowles, whom Mrs. Hauge had found "a little bit bitter" a few months earlier. "Nice house, good bunch to work with, good boss, and a chance to make a paying proposition of this set-up—that's a lot to get."

The reporter was entranced by what she saw. "If you want proof of what this farm can do to a family," she wrote, "you should have seen one come in here. There were nine, the woman was defeated, her head hanging. They were all defeated, depressed. They'd been kicked around the country during the depression, lost their farm, everything. Not a hope anywhere except for an occasional day of labor for the father. You should have seen them 30 days later. It takes only a month to turn the trick for any of 'em. The woman's head was up, the kids were clean and wore bright-colored dresses. The man's back was straighter and he had a new look in his eyes."

Ordinarily the men worked on the farm ten hours a day six days a week, with an hour allowed for coming and going to work because their jobs were scattered over 4,000 acres. The pay was $60 a month, with free rent—the value of which varied with the size of the houses from $10 to $14 a month.

Some jobs, like irrigating and tractor driving, had to be done 24 hours a day so on these jobs the men worked in eight-hour shifts. When the pressure of work was great, all of the men were expected to put in overtime. This was credited to them, and they were allowed to make it up by taking extra time off.

Faul was both the government's supervisor (or creditor's representative) and the cooperative's manager. Regional Director Garst had intended that he be paid in the latter capacity by the association as soon as it was in operation, but, in view of the water shortage which was severely hampering the farm, Garst decided it would be best to continue him on the FSA payroll until the cooperative was safely through its first period of trial. In his dual capacity, representing both the government and the association, Faul was in direct charge of every aspect of project administration and farm operation.

Faul was not a man to slight any of his duties or authorities. At seven each morning he climbed on the tailboard of a wagon, the men crowded around, and he bawled out the day's assignments. "He used to swear like hell," one of the men recalled later. "He said he sure admired Hitler and Mussolini, and that was the way he ran this place."

No detail of the day's operations escaped him. Almost never in his office, he appeared first in one field and then in another, giving detailed instructions in the smallest matters—"snooping," some of the men said. One of the settlers, speaking quite literally, said later that Faul would come around to tell a man how to hold a shovel. Despite this close supervision there was some shirking, Faul believed, and this he handled—he once told a reporter—"very well by having a talk with the man's wife. Somehow the woman folks manage their men pretty well. The men stop shirking, and I don't ask how it came about."

The women were also under Faul's supervision. He required for example, that all clotheslines be strung from north to south. The purpose of this ruling, he explained, was not so much to create an orderly appearance as to prevent sheets from flapping against other laundry in the wind.

Faul did not forget that when 13 settlers were called together early in February to amend the by-laws there was some danger that they would try to take control of the association into their own hands. One of his first acts, after his authority was firmly established, was to fire two settlers who had been ringleaders in the movement to displace him, and, although the by-laws required quarterly membership meetings, he permitted none to be held during 1938. When the Board of Directors met, Faul usually stayed away and then made a point of doing the opposite of what the Board had recommended. Not only Faul, but Waldron and Garst also, were inclined to think that there had already been too much idealistic talk about cooperation. The settlers would have to reconcile themselves to government management for a while; the thing they needed most to learn was not cooperation or self-government, but to accept the discipline of management—first the government's management, then later their own. This was a lesson which Faul was well suited to teach.

The *Star* reporter found only one settler who was dissatisfied with the project early in August, 1938. He was a native of Arizona who complained that too much tractor driving would be bad for his kidneys. Although the reporter made no mention of it, many of the settlers hated and feared Faul. But there were others, among them Perry, who agreed that the cooperative needed a hard taskmaster, and even those who disliked Faul had to admit that he was a man of great force and drive—it would be hard to fail under as tough a driver as Faul.

Despite Faul's nagging and the hard work of the farm, life at the project was very pleasant and full of excitement. There were "sings," picnics, pie dinners, dances, home demonstration classes, a vacation camp 80 miles away at Peppersauce Canyon, and, of course, the novelty of the new houses with their plumbing appliances and the new neighbors. The principal of the Kennilworth school at Florence recalled three years later that when the project children first enrolled they seemed to expect a picnic or something special every day. That was the way it had been, for the grown-ups as well as the children, on the cooperative farm in the summer of 1938.

Late in the summer the general satisfaction was dissipated by an event from which the settlers would date all subsequent happenings—wages were cut from $60 to $52 a month.

As Harry Olivier, one of the most articulate of the settlers, described it three years later, this is what happened:

"Mr. Waldron came down and suggested that we give a big feed for some FSA people who were coming. We did. I sat at an end table (that was my fault, I guess) and there were nine of us with three water glasses and a couple of dishes of fried potatoes. Up at the center was a table with Mrs. Hauge, Waldron, Shelly (Waldron's assistant), and others. That table was just loaded down with food—running all over. But did they ever think of passing it? We passed water glasses and fried potatoes.

"Then Waldron got up and announced a wage cut of $8—for rent, he said. Mrs. Hauge said that would be taken care of on the books. There was no discussion. It was simply announced."

Until the cut, the settlers received a "basic monthly allowance" of $60. The allowance was still $60, but now the settlers were to be charged rent which up to this time had been free. The rent of a three-room house was $8, and this would be deducted from his allowance before the settler received it. (The rent of the four and five-bedroom houses was $2 and $4 a month more, but these extra charges would be carried on the books of the association and deducted from the householders' future dividends.) Thus the cash income of the settler would be $52 a month. From this he would have to pay $2 a month for the rent of his furniture.

The reason for the change was that FSA had not charged the association any rent until June, when its lease became effective, and so the association had not had to pass any house rent charge on to the settlers. When the association began paying rent under its lease, Waldron thought for a time of having it carry the settlers' house rent on its books as credit to be deducted from future dividends. This had been the original plan, but now, in view of the water shortage, it seemed wiser to have the settlers pay their rent in cash. Since the association's earnings for the year would be distributed among the settlers anyway, it made no difference, in Waldron's opinion, whether they were distributed as a monthly allowance, house rent credits, or dividends—except (and this was very important) that if the monthly allowance were set too high the settlers might easily be paid more than the association earned. It was important to the FSA for public relations reasons that the association should meet its obligations to the government in full and on time, and it was even more important that the settlers should learn the necessity of keeping the allowance well under the cooperative's probable earnings. To be soft on this point now might cause serious trouble later.

Had he realized how his announcement would shock the settlers, Waldron might have taken pains to explain it. He supposed that they realized that the amount of the allowance had not been definitely fixed. The Work and Occupancy Agreement which they had all signed guaranteed only that they would be paid not less than $1.50 a day. Moreover, Mrs. Hauge had warned all of the families at their first interview that while wages would be $60 at the start they should not come to Casa Grande unless they could get by on $50, if that should be necessary.

There was no doubt that Mrs. Hauge gave the warning conscientiously, even though Faul had not. All the same, the news of the cut came as a surprise to the settlers, and they looked at it through quite different eyes than Waldron. Some of them had worked at 35¢ an hour for FSA before the association began operating; after eight or ten months at $60 or more, $52 seemed very little. As for the theory that they would eventually get all of the association's earnings in dividends, if not in allowances, the settlers distrusted it. To Waldron's exasperation, they always referred to the allowance as their wages—if they understood the difference, which was doubtful in most cases, they refused to recognize it. As they viewed the situation, this was an arbitrary and unjust wage cut. It was the kind of a thing one might expect from a private employer, but not on a government project like this.

Of course, even if the prospect of a labor bonus was not taken into account, the settlers were still far better off than the migratory cotton pickers in the community and considerably better off than the year-round workers who were the aristocrats of Pinal County farm labor. At $52 the cash allowance equalled, or very nearly equalled the prevailing wage for year-round workers, which was $2 a day. The settlers had housing which was incomparably better than any private employer provided. They received vegetables without charge from the community garden, and, if they wished, had the use of a team to plow and cultivate their individual, home-plot gardens. Most farm laborers who had year round jobs could keep a few chickens and a family cow, whereas the settlers had to buy their milk, eggs, and butter, but of course the settlers were being paid to produce this food for their own consumption. Moreover—and this was unheard of among farm laborers—the members of the cooperative received two weeks vacation with pay and whatever sick leave they required.

Still, as the settlers saw it, a wage cut was a wage cut no matter what anybody said to the contrary. "If they're going to pay $52, they'll get $52 worth of work," one man said, and there were many who felt the same way.

Fifty-two dollars worth of work was not enough to satisfy Faul or Waldron. When the settlers showed their reaction to the wage cut in their work, Faul proposed to abolish the monthly allowance entirely and put the men on an hourly basis or, where possible, on piecework. This was common practice on most big farms, and, as Faul pointed out, it gave management a whip hand—a man who loafed for an hour or who wasn't needed for an hour wouldn't be paid for the lost time. Waldron agreed that some changes was needed; morale was at a very low ebb. However he thought Faul's remedy was too drastic—it might leave some families without the necessary minimum of cash for subsistence. He proposed instead a system of graduated wages in a letter to Faul:

"I have been giving the matter of the wage-scale problem very careful thought, and I am firmly convinced that we are using the wrong policy. The paying of the same wage scale to all people on the ranch has a deadening effect that I do not believe can be overcome, as there is no incentive for a man to work for advancement. Consequently the morale is, and always will be, at a very low ebb. I fully appreciate that under any system that may be used there will be disgruntled members, but I am likewise firmly convinced that there will be fewer disgruntled members where there is some reward for real merit than where merit and ability are in no way recognized.

"We have given the present policy a good trial, and, without question, it is going to lead to a final breakdown of our cooperative. Our good men will gradually move out, leaving only the dregs, and instead of a cooperative we will have, in fact, nothing more than a Fascist concentration camp under the iron hand of a dictator. You noticed yesterday that the better men are getting discouraged. I fully appreciate that the plan we have to follow is much the harder way. However, in my opinion our big job in operating the Casa Grande Valley Farms is not building buildings, leveling land, putting in street lighting, or even making the mechanics of the ranch operation move smoothly, important as these are; but it is developing people, and that is always a long, hard, discouraging job. I do not believe that holding out future dividends is a sufficient inducement to keep up morale.

"I think without question the answer to the present problem is the adoption of a graduated scale of wages. In others words, classify the jobs and fill them gradually with men who have proved themselves. You, as farm manager, will have plenty of opportunity to exercise judgment in the selection of your individuals, using a firm hand and handling the matter on an impersonal basis. I am firmly convinced that there will be very little criticism of a program of this kind.

"Jobs requiring no responsibility, such as irrigators, hay pitchers, sack handlers, or manure haulers will simply draw the straight $50 a month and furnished house.

"As regards cotton-picking, which serves as a very good example of the lack of effort put forth by the individuals because of lack of incentive and of the deadening effect of the standard wage scale, I believe that instead of discarding your monthly wage entirely and putting them on a contract basis it would be much wiser to maintain the families on the regular $50 wage scale, but send the men who are available for that purpose to the field to pick cotton with the understanding that all cotton picked by each individual will be weighed; and if the head of the family is able to pick, for example, 300 lbs. of cotton a day, 200 lbs., or any other satisfactory figure, the 300 lbs. will be paid for by the regular monthly wage, and for all cotton above that amount he will get the established contract price for cotton picking.

"In this way good cotton pickers will be rewarded for their effort, and those who simply cannot pick cotton because of lack of experience will still be able to earn their monthly wage, and not jeopardize their family incomes. I do not think it would be fair to say to an individual that his family monthly wage is going to be stopped and that he is going to pick cotton on a contract basis when he never has picked cotton and, through lack of experience and ability, cannot make as much as his monthly wage. The man is there, ready to work, and I think he has the right under our by-laws to receive a reasonable reward for honest effort. Likewise, this method does reward the man who can excel. Of course the contract price would apply to cotton picked by other members of the family.

"This sort of a system gives you a chance to reward your good men and a chance to discipline those who will not work for the benefit of the cooperative. Under your present method, you cannot discipline a member, for, by so doing, you will take food from his family because the wage scale is so low."

Waldron's plan was adopted, and Faul appointed a general foreman and several sub-foremen, not because he felt he needed assistance in running the project but because it seemed logical to accompany the extra pay under the graduated wage system with some kind of title which would suggest added authority or responsibility. The foremen got very little authority, but neither did they get much extra money, for the bonuses ranged from $2 a month to $8 for the general foreman.

Faul had never troubled to conceal his contempt for the settlers, and, as the year wore on, his manner toward them became more and more harsh. He seemed to enjoy being feared. Garst, who believed in great firmness, had not bargained for this senseless bullying and he saw that as long as it continued the settlers would learn nothing about self-management. Besides, there was danger that Faul might do something that would seriously embarrass the administration. He had, in fact, built a warehouse without asking approval. The building violated the architecture of the project and since Faul had ignored the government's purchasing procedure there was some question whether FSA could pay the bills he had contracted. Highhandedness could be carried too far. In December, 1939 Garst asked for Faul's resignation.

"Faul took the position of a dictator," Garst explained in a letter to the Administrator. "I had thought he would last about two years because I knew he was a dictatorial type, but we really should have got rid of him about last September. He did a very good job on organizing a co-op and carrying it through the original land leveling and construction stage, while it was getting started. He turned out to be a most peculiar individual. He admitted that if the co-op were ever to take over the management, they would never do it under his direction because he had them all so scared of him that they would not even talk to him."

Faul's resignation was news from coast to coast because of an interview he gave the Associated Press.

"From my knowledge of the Soviet economic set-up, I would say about the only difference between this cooperative farm plan and that operated in Russia is that the government is paid its share of the gross income in cash instead of in kind," Faul told the AP. The farmers, he conceded, were "conservative minded and probably don't realize or care that the project is basically communal."

When the AP called him for comment on Faul's charges, Waldron tried to explain and justify the project by describing improvements in the settlers' level of living. "Most of the project's tenants," he said, "came from cotton-pickers' shacks right here in the Gila Valley. Good food, hard work and decent living conditions not only have filled these people out physically, but it has broadened their outlook."

The AP story provoked a flurry of editorial comment from newspapers all over the country, most of it sympathetic to Faul. This was the first notoriety the cooperative farm had received, and it was a matter of concern to the FSA Administrator in Washington. Garst, who was amused by Faul's outburst, wrote to reassure the Administrator: "My own answer to that statement is that I have never been able to find out about a Russian cooperative farm, but I think we pattern closely after Allen Hoover's farm in the San Joaquin Valley. Faul's statement had no effect whatever in Arizona; as a matter of fact, I think the reaction was rather favorable."

Leonard Tompkins, one of the settlers, took much the same view as the Regional Director. "I'm no Communist," Tompkins said, "—but more of a hired hand."

Faul's successor had to be chosen at once. The farm was too large and complex a business to be without a manager for even a few days, and if there were delay in filling the position the settlers might use the interval to seize control of the association. Fortunately a suitable man for the position was already on the FSA payroll as a rehabilitation supervisor. Waldron was able to introduce him to the settlers as their new manager even before Faul had departed.

Ralph E. Beatty, a calm, quiet man of 45 who had graduated from Ohio State University and operated a 550-acre Ohio stock farm before coming to Arizona in 1933 as agriculturalist for a Federal transient camp, made a good impression on the settlers in his first appearance before them. Waldron had told Beatty of the mistakes Faul had made, and the new manager took pains to assure the settlers that henceforth their Board of Directors would be consulted and no one would be fired without a hearing. Beatty said he was aware that there was some feeling that the foremen should be elected by the membership. He could not agree to this, but if the men he appointed did not work out well he would change them. "It was a swell speech," Harry Olivier said later.

Garst regarded Beatty as a very happy choice. His college training and his practical experience were in animal husbandry; since livestock was to be the most important of the farm's enterprises, this was the background needed in a manager. To be sure, Beatty had no practical experience with irrigation farming or with row crops like cotton, but his general training in scientific agriculture outweighed this lack, and, after all, no one could be a specialist in everything. And, whereas Faul had been paid $3,000, Beatty was to get only $2,300.

The Administrator, anxious to avoid another mistake in the choice of a manager, asked for a special report before confirming his appointment. "He is a rather slow, unexcitable individual," Garst replied. "My first impression was that he looked a bit leaded. However, I think I was really wrong in this analysis because on talking over the problems of Casa Grande with him he showed plenty of energy. Our real problem at Casa Grande is going to get to be to keep it from getting out of hand. There is likely to be a tendency on the part of all homesteaders, with Faul removed, to try to manage the co-op themselves, but as I have always pointed out to them, I am sure the essential feature of a cooperative production organization is that the individuals give up their right of management. I feel sure that Beatty will get this in hand. I really think you need have no concern about Beatty."

When the books were closed at the end of 1938, they showed a loss of $3,069 on the first year's operations. The farm had made a small profit in cotton and grain, but this was more offset by losses on the dairy and poultry enterprises.

On the whole, the first year's financial record was encouraging. It takes time to bring a new farm into profitable production, especially a farm the size of Casa Grande. The cooperative had been operating only ten months at the end of 1938 and with only 2,432 of its 3,200 irrigable acres leveled and available for use. On much of this land it had been necessary to plant alfalfa, from which there would be no return for nearly a year. The beef cattle on which the farm would depend heavily in a normal year could not even be purchased until the feed had been grown to fatten them. In the case of the dairy herd, it was necessary to assemble the cows and acclimate them to their new surroundings before any profit could be expected. The poultry was being raised from chicks, and that too was a matter that couldn't be hurried. Even under favorable circumstances, an experienced farmer would not expect to make a profit from an enterprise like Casa Grande in its first two or three years.

And in 1938 circumstances had been far from favorable. Because of the drought, the San Carlos Irrigation District had supplied only 2.49 acre-feet of water—about a foot less than it had supplied to the same land in each of the three previous years. The project planners had foreseen the possibility of a water shortage and they had provided a deep well to supplement the surface supply. However the Indian Service maintained that the well infringed the water rights of a nearby reservation, and the cooperative had not been able to use it. Although it had an allotment of 1,300 acres, the association could plant only 925 acres of cotton because of the water shortage—and cotton was to have been the main cash crop in the first year.

Despite these handicaps, the farm had met its payroll—$30,904 to members (an average of $475 per family for the ten months) and $541 to non-members, and it had paid $16,740 in rent to FSA, which was almost double the minimum rent called for in the lease. By the end of the year most of the rough land had been leveled, 450 acres had been seeded to alfalfa, and a dairy herd of 66 cows (42 milking) had been built up to the point where it was producing 110 gallons of milk a day with an average butterfat content of 4.25 percent. The 1988 cotton crop averaged two bales to the acre, almost twice the ordinary yield in the vicinity, and, toward the end of the year, 900 white leghorn pullets were producing eggs. Even so, the farm was not yet fully developed; it would be necessary to buy hay to feed the cows through the winter and there was still more land to level. Not until well into 1939 could the farm be expected to reach its normal level of operation.

When the *Star* reporter returned to the farm for a visit in the first days of January, 1939, she decided that lack of irrigation water and government red tape—"far more than any sociological problems among the farming population"—might cause the project to collapse. The danger of water shortage was real enough; the drought had continued and it was already evident when the reporter visited the farm that it might get even less water in 1939 than in 1938. As to the red tape, the reporter was unduly alarmed. A window pane in the community house could not be replaced because the proper government requisition form could not be found, and, some months ago, a crop had not been sown because a tractor got caught in red tape. These matters were not as serious as she supposed, for the association was not restricted by government procedure. The window and, at that particular time, the tractor were rented from the government. If, like most landlords, the government was slow about making repairs, the matter was certainly not crucial.

The reporter felt that the government had relaxed its control over the project somewhat since Faul's departure a few days earlier. "Since the cooperative was established by the government, it [i.e., the government] has some dictatorial powers in the management of the farm," she wrote. "That management has just been relaxed to a certain extent with the change in administration from R. A. Faul, who was with it from its inception, to R. E. Beatty. The government now wishes to test the ability of the farmers to cooperate and direct themselves to a greater extent than before."

Stopping at a house she chose at random, the reporter found Mr. and Mrs. Tompkins and their children, Ann, six, and Wilma, four, preparing for supper. Mrs. Tompkins was stirring frying potatoes and putting corn meal in the oven. The house was clean, neat, lived in, happy.

"We didn't live in a shack before we came on this project," Tompkins, a native of Arizona who had earned $375 in 1937 by working on his father's farm, told the reporter with feeling. "Our home was comfortable, as nice as anyone's. We came on the project because it was painted rosy to us. It's not as rosy as we were told, but we still think we have a chance of working things out."

5

Progress Report

From Regional Director Garst's point of view, Ralph Beatty turned out to be just the kind of manager the project needed. He had none of Faul's harshness or his egocentricity. He was in fact an exceedingly quiet, mild, and unassuming man. Yet there was an unyielding quality about Beatty—the firmness of a professional who doesn't argue because he knows.

As a professional, Beatty knew the rules of the farm management game and adhered to them painstakingly, expecting others would do so also as a matter of course. The rules contained nothing complicated or subtle. A manager's job was to run a farm as profitably as possible, to give the workers fair treatment, and to carry out the orders of his employers. A worker's job was to take orders from his boss and carry them out as well as he could. If he felt he was not being fairly treated or well enough paid, the worker could quit. If he didn't do his job willingly or satisfactorily, he could expect to be fired. "Mr. Beatty is down to earth," an interviewer for the *Christian Science Monitor* wrote, ". . . the kind of a man who might have made Brook Farm in New England, a century ago, an agricultural instead of a literary success, if Dana and Dwight and Ripley had hired him."

Since it was an agricultural instead of a literary success that the Farm Security Administration was seeking at Casa Grande and since, presumably, the farm laborers there held to the same code as Beatty, there was every reason to expect good results from his management. It was true, Garst would probably have conceded, that eventually the Casa Grande community should have some of the attributes of the literary conception of a cooperative. But the first essential, the *sine non qua*, was to do a businesslike job of farming. If that were done, the settlers would in time learn a different code—and so would Beatty. Meanwhile Beatty was to manage the Casa Grande farm as he would any other big farm.

As he would on any other farm, Beatty appointed foremen and delegated responsibility to them. He named a foreman for each of the farm's enterprises—livestock, dairy, poultry, and field crops—, a machinery foreman, an irrigation foreman, and, to supervise the others, a general foreman. If there was a question about the work to be done or a suggestion to be made, a settler went to his immediate foreman or, if he liked, to the general foreman, a settler named Coker. Beatty himself was seldom seen in the fields or barns, and no one could ever accuse him of snooping or cracking the whip. In fact it was difficult for a settler who was not a foreman to see Beatty at all. Conversations with him were rare and always brief, for he was lonely (his wife had recently died) and shy and he believed, professionally, that contact between the manager and the workers should be avoided lest it weaken the position of the foremen.

From the beginning the management staff had included a bookkeeper and a typist. After the first year, a year of development, more assistance was needed. Under the title of project clerk a young man named Wildermuth, a recent graduate of an agricultural college, functioned in a capacity which was almost that of assistant manager. He bought supplies and with very little direction from Beatty took charge of the dairy and poultry enterprises. Beatty himself took direct charge of the livestock enterprises and most of his time was taken up with the buying and selling of livestock.

The importance of the livestock enterprise in the farm's economy grew steadily because that was Beatty's specialty and because continuing drought limited the acreage that could be planted to cotton. In 1939 the San Carlos Irrigation District delivered only 2.53 acre-feet and in 1940 only 2.46. The dispute with the Indian Bureau continued, so that the deep well on the project could not be used. Under the circumstances there was no alternative but to put more land in grain and pasture, and to depend on shrewd buying and selling of stock to supplement the reduced income from cotton. This suited Beatty perfectly, for he had very little experience with cotton and he was tremendously interested in stock—a fact which may have helped to convince him that the future of the farm, even in times of normal water supply, lay chiefly in the development of the hog and beef cattle enterprises, a task to which he devoted most of his attention.

Because of the drought, FSA refrained from requiring the association to pay the salaries of Beatty, Wildermuth, and the bookkeeper. Strictly speaking, Beatty was paid, not for managing the cooperative, but for seeing to it that the terms of the loan agreement were carried out—a position in which he had authority "to conduct the business of the borrower in all its branches." Although it did not pay any part of his salary, the association, by vote of its Board of Directors, "employed" Beatty as its manager, so that he was also responsible, if only technically, to the Board. In this nominal capacity he attended meetings of the Board and gave careful, detailed reports whenever called upon. He accepted recommendations from the Board and gave them his consideration, but he did not accept instructions from the Board, nor did he engage in discussions with it. Discussion was not his way, and, manifestly, the Board was not his employer.

Waldron, Beatty's immediate superior, had been a farm manager himself and the two men got along well together, which was one reason why Garst, who valued Waldron highly, had selected Beatty. Although he rarely interfered in the day-to-day management of the farm, Waldron made the policy decisions in matters affecting the project and he also made whatever explanations were considered necessary to the settlers. Beatty had made it plain from the start that he was not much of a man to make speeches or to expound social theories; that kind of thing might have its place, but it was not part of a farm manager's job. If he wished, Beatty could ask Waldron's advice on technical matters or he could have the regional farm management specialist visit the farm to work out some special problems. In the fall of each year he was required to work out a detailed farm budget for the coming year. This was submitted to Waldron, to the regional director's staff in San Francisco, and to Washington, but changes were seldom required from any of these sources, although some might be suggested. On the whole, Beatty was free to run the farm pretty much as he would any other farm.

Judged by the usual standards, he ran it well. In 1939 the farm's average per-acre yield of cotton was 725 pounds, which was 113 pounds more than the average for the county as a whole; the barley yield was 2,031 pounds per acre, as against 1,500 for the county as a whole; the wheat yield was 1,926 pounds, as against 1,200 pounds for the county as a whole, and production of hegari silage was 11½ tons to the acre, as against a county average of 8½ tons. At the end of 1940 the farm had 1,244 head of beef cattle, 698 hogs, 138 mature dairy cattle and 89 head of young dairy stock, and 1,520 chickens. All of the stock was producing well—far better than the average. The cows, for example, produced an average of 371.6 pounds of butterfat in 1940, an amount which kept them usually at the top of the

Arizona herd-testing association's list of more than 50 herds. The hens laid an average of 13½ dozen eggs in 1940. The pigs averaged 8.44 to a litter and of these 8.03 survived. These were all indications of a well-run farm. Perhaps only a few "showplace" farms in Arizona could point to such good records.

The profit from the farm was very small nevertheless—$1,513 in 1939 and $7,274 in 1940—and, although the association's assets had increased to $228,980 by the end of 1940, its net worth was only $4,075. The dairy and poultry enterprises had incurred losses in both 1939 and 1940. There had been a good profit—$12,704—from crops in 1939, and a small loss from the newly-established beef enterprise. In 1940 it was the other way around— there was a small loss on the crops, while the livestock enterprise made $12,375. Commenting on the 1940 operations, Beatty said that the dairy would have broken even if it had not been for death losses, a high rate of depreciation, and the problem of finding and keeping good milkers among the settlers. The death loss among the chickens was 35%, a figure he said was not above average for hot climate areas. With characteristic brevity he explained the loss on the 1940 cropping program: "Operations show loss of $3,312.59. The entire amount of this loss was on alfalfa. Chief reason for loss was lack of water for irrigation. Barely enough to make one cutting. All crops had to be charged with full water assessment, which practically doubled cost for the actual water run."

While it had only a very small profit to show after three years, the cooperative was at least solvent, which was something of an accomplishment in view of the drought and the difficulties inherent in bringing a new farm into production. It had paid its rent to the government in full and on time—$13,633 in 1939 and $18,151 in 1940, and it had met its payroll.

The settlers were still receiving $52 as their cash monthly allowance at the end of 1940, and of course there had been no labor bonus. Although the wage rate remained disappointingly low, the association's payroll was considerably higher than its circumstances justified; the drought and the consequent shift from cotton to cattle had reduced the farm's labor requirements, but there had not been a corresponding reduction in the number of settlers. Even in the planning stage it had been impossible to show how the full quota of members could be kept profitably employed all year around. Now the problem was greatly accentuated. On another farm Beatty would have been at liberty to discharge workers who were not really needed; indeed, it would have been required of him. Here, on the contrary, he was obliged to keep all those who wanted to stay, even though the expense of their unneeded labor reduced the farm's profits and therefore the wage rate of all the members.

Some settlers had chosen to leave the project, and this eased the problem. In 1939 five settlers (including Tompkins, who had told the *Star* reporter earlier in the year that he still thought there was a chance of working things out) withdrew, and in 1940 seven more left Casa Grande. Waldron and Beatty would have been content to leave the vacancies unfilled, for the 45 remaining members were about twice as many permanent workers as were really needed. Unfortunately (but probably not by accident, since they were the only skilled workers on the farm) many of those who withdrew were milkers whose places could not be filled from among the remaining settlers whose experience, in most cases, did not go beyond cotton picking. Beatty had been obliged to recruit three or four new members to fill out the dairy crew, so that at the end of 1940 the membership of the cooperative stood at 48. Considering that the dairy enterprise had been established chiefly to provide work for the settlers, that it had incurred a loss each year, and that the payroll, which was already too high, had to be further increased to maintain it, there was some irony in the situation, an irony that was not altogether lost on the settlers.

Although they still received only $52 a month in cash, the position of the settlers remained better than that of most year-round laborers in the vicinity, for the prevailing wage in Pinal County was still $2 a day late in 1940. Compared with what it had been before they came to Casa Grande, the situation of the families was much improved, although they were still far from prosperous.

In 1940 the average family (there were seven who had been members eight months or less) had an income of $804. Employment on the cooperative farm accounted for $692 of this, and other farm employment (of family labor, chiefly) accounted for $73. The value of food produced for family use on the home plots was very small—only $6 on the average. "Other income" was $33. The expenses of the average family (which FSA, the source of these figures, reported skeptically because some families kept inadequate records and others padded their expenses) were $1,018.

The chief items of expense were food, $434, clothing, $83, purchase of capital goods, $40, payment on old debts, $38, and health care.

The debts of the average family amounted to $114. Debts for medical care—$58—were the largest item; automobile debts (12 of the 41 members who owned cars at the end of 1940 were in debt for them) were $18, debts for household goods $15, and other debts, $23.

The relatively large amounts owed for medical care reflected the fact that the families were now securing the health attention they needed. Virtually all of the families received some kind of health care during 1940 and the total for the group was very large:

Home Calls by nurses	31	14
Office Calls by nurses	153	22
Home calls by doctors	69	23
Office calls by doctors	431	37
Teeth filled	24	4
Teeth extracted	161	26
Sets of false teeth procured	4	4
Pairs of eye glasses procured	14	12
Days hospitalization	238	25

The settlers required most of this care to repair the neglect of former years, but, despite the attention they were now receiving, the signs of that neglect were still visible. Mrs. Hauge noted a general and very decided improvement in health after three years of project life; the families were no longer emaciated, as they had been in many cases on arrival at Casa Grande, but the contrast between the older and the younger children was striking—those who had lived at the project since infancy were vigorous, normal children, while their older brothers and sisters, whose early years had been spent elsewhere, were noticeably weaker.

Because of the water shortage, the farm's financial record had been disappointing in the first three years. Yet, despite handicaps, the farm was paying its bills and supporting its members—supporting them more dependably and at a better level than most of the other farms they could remember. If it was too early for FSA to claim success for the project, it was not too early to point out the advantages of large-scale, cooperative organization which had already proved themselves over three difficult years. These advantages were described to a Congressional committee late in 1940 by Laurence I. Hewes Jr., who had succeeded Garst as regional director early in the year:

"The figures indicate that large savings have been effected through pooling the buying and selling power of the 50 or more families involved. This is especially evident in the livestock enterprise. During the past year 679 head of hogs have been marketed in the Los Angeles market, approximately a carload being shipped at a time. These hogs have consistently topped the market by 10¢ to 15¢ per hundredweight.

"Theoretically the ranch is supposed to support 60 families, or, since the size of the project is 3,600 acres, one family to each 60 acres. Farmers operating individual units of this size and producing in small quantities could not have shipped in carload lots and, unable to meet the proportionately higher freight costs, would have sold to a neighborhood buyer, and so would have been unable to obtain the higher prices of a terminal market.

"While there are 775 head of beef cattle on the ranch, most of these are mature animals being carried over a long feeding period on pasture. Approximately two carloads of cattle were marketed during the year and topped the market for the grades involved. After deducting all expenses, a gain of 70¢ per hundred pounds was realized over prices current at local packing houses, again showing the advantage of being able to ship cooperatively to a terminal market.

"The association sold 400 bales of cotton in one lot in the fall of 1939, at $10.60 per hundred pounds. No report of higher sales has been obtained in the community, but this is much above the average received by small operators at the time when this cotton was being sold. Undoubtedly one half cent more per pound was realized because of the quality of the cotton and the size of the lot. Any one of the members of the cooperative, if he had sold his eight or ten bales of cotton individually in the open market would have been greatly handicapped and probably penalized at least a cent or more.

"The farm operates a Grade A dairy, the herd consisting of approximately 135 milking cows with about 90 head of young dairy cattle. The size of the herd and volume produced makes it possible to provide the refrigerating equipment necessary for marketing high class produce under the desert weather conditions that prevail during most of the year. These facilities, together with the volume produced by as large a herd as the one at Casa Grande, makes it possible to obtain a market for Grade A milk at Tucson, 65 miles distant where much of the milk is marketed. The balance is being more and more sought after by local distributors in the nearby towns of Coolidge and Florence. Practically all of the milk during the past year has been sold as Grade A, realizing from 15 to 20 cents more per pound butterfat than for manufacturing milk. It is very doubtful that any individual farmer operating on a 60 acre farm could meet the requirements of production and competition that govern the selling of Grade A milk.

"The buying power of these families is materially increased through the cooperative association. All machinery was purchased at 15 percent discount through local dealers. The feed concentrates necessary to balance the farm-produced rations are purchased at carlot prices. There is a saving of at least 50 cents per hundred pounds on mixed poultry feeds because of the volume bought.

"In the physical operation of the property, men can be selected according to their ability to do certain types of work and their time and efforts used to a maximum, effecting a continuous economy. Another saving is very apparent when it is noted that the ranch operates with twenty head of mules and horses, including three saddle horses used in handling the beef cattle. Heavy mechanical equipment consists of two Diesel tractors, one four-wheel tractor and three row-type tractors. If the ranch were cut into 60 individual 60 acre farms the number of machines would be much greater, increasing capital debt as well as operating costs.

"During the serious droughts of the past two years it has been necessary to make the maximum use of irrigation water. Because the size of the farm makes quantity use possible, there is a rate advantage and ability to shift the water from one part of the farm to the other has made it possible to get much more effective use of irrigation water than would have been possible if all the families operated on 60 acre farms. It is conservatively estimated that the increase in production brought about by this type of water is approximately one-third.

"One of the larger values of this type of farming in my opinion, while difficult to evaluate in monetary terms, is the educational training the farmers and their families get by working in a diversified and completely organized cooperative farm enterprise. This is just beginning to show results. Recently the herdsman who had been handling the dairy herd for the past two years, got a job as herdsman with a large dairy in the locality at 50 per cent increase in salary and with house furnished. He came to the Casa Grande project without any special experience in dairying except as a milker in one of the dairies in the Salt River Valley and was formerly a cotton picker.

"The man handling the poultry plant has shown unusual development. He knew nothing of poultry when he started working in the plant about two years ago.

"The farm is proving to be a very fine training institution for young people, since they are able to gain experience in the handling of machinery and livestock in a much more effective manner than would be possible on small individually operated farms. A young couple from two of the families on the ranch recently married and asked to become members of the Association. This was not granted because the Board of Directors felt it was not desirable to have too many members of the same family on the ranch. However, due to the young man's experience with the project dairy herd he got a job as milker with one of the high-standard dairies in the Salt River Valley at a good wage."

Hewes had been regional director somewhat less than a year when he made the statement quoted above. In this time he had visited the project at least twice and, although he could not be called familiar with it, he had seen enough at Casa Grande to convince him that FSA's policy there should be changed. Unlike Garst and Garst's predecessor, Packard, Hewes had no background as an agriculturalist. He had been in the investment banking business before he joined the California Emergency Relief Administration and, later, the Washington staff of the Resettlement Administration. Having no technical interest in agriculture and, as a militant, urban liberal, having many suspicions of the agrarian point of view, Hewes was by no means content that Casa Grande should promise good success as an agricultural venture. It might succeed agriculturally and yet fail dismally in other more important respects—in the creation of democratic social values, for example, an objective which, while it could not be obtained apart from financial success, was by no means subordinate to it. Whereas Garst had seen the cooperative chiefly as a device through which the government could demonstrate a method for distributing the earnings of a large-scale farm among the farm laborers, Hewes conceived it as an experiment in economic democracy.

Hewes was not committed to the orthodoxy of the cooperative movement, but he had a great deal more respect for it than did his predecessors. He believed that a cooperative should be run in democratic fashion by its members; that it should offer them a wide range of educational advantages, and that fundamentally, since its purpose was as much moral as economic, a producers' cooperative should represent a challenge, a more or less conscious and deliberate challenge, to the predatory spirit of the times. As Hewes thought of it, cooperation was not merely a convenient form of organization—it was an enlightened principle of conduct, which, at Casa Grande, should be exemplified in ways that would create a superior, if not a model, community. The success of other big farms might be a purely pecuniary matter, but Casa Grande, to be a real and significant success, would have to demonstrate the moral superiority of cooperation as a basis of group life.

On his first visits to Casa Grande Hewes saw plainly enough that the project was demonstrating nothing of the sort. The cooperators were merely farm laborers working under Beatty's direction. They were better off than other farm laborers, it was true, but they had made no progress toward self-management in business affairs or self-government in community life. It was even doubtful that they understood the first principles of cooperative organization; there had been rumors from the project that some of the settlers were considering a strike, or a demonstration of some kind, to force higher wages from the management. In Hewes' eyes the threat of a strike made it perfectly plain that Waldron and Beatty had failed to teach the settlers the most elementary lessons about cooperative organization, for surely if they realized that they were their own employers the settlers would not strike against themselves.

Since he was a practical man and a responsible administrator, Hewes did not suppose that the character of the cooperative could be changed overnight or that the settlers could safely be trusted to manage so large an enterprise. He was not inclined to take any action which would jeopardize the financial success of the farm or the security of the government's loan. He respected Beatty's abilities as an agriculturalist and he knew that Beatty took the job as manager on the understanding that he would not be expected to look after social or educational matters. All the same, Hewes was determined to start the Casa Grande project on the way of becoming a moral, as well as an agricultural, success.

What was needed was a thoroughgoing educational program to teach the settlers the real meaning of cooperation and to stimulate and direct the development of democratic community life. It was unlikely that any man could be found who had the right combination of abilities and experience to do both the educational and the farm management job, and, in any case, it was clear that the management of the farm business was a full-time job. Hewes decided to appoint an assistant manager or a co-manager to look after the "social side" of the project. The kind of a man he had in mind, he explained later, was "a high-type educator—someone worth around $6,000 a year." This plan was referred to a United States senator from Arizona who had followed the project with interest. The senator approved the idea—on condition that Hewes choose the educator from among the residents of Arizona, a condition which caused Hewes to drop the idea because he was certain that a man with the necessary qualifications and point of view was not to be found in Arizona.

Toward the end of 1940, while he was trying to decide what should be done there, Hewes visited Casa Grande. He found the community house littered with dirt and rubbish. It was a mess, he wrote Waldron on his return to San Francisco. Why?

"The present condition of the community house is more or less a symbol of community activities at Casa Grande," Waldron replied. "During the first year of operation, community activities were quite flourishing but since that time they have lagged. While there may be many causes for this, I think the fundamental one is that there is a definite split in the membership and very strongly opinionated, in fact almost bitter, groups have developed.

"I do not know as it is possible to put down the real point of issue between these groups. However, very briefly, it may be said that one group wishes to get everything possible from the government in the way of wages, benefits, subsidies, etc. and also to control association on a political basis. The other group, in our opinion, has a more fundamental outlook.

They look to the future of the organization rather than to the immediate benefits to themselves.

"I am sure you realize that during the first two or three years of setting up as large an enterprise as the Casa Grande Farms, especially when it is beset by such an emergency as the present drought, changing of managers, etc., matters that do not seem to be quite so pressing are in the natural course of events delayed, even though their importance might be fully recognized. As State Director I appreciate fully the desirability of well organized and effective community activities, but unfortunately my efforts were badly diluted because of other duties.

". . . Mr. Beatty, because of his training, experience, and temperament, does not do community organization and educational work easily, and while he always gives a very fine, precise and complete report of the operations of the ranch at all community meetings and proposes many constructive plans for the operation of the ranch, he is not so interested in the social activities and the philosophy of cooperative living . . . as a person engaged more directly in educational work properly should be. He always inspires confidence, but may lack a little in inspiration."

Beatty, meanwhile, was replying to a questionnaire which had come to him from the National Office. It was a hectographed list of the activities which the Washington people believed should be carried on in resettlement communities. Beatty was supposed to check yes or no against each item on the list.

On the positive side he reported that there were committees of settlers to study the farm's budget, a women's club, a Sunday school and church services held in the community house, and a playground—a meagre list, and not quite accurate, for church services were no longer conducted at the project, the Sunday school had recently been discontinued, and the playground—only a bare plot—had been plowed and planted that Spring because the men had been slow to leave it for their work after the lunch period. On the negative side, Beatty's list was long: the association had no budget for recreational and educational activities, the nursery school had been closed, there was no parent education program, no study or discussion groups, no recreational activities, no special interest groups (such as a garden club, dramatic club or camera club), no health program (such as a well baby clinic, inoculation or venereal disease clinic, study

group, or ladies' health committee), no cooperative other than the association itself, no project newspaper, and no "other activities."

6

Factionalism

The definite split in the membership which Waldron believed was the fundamental reason for the project's inadequacy on the "social side" could be traced back to that rainy day in the late fall of 1937 when the first 13 settlers, finding themselves with nothing else to do and having read the by-laws assiduously, met in the dairy barn and elected one of their number, Fortas, manager in place of Faul. The vote at that time was not unanimous; some of the men believed that FSA's management would be essential to the success of the farm for a long time to come, and only by promising his special cronies favored positions as heads of the various enterprises had Fortas been able to win enough votes to be elected manager.

As soon as he could, Faul fired Fortas and another settler. That action, and Faul's subsequent actions—his refusal to allow membership meetings or to heed the Directors' recommendations, his failure to appoint foremen with real responsibility and authority and his daily whip-cracking—forestalled any further combinations against him. Late in 1938, at Waldron's insistence, Faul inaugurated the system of graduated wages and appointed several settlers foremen. These, of course, he chose from among the settlers who had shown no hostility toward him. No doubt his choices caused some resentment among the others; even if he followed Waldron's advice—"use a firm hand and handle the matter on an impersonal basis"—jealousy would probably have been inevitable. All the same, the cooperative's first year, as the settlers, including those who had been Faul's antagonists, later recalled it was an era of harmony and good feeling, and, as Waldron told Hewes, community activities had flourished. "We haven't got the time to fight," one of the settlers told the *Star* reporter that first summer. "We can leave the wrangling to the womenfolks. They'll do enough of it, I suppose."

But when the time came, soon after Faul's departure, to hold the first annual membership meeting, there were two factions engaged in a bitter contest for political control of the association. Harold Bowles, whom Waldron had appointed president pro-tem of the association the year before and who had supported Faul's administration, was a candidate to succeed himself. He and his supporters constituted one faction. Opposing Bowles was a settler named Julius S. Mott who claimed that Bowles and his crowd were FSA's tools. Mott argued that the settlers, not the government, should control the association, and he promised that if elected he would restore the wage cut and give the settlers the right to elect their own foremen.

Since the by-laws provided that the top men from a single slate of nominees would be elected to the Board of Directors and that the Board would elect the president, it seemed quite likely that both factions would win places on the Board and that either Bowles or Mott would be chosen president. But somehow the election rules were not followed. There were separate ballots for each position on the Board and the Mott faction took every place. The Board immediately elected Mott president.

Bowles protested to the County Attorney that the election should be set aside. The attorney agreed that the election had been improperly conducted but he ruled that since Bowles had not made his objections a matter of record during the meeting nothing could be done. Not long afterward Bowles resigned from the association.

Now Mott, who at once found he had no power to overrule or even to influence FSA, was accused of stirring up dissatisfaction among the field workers. A committee of settlers came privately to Waldron to ask how Mott could be expelled from the association. Waldron explained that under the by-laws a member who failed to cooperate in the purpose and objects of the association could be expelled by a majority vote of the membership if his expulsion was recommended by the Board of Directors. The matter was entirely in their hands, Waldron told the settlers; FSA would not interfere.

"After they left, thinking the matter over," Waldron wrote later, "I decided that any such action, although it might be successful, would probably tend to split the association more than ever, so I asked Mr. Beatty to contact them and suggest that all activity of that kind be dropped. I contacted a member of Mr. Mott's faction and frankly told him of our concern regarding the situation. He expressed appreciation and said he would cooperate with us in trying to work the matter out without an open break."

Waldron was showing forbearance, for both he and Beatty considered Mott a worthless troublemaker. Mott and his chief lieutenant, Harry

Olivier, were among the "strong-headed" individuals who had tried to oust Faul and who were now trying to get all they could out of the association without regard for its future stability. "They have the wrong attitude," Waldron said, ". . . in fact they want immediate returns rather than future security."

The settlers who sided with FSA against Mott, Olivier and the others of their opposition faction were mostly foremen. They were men who believed that the cooperative needed FSA's management, who had got along well with Faul, and who had been recommended to Beatty by Waldron. Under Beatty's system of management these foremen had a good deal of authority; next to Beatty and Wildermuth, the general foreman, Harry Coker, was the most important man on the farm. Hennesy, the livestock foreman, was only slightly less important. It was natural that Coker, Hennesy and the other foremen should defend the management of which they were a part, against the attacks of Mott and Olivier. With two or three other settlers—Perry, who came to Casa Grande because he liked cooperation, and Cecil Hopkins, a young farm laborer fresh from Oklahoma— these men shared the leadership of the pro-government faction.

Most of the settlers were not dependable supporters of either faction. On one issue they would divide in favor of Mott and the opposition, while on another issue the majority would be with Coker and his pro-government group. At elections they could usually be depended upon to turn out the faction in power.

At the second annual election early in 1940 the majority sided with the pro-government faction and elected Cecil Hopkins president. Mott had not been able to keep his campaign pledges, for a wage increase was out of the question and Beatty flatly refused to allow the settlers to elect foremen. Again the election was a source of bitterness. "Two of our foremen called on over half of the members, threatening, coercing, and instructing them how to vote, promising these men a raise in pay if they voted right and lower wages combined with disagreeable working conditions if they did not vote right," Mrs. Mott complained in a letter to Mrs. Eleanor Roosevelt. "We people came here in good faith," she went on, "believing what the government employees told us about our treatment here. We came to make this farm a successful cooperative, but it is far from that, as the people are discontented and discouraged. . . . not one of the promises made to us before we came has been fulfilled. A number of the families have moved away and many more will leave as soon as possible. Our nerves cannot stand the constant discord and unfairness. We have many fine families on this project—good workers who would gladly pull together to make this project a success if there was anything but a bare existence, unfairness, and discouragement in the future."

In the spring of 1941 the opposition faction again won a majority and one of Mott's lieutenants, Thomas, was elected president on a platform which called for a wage increase, election of foremen, and elimination of the system of graduated wages.

The tension between the two groups had now reached a high pitch. Tom Goody and his family had needed a three-bedroom house for a long while. But when one finally became vacant in the spring of 1941 the Goodys didn't take it because it was down at the "tough south end" of the project, the neighborhood of Mott, Olivier and others who "just wouldn't cooperate with the main street" where Beatty and most of the foremen lived. In words almost the same as Mrs. Mott had used the year before, Coker now complained to a visitor, "I can't take it much longer. It's too much to take . . . being all stirred up on the inside all the time. I'm going to leave."

The chief leaders of the opposition—Mott and Olivier—were among the settlers who had lived in Arizona for several years before joining the project. Between this group and the Dust-Bowl migrants there were manifest differences—the Arizona residents had better health, better education, a higher standard of living, and a more urban outlook. Within this favored Arizona group, Mott and Olivier stood out among the most advantaged.

Mott, who was in his early fifties when he came to Casa Grande, was born on his father's 160-acre farm in Illinois. His family moved to Kansas when he was a child, and Mott finished the eighth grade of school there, got a job as a telegraph operator, and married an Iowa farm girl. In 1924, after an attack of pneumonia, Mott and his family moved to Arizona. For the next seven years he worked for an irrigation district as a ditch rider—a semi-skilled, supervisory job which paid $155 a month with a house and a space for garden, chickens, and a family cow provided. When the Depression came, the company cut wages several times. Mott helped organize a union, became its secretary, went on strike, and was fired. After that the Motts were on WPA—$30 a month for a family which now numbered nine. When they were referred to Casa Grande, after Mott had applied to FSA for a loan to operate a rented farm, Mrs. Hauge noted that both Mott and his wife were intelligent and that they had tried to maintain a high standard of living. The children, Mrs. Hauge thought, were exceptionally well brought up.

Olivier was 27 when he joined the project. His father, a Phoenix physician, died in 1931, leaving Olivier, who had eight grades of schooling, an interest in a small citrus ranch. Olivier operated the ranch and did piecework for a copper roofing company—an arrangement that brought him an income of $1,050 in 1937. Despite this income, when Olivier, his wife, and their two children moved to Casa Grande their assets consisted of a refrigerator and a car on which they still owed $217. "An exceptionally intelligent and responsible person and very interested in the project," Mrs. Hauge wrote of Olivier at that time. Olivier himself said, some time later, that he was attracted to the project because "it looked like an opportunity to learn farming on a large scale, using modern technology, and to have a permanent home and a good way to live." He was a dues-paying Technocrat.

After a year, Mrs. Hauge could see that she had made a mistake. Of the Motts she wrote early in 1939, "They have proven to be too individualistic to make good homesteaders. Because of their previous standard of living, they have become more dissatisfied as progress on the project is slower than they thought it would be. The wife and children have been fairly cooperative, but the man has been a disturbing factor." Of Olivier Mrs. Hauge wrote at the same time, "The man is an excellent worker and a good manager as far as work is concerned. But the whole family attitude is very poor. Nothing pleases them. They are too individualistic for project life."

Early in 1941 Mott and Olivier had a chance to tell a friendly interviewer their side of the story. They responded eagerly with statements which defined the opposition faction's point of view and revealed more about themselves than Mrs. Hauge had discovered.

"At first this was fine," Mott told the interviewer. "During the first year everything was fine. The people were enthusiastic and they cooperated and everyone was happy. The first 17 families here were all of the same type and got along well together. Then another type of family was brought in and the two groups have never gotten along together very well.

"But the real trouble here is that the management never keeps its promises. It runs the place like a peon camp and pays peon wages but advertises it as a great cooperative democratically run. All FSA officials are plain no good and liars. I formed that opinion soon after coming here, and I doubt very much that it will ever be changed. Not one of them knows anything or can answer any question. They are all great fellows for saying that they don't know or someone else handles that. But they won't let the Board decide anything.

"Take the case of the hay-baler. The Board is supposed to sign all orders and checks. They are held responsible for any losses. But when they decide they need a baler to handle their hay crop, Mr. Waldron vetoes it. Now they lost a couple of thousand dollars on that deal. Why shouldn't Waldron or the FSA be held responsible for it? We're going to settle that question. In fact, we're going to settle the whole question of who is running this co-op if we have to get our own lawyer to represent the Board and if we have to go to the state corporation commission. Either we are going to run it and make the decisions and the manager is going to work for us, or we are going to leave. But before we leave, we'll fight it through the courts of Arizona if necessary.

"Of course the government needs its manager to look after its interest, but that is not the same as having the manager and a couple of his pets run the place. In the 1940 Board election Hennesey and Coker went around and visited all the people they thought they could intimidate. They won that election as a result. But they didn't win this last one, and now there's going to be a showdown.

"Two men, Hennesey and Coker, are going off this place whatever happens. Furthermore, I may yet take Hennesey to court for threatening to cut the head off my boy and waving a knife at him when he was on one of his drunken sprees. He has not drunk so much this year—in fact, he seems to have pretty near quit—but he is still a bootlicker and a drunk.

"We can manage this place without any FSA help. So far they have given us no help. They have mis-managed for us and put in a bunch of incompetents as foremen. We know enough about farming to run the place, except, possibly, the business end of it. If we could get help on actual farming from men who were practical farmers, not college boys, that would be fine. We would welcome it. But right now we have a manager who knows nothing about crops and cares nothing about them. Our general foreman, Coker, knows nothing of machine farming or irrigation—but he is supposed to be in charge. He can't organize the work, labor is wasted, and we just lose money.

"We can't live on $52 a month. Nobody can. We want and need higher wages, and we are going to get them. If we got higher wages, and if the manager would cooperate with us in managing the place, and if the men could select the foremen, why then the attitude of everyone would change and the work would be done. No one is going to work his fool head off for $52 a month.

"I would like an individual farm better. Of course, you might have a hard time making a go of it, but that's the way it is under a price system. This country can produce enough to support its people at a high standard of living but with this cockeyed price system, where are you? I don't like to live in the past, but I can remember my father's farm. He had security. No matter what happened, he had food and a living. There was something to that. On an individual farm, too, if you want to quit early in the afternoon and come in and say to the wife, 'Let's take in a movie', you can. Here on the co-op, you're stuck. You can't go to town, or if you do you have to ask somebody. There's no freedom in a set-up like this.

"Some of the people here are not much good. That class of people—not that we have any right to think we are better than they are, although we do think so—just doesn't fit in with the rest of us. You can't mix the two on one project. They love this. They have never been as well off before and they bring all their relatives out here. They stick together like flies.

"We are sorry we came. Our children can't go to college here. If we had lived in Phoenix, they might have been able to go. One boy went to the Navy. He likes it pretty well and is doing all right. Before the war the Navy was a place for bums and criminals. Now they attract a different type of boy. There is no opportunity here for youngsters. They can dig ditches, but they are never taught anything unless they are the children of the manager's pet. That is one of the main troubles here. If there were more opportunity for the children we might stay if they raised wages to $75. But we may leave anyway.

"If wages were raised you would see a tremendous difference in the way people feel here. The entire spirit would be changed. And if we could get a little cooperation from the management and get the place managed decently; this would be a good place to live. But our own farm would be still better."

"When I came here I started right in to fix the place up," Olivier told the interviewer. "I planted citrus trees, grapevines, and so on. Leveled the land with pick and shovel and did other work. Everything seemed fine.

"The manager then, Faul, was a stubborn man who would go out of his way to disregard suggestions from the men. He had a couple of yes-men on his Board and he was called 'Hitler.' Well, he was removed—the FSA people knew the men objected to him.

"Then the wage cut was announced. That was the beginning of knocking the underpinnings out from under us.

"Then Beatty came. Well, he's a pretty fair stockman, but he doesn't know much about farming. He gave a nice speech and we were taken in. Said he wanted an advisory group. Then he picked them. They were the last ones the men would have picked. Coker was put in charge as general foreman. He knows nothing about this kind of farming with machinery. He can't even crank a tractor. An irrigation foreman was appointed. He knows nothing about irrigation—he had done a little part-time farming, probably as a cover for bootlegging. Then Hennesey, a drinker and a stool-pigeon. He doesn't work, uses the best horses, spies on the men, and reports to Beatty. Beatty must like it or he'd stop it.

"They mismanage. There is no management. Crops aren't planted in time. Hay isn't number one because there isn't adequate equipment. Beatty ordered a baler. Waldron cancelled the order. Not enough stock to pasture the stuff down. Management is poor. Men have no fixed assignments, except for the milkers. We go down every morning for assignments and some men are still at the warehouse at 8:30. There is no organization. Men are sent out on jobs just to keep them busy when we have equipment that could do the job with less labor.

"There is no discussion of how or when things will be done. We are told, and always at the last minute. When regional office people are here, Beatty gives a little presentation of the general plan but that's all soft-soap.

"When anyone comes here to get information a barrier comes up. That's because we have so damn many pep talks and promises and lies that we just don't care anymore. Morale here is gone. I have none. I don't care whether I do a day's work or not, or whether my neighbor does. This past year I got so discouraged I let my garden go, and it was overrun with weeds and looked pretty terrible. When friends come to visit, I am ashamed to take them out. They're farmers and know how a place should look. I've got to stick in the house then.

"There are two factions here and they (the other faction) are a different kind of people. Some can't express themselves. Some are getting old and have large families. They're afraid they can't do better somewhere else and afraid to get in bad here. Some have never had anything as good as this— some from Oklahoma, they think this is O.K. They're not really satisfied either, any of them, but they're afraid to say anything.

"What would it take to restore my morale? First, the wage increase. That would be evidence of good faith and give some assurance of the future. We don't want a new manager. That would cost us money. We could make a manager out of Beatty if he will cooperate with the new Board and the people. Change some by-laws. Stop Waldron from making rules. Get more equipment. Stop buying horses and secondhand machinery."

* * * *

Coker, like Mott, was a native of Illinois and in his early fifties. He finished five grades of school in Illinois, married a farm girl with eight grades of schooling, and in 1911 moved with her to a farm in South Dakota. Later they went on to Montana, where Coker became a wheat farmer—first as manager, then as sharecropper, and finally on a contract to purchase 2,000 acres. Drought, grasshoppers, and low prices stuck him in the early 'thirties and he lost what he had paid on the farm. The family came to Arizona in 1937 with assets—a car and some household equipment—worth $305, and debts of $15. Coker and his 20-year old son picked cotton and fruit in the Salt River Valley, and Mrs. Coker, a practical nurse and good seamstress, found occasional housework and nursing jobs. In 1937 their income was $1,375, the highest among the settlers, and they lived fairly comfortably in a frame house in the suburbs of Phoenix for which they paid $10 a month rent. Mrs. Hauge was well impressed by the Cokers. "They seem to be very solid, substantial citizens," she wrote.

Shortly after he came to Casa Grande, Beatty asked Mrs. Hauge to recommend one of the project women for employment as his housekeeper. Not anticipating that Beatty would choose Coker for general foreman, she suggested Mrs. Coker. Later the Coker boy, who was older and perhaps better qualified than most of the other boys, was employed on the farm steadily at the same cash wage as the settlers, although the other boys were given work only intermittently and at wages considerably lower. As general foreman, Coker received $60 a month; his wife earned $15 a month as Beatty's housekeeper, and their son earned $52. This brought the family's income to well over twice that of any of the other settlers, and, of course, both Mr. and Mrs. Coker's association with the management was by far the closest.

Coker's attitude toward the others was naturally that of a manager, rather than a fellow-settler. "Just 16 men do all the work," he told an interviewer early in 1941. "The rest are good for nothing. They criticize all the time, and they don't know a damn thing about farming or doing most types of farm work. Not a man on the place can handle a team of horses. The 16 who do work are all fine fellows. The others are just so much money lost to the cooperative. Generally they're placed together so they won't bother the others."

Hennesey, the livestock foreman, who ranked next to Coker in the managerial hierarchy and in the leadership of the pro-government faction, was in his forties, a native of Oklahoma, where his parents were tenant farmers, and a veteran of the World War. He had gone to school eight years and, after his war experience, had been a truck farmer on ten acres in Texas, a policeman and a restaurant operator in El Paso, and, finally, a farm laborer in the Casa Grande Valley. When the Henneseys joined the cooperative in September, 1937, they lived on the outskirts of Phoenix in a one-room cabin without electricity or a kitchen sink. The Henneseys had a daughter who would soon be of school age and they moved to Casa Grande because, among other reasons, they felt that project life would be advantageous for her. Shortly afterward Mrs. Hennesey died. Hennesey was much affected by her loss; his work and his relations with the other settlers may have suffered as a result.

Cecil Hopkins, another leader of the pro-government faction, was 30 years old when he came to the project. Part Cherokee, he was a native of Oklahoma and had finished the tenth grade there. Hopkins and his wife (they had no children) came to Arizona as cotton pickers in 1937 and lived in a one-room shack on the edge of a cotton field until they joined the cooperative. They were accustomed to working in the fields together and both (Mrs. Hauge noted) were hard workers. Although Hopkins had done nothing but common farm labor, he had a knack for figures and was soon assigned to help with the bookkeeping, a job which he accepted reluctantly because he knew that many of the other settlers would be jealous of his position as an office worker.

It puzzled Hopkins that Mott and Olivier should be in rebellion against FSA. "Some men want to run things their own way," he once remarked, "—they want to 'lick the government,' you might say. They seem to think the government should have put us out here and said, 'Go to it—you're on your own.'" For his part, Hopkins believed the association should welcome all the help and direction it could get from FSA.

Ernest Perry was another who consistently supported the FSA and opposed the Mott faction. Perry left an Arkansas sharecrop farm in 1924 to come to Arizona for his health. He worked in a copper mine until he was fired for union activity during the Depression. A quiet, gentle, gray little man, Perry kept himself above the factional fights as well as he could. He and Mrs. Perry, a woman of much good sense, had come to Casa Grande because they wanted to cooperate.

Feeling that a man was either a good worker or a poor worker, Beatty was not much inclined to analyze the differences among the settlers or to account for their division into factions. Early in 1941, when a visitor to the project pressed him for an explanation, he said he thought two or three troublemakers, whom nothing would satisfy, were chiefly responsible for the discontent of the others. "Those who fit in worst," he went on, "seem to be the ones who have worked in the cities or on WPA. They have a different standard—agricultural standards are lower, of course—and once they've had the other they don't want this anymore. I had the same experience when I was managing private farms. Fellows who had been excellent workers would go to the cities and work for a while. When they came back they weren't worth anything as workers. Those who had farms and who had some experience in managing money are generally the most industrious. They understand that they can't get more than the place makes."

Although he was probably not aware of it, there was some evidence in support of Beatty's opinion. In 1940 an FSA survey of settler opinion showed that seven settlers were critical of the project and six were openly antagonistic. The six who were antagonistic were all men who had done other things besides farming and who had at some time earned higher wages than were paid at Casa Grande. As a group the antagonistic settlers were better educated than the others—all of them had graduated from grammar school and four had gone to high school for two years. None of the seven critical settlers had ever operated a farm, and four of the seven had occupational experience that went beyond farm work.

Another study, made early in 1941, gave results that were consistent with the earlier analysis. Comparing 18 members of each faction, a careful student found that a majority of the Mott faction were under 40 years of age, while most of the pro-government group were over 40. All of Mott's faction had completed at least five years of school and seven had gone to high school. Only two of the pro-government faction had gone to high school and six had less than five years of school. Among the 18 pro-government settlers there were only three with non-agricultural experience. Eight of the Mott faction had worked as skilled or semi-skilled industrial labor or had owned farms.

The settlers themselves saw other differences between the adherents of the two factions, or, more precisely, Mott and his supporters saw differences which set them apart from the other settlers and gave them a feeling of superiority. Referring to the migrant cotton-pickers, Mott, in the interview quoted above, said that "that class of people . . . just doesn't fit in with the rest of us." Olivier also said there were "two kinds of people," and he described the other kind: "Some can't express themselves. Some are getting old and have large families. . . . Some have never had anything as good as this—some from Oklahoma. . . ."

John Hinton, one of Mott's prominent supporters, gave a fuller explanation of the supposed differences between the first 17 families and the others who came to Casa Grande a few weeks or months later:

"There were 17 families at first and we did a swell job—we really pitched in and worked. Then they had a lot of transients they wanted to house so they sent them down here. There are two classes of people here, and a lot who came that summer are the other type.

"They are the ones who never made much in their lives before and they're satisfied if they have their bellies full and can lie around on Sunday and booze. Some of us have had more and want more. We're all failures or we wouldn't be here, but we try to do better. That bunch thinks this is great.

They've always lived that way. They're all from eastern Oklahoma; they had to leave everywhere else and wound up in the last place, the Indian Territory, with a small farm where they had a few beans and could take it easy, with one horse and booze on Sunday. Imagine playing poker here, where no one has enough to live on! One man lost his wife's cotton-picking check for $14.

"We have nothing against those people. We don't think we're any better than they are (I guess we do, too), but they just don't fit in with the rest of us. Another thing, they've always got kinfolk with them—in their houses, parked in their yards, and using electricity and gas. That runs up the utility cost for all of us.

"We don't want our kids associating with them because they're liable to marry those they associate with."

None of the generalizations that were made by Beatty, Hinton, or the others entirely fitted the facts. There was an element of truth in all, perhaps, but all were fatally weak in some respects. It was true that adherents of the Mott faction tended to be younger than the others, but Mott himself was one of the oldest settlers and Hopkins, a leader of the other side, was one of the youngest. Some of the pro-government faction did put a high value on security ("I don't want to go out and buck the world for a job," Fred Telson said, "I did that for 20 years. Here I have a job as long as I do my job right, and my kids have a place that they can call home. I want to stay,") but so did some of the opposition—the very fact that they remained at Casa Grande despite their acute dissatisfaction showed that clearly enough. It was true, too, although with many qualifications, that the background of the first 17 settlers was different from that of the others, but it was also true that there were first-comers, and late-comers, Arizona residents and "Okies" in both factions. Coker, Hennesey and Perry, for example, were all among the original 17, while Olivier was not.

When the dividing line was drawn, as Hinton drew it, between Oklahomans and the others the case became even weaker. Hinton himself came from a share-crop farm in Oklahoma. He and his wife came to Arizona in 1936 to pick cotton, just like the others whom he despised. His best job—which lasted only six months—was as a garage mechanic in Marlow, Oklahoma, and his assets when he arrived at Casa Grande consisted of an old car worth $50.

Weak as these explanations of it were, the factionalism was real enough and it seemed to be a clear indication that there were indeed "two types of people" at Casa Grande. Perhaps, if generalizations are possible at all, it can be said that the more advantaged settlers held to value standards and ways of living which were objectively different and that accordingly they felt themselves set apart as a "higher-status" group. These advantaged settlers were men like Mott, Olivier and Coker, who came from prosperous farming areas and from families Mrs. Hauge would have called solid and substantial, and they were men like Perry and Hennesey who had been urbanized by city life, industrial employment, or long residence in Arizona. With some others the advantage, if it existed, was not discernable, but their adherence to higher-status standards was nonetheless real. Hinton, for example, might base his claim to higher status on nothing more than the fact that his father had been a farm owner in Texas before slipping into sharecropper status in Oklahoma, but the claim was nevertheless real, and probably it was valid, for Mrs. Hauge described the Hintons as "very neat and clean, with a high standard of living."

To these "higher-status" settlers who had known better days (or who liked to think that they had), it was embarrassing to be thrown together with a lot of "Okie" cotton-pickers, some of whom had never used a flush toilet before, and to be lumped with them into the category "low-income farmers" by the FSA personnel. Olivier, for example, might pick cotton—but he would never be a "cotton-picker," and it irked him to sit at the foot of the table, passing water glasses and fried potatoes, while the FSA people treated him as if he were. The project, and particularly FSA's management of it, was a continual reminder of failure to these "higher-status" settlers; it gave rise to feelings of guilt and shame, and it aggravated their need to assert claims of superiority. "We are all failures or we wouldn't be here. But *we* (the "higher-status" group) try to do better," Hinton had said. But the charge of failure could not be set aside; it was implicit in the presence of these "higher-status" settlers at Casa Grande. "Some of these fellows try to say they used to own farms of their own or they earned $6 a day," Martin King said. "I tell them right to their faces they're lying."

The case was quite different with the so-called "Okies"—the settlers who were fresh from the degrading poverty of the Indian Territory and who had never known anything better until they came to Casa Grande.

To them the project represented not failure but success. Their search and struggle was not to recapture some real or fancied status they had lost, but to enjoy the fruits of their success—security, good housing, a regular cash wage, fair treatment from the boss, and the opportunity to drive big tractors over the soil of the Casa Grande Valley. "I'd like it fine anywhere where we're not out of work," one of them said.

But to the "higher-status" group questions of status were paramount, and, since at Casa Grande there were no other avenues to status, the settlers' quest for it took the form of a quest for power—real power, not merely the nominal power of elective office in the association. Coker, Hennesy, Perry and the others who were foremen or leaders of the pro-government faction achieved a large measure of real power by associating themselves with the management. Others like Mott and Olivier either chose, or were forced into, the role of contestants for power. They did not seek power by currying favor with the management, for they realized from the start that they could not succeed in this way. Instead they attacked the citadel of power, FSA itself. This course gave them some of the power and status they sought, for to make FSA squirm and twist by threatening to strike or to appeal to the Arizona corporation commission demonstrated power even superior to that of Coker, who could ride around in a pick-up truck all day, or of Hennesey, the livestock foreman for whom the best saddle horse was always reserved.

If Beatty and Waldron had interpreted the factionalism in this way, they might have concluded that no gestures of conciliation, short of an actual transfer of power, would satisfy Mott and his fellows, and that if the pro-government leaders—Coker, for example—were to be shorn of their power they would either leave the project in disgust or eventually assume the role of opposition leaders. Waldron might have decided that his system of graduated wages provided incentives that were actually destructive, and that Faul's system of one-man rule was more likely to secure harmony and efficiency than Beatty's dependence on foremen.

If this had been his understanding of the settlers' motivations, Waldron might have wondered whether after three years of project life the "Okies" were beginning to accept new standards of value—standards which would make the project seem like failure to them and which would cause them to rebel, like the others, against the idea of failure and against its symbol,

FSA's management. There was evidence early in 1941 that the "Okies" were indeed adopting the psychology of the "higher-status" settlers.

For one thing, it was becoming harder to get them to take on low-status jobs like cotton-picking and irrigating; more and more non-member labor—Indians, Mexicans, and other "Okies"—was being hired for these jobs which, as the project was originally planned, were intended to provide supplemental income for the settlers by using their family labor. Harry Church, for example, complained to an interviewer that his wife was expected to pick cotton, something she and the children had done as a matter of course back home in Texas, and he went on to say, in Mott's manner, that it was a shame the settlers were not consulted more by the management. This was a change in Church's point of view, and, as the interview continued, it could be seen that the change went pretty deep and was somehow associated with the idea of failure, a new idea to Church:

> Mrs. Church: Mr. Church has changed a lot. He has become radical since being here.
> Mr. Church: Well, I've hemmed around for 40 years and not gotten anywhere. I might as well stay here . . . if we can passably . . . and devote the next 40 years to getting my kids an education. We have nothing else to look forward to.
> Mrs. Church: I didn't know that you knew that.
> Mr. Church: Well, I do.

If the essential bases of the factionalism were indeed the status feeling of the settlers, their association of the project with the idea of failure, and their impelling need to express feelings of guilt and to achieve status and recognition by capturing power, then Regional Director Hewes, even if he should have succeeded in hiring a high-class educator, might have found some unexpected difficulties in the way of creating a more democratic community at Casa Grande by giving the settlers greater freedom, responsibility and power.

7

Dissatisfaction

"The most striking fact about the Casa Grande project is that it seethes with dissatisfaction," Dr. Bernard Bell, a researcher for the Bureau of Agricultural Economics, concluded after a month's study of the community early in 1941. "In spite of the provision of housing facilities superior to any the settlers had before and cash incomes ranging in 1940 around a median of $730 with none under $600, discontent is widespread. Over three-fourths of the settlers interviewed expressed dissatisfaction with life on the project."

Bell interviewed 30 of the settlers and found only six who would say categorically that they were glad they had come to the project. An equal number said categorically they were sorry they had come. "The remaining 18 expressed ambivalent feelings or seriously qualified their statements," Bell reported. "Most of them indicated they would be 'not sorry' if certain conditions were met, ranging from virtual elimination of FSA control to expulsion of half the membership. Only three settlers of the 30 interviewed were able to express unqualified intention to remain permanently on the project. Five expressed definite intention to leave in the near future. Twenty-two made qualified statements. Of these, 12 stated they would remain permanently if they made more money. This was their only condition. Ten others expressed this and other conditions involving better cooperation on the part of the management of other settlers or both.

"In answer to the query, 'What would you consider a better proposition than this?' 12 of 30 settlers indicated that they would prefer to be operating individual farms. Ten indicated that they would consider jobs paying from $75 to $100 per month better propositions. Of the 10, however, seven indicated that they would prefer the project to such jobs if cash income on the project were $75 a month. Eight thought the project the best proposition they knew, provided it were to function with less dissension and conflict. Only a few settlers were actively seeking alternative economic opportunities."

That some of the settlers should prefer individual farms or better pay-ing jobs was not at all surprising, although it was somewhat irrelevant as a criticism of the cooperative farm, which was organized to benefit peo-ple who in all probability could not obtain individual farms or good jobs. Whatever their preferences, the settlers had to reckon with real, not ideal alternatives, and for most of them the only real alternative to life on the cooperative farm was gang labor on some private farm, sharecropping in the Dust-Bowl or, possibly unskilled labor in the cities. The fact that they remained at Casa Grande showed clearly enough that, dissatisfied though they might be, they considered the cooperative better than any of these real alternatives.

Martin King was one of those who thought that an individual farm would be a better proposition. One day in 1939 he and his wife decided they would quit the project and go back home to Texas.

Martin had written letters to the home folks in which he had used the word *we* repeatedly—*we* have 100 dairy cows, *we* have 300 acres of alfalfa, and so on. It never occurred to Martin (so he said later) that the pronoun might be misunderstood. But shortly before leaving Casa Grande he real-ized that the folks in Texas had never heard of cooperatives and so there might be some misunderstanding on account of the letters he had writ-ten. This being the case, the Kings needed a different car. They had a 1928 Chevy—"a runnin' sonafagun"—for which he had paid $25. The windows were broken, the roof was ripped, and a fender was off. The Chevy just wouldn't do, after all those letters.

"I traded in a hurry in Tucson," Martin recalled later, "paid a little too much probably but I got a Nash that had good tires and looked pretty good. We got every cent of our money together—$36—and we started."

Texas didn't look so good to the Kings after all. Martin's brother-in-law said he had some fine cotton—the best in the country, the best in the whole state maybe. "I went out to look at it. It was just about a foot high with three bolls. I said, 'Yeah, you sure got some fine cotton'."

The Kings went over to see their old house. It was sure run-down. The garden was overgrown with weeds. The fence was down. That was enough for Mrs. King. She'd been in Texas only two days but she was ready to leave.

After two weeks they started back to Casa Grande with $12. At Tucson they had 70 cents left. They bought breakfast and three gallons of gas and

Martin still had a nickel. Right at the head of the lane on the edge of the project they ran out of gas. Martin borrowed a quart and saved his nickel so that he could say he had come back with some money. But he lost the Nash. The payments were $11 a month—more than he could find.

"Last summer we stayed home and got another car and if we can save enough we'll go to Texas on our vacation this year," Martin said early in 1941. "I like to visit and kinda tell them what it's like here and look at their poor stuff back there. When I tell them that I get $52 a month regular they say they wish they had a job like that. That's pretty good money back there."

If the project was better than an individual farm in Texas, it was also better than a good-paying job in the city. Joseph Buntz and his family, who had sharecropped on the rim of the Dust-Bowl in southwestern Kansas before joining the cooperative, went to San Diego on their vacation in 1940. "We sold all of our stuff here—our linoleum, drapes, lawnmower, and everything else. He (Mr. Buntz) could have got a job in the airplane factory where my brother-in-law works, but we didn't want to live there. By the time we paid the rent we might not have much more and this is a better place for children. It's not as good as an individual farm but it's better than San Diego."

But although the settlers might decide that Casa Grande farm was better than any real alternative, that did not prevent them from being dissatisfied with it. Martin King, when he returned from Texas, complained bitterly that in order to get by on the project wage it was necessary for his wife to pick cotton. He and his wife and step-daughter needed two gallons of milk a day, Martin said, but they could afford to buy only one. That they probably would have had no milk at all anywhere else was beside the point, as the Kings saw it. In this, as in everything else, the cooperative was bound to fall short when it was measured against an ideal, rather than a real, alternative.

In part the settlers' dissatisfaction was attributable to the fact that Casa Grande was an industrially-organized farm, rather than to the fact that it was a cooperative or a government project. Most of them had been 40-acre sharecroppers or seasonal farm laborers and their new positions as year-around workers on the big farm imposed new requirements on them, requirements which were inherent in the technology and organization of industrial agriculture. In their answers to Bell's questions the settlers did not distinguish between the causes of complaint which were unique to Casa Grande and those which were common to all other industrial-type farms.

Any big farm would have imposed new disciplines on the settlers. One of the hardest disciplines to accept was regular work hours. At Casa Grande the work day began at 7 in the morning and ended at 6 at night. A man had to get to his job on time and if he wanted to take time off he could do so only with Beatty's consent. Sometimes irrigating had to be done on Sunday or at night. On an individual farm it was different; as Mott had said, on an individual farm "if you want to quit early in the afternoon and come in and say to the wife, 'Let's take in a movie,' you can." Two weeks vacation with pay did not take the place of that kind of freedom, nor of the long season of inactivity that the individual farmer could look forward to each year. Those settlers who had been farm laborers, rather than farm operators, also found the routine of a year-around job hard to accept. As migratory cotton-pickers they had worked on piece-rates, if they were absent from the fields for an hour or two or for a day or two no one knew or cared. And of course as seasonal workers they had had long periods of unemployment which, although they were a hardship, served to break up the work routine.

For another thing, work on a big farm like Casa Grande was so specialized that the worker had very little opportunity to use his own judgment or initiative. It was not feasible to allow the men to choose their own jobs; a man's experience was taken into account more or less in making assignments, but not often his wishes. Sometimes a man would have to do just one thing, like driving a tractor or being a night watchman, for months at a time. "This cooperative farm is all right for some people—people who never farmed for themselves," Dewey said one day. "I'd like my own farm because I could be my own boss. You know, a farmer does all kinds of things. Here you just have the same thing and it gets monotonous. They ought to let the men do all kinds of jobs." Not only the monotony of doing the same job but the obligation to do it in a prescribed way was hard to accept. To feed cows without having anything to say about the ration or to irrigate without being able to decide for oneself how much water should be applied robbed a man like Dewey of a satisfaction that was important to him. Yet specialization and routinization of this kind was inherent in industrial-type organization, and if the cooperative differed from other big farms in this respect it was in giving the men somewhat more freedom.

Cecil Hopkins, who had been both a farm laborer and a sharecropper, thought that the greater a man's freedom to make decisions the stronger was his feeling of ownership. When he rented farms the owners had always said to him, "Go ahead and use your own judgement. What's good for you is good for me." Being able to decide things for himself made Hopkins feel as if he owned the farm he was sharecropping. At Casa Grande he didn't feel so much like an owner as he had when he had sharecropped, but he felt more like his own boss—and therefore more like an owner—than on any farm where he had been merely a laborer.

Some of the men were disappointed at not being able to learn more at Casa Grande. There was Warren Nelson, for example, who was hardly more than a boy and who had come to Casa Grande because he wanted to learn farming on a big, mechanized ranch. Well, Casa Grande was a big, mechanized ranch all right, Nelson said three years later, but he couldn't think of a damned thing he had learned, and he didn't believe that any of the other men had learned anything either. He wanted to learn how to operate a tractor, but he hadn't had a chance. He realized that when you needed work done you naturally took men who knew how to do it. But all the same, Nelson said, it seemed as if they could have worked a little teaching in on the side in slack times here and there if they had stopped to think about it.

These were all causes of complaint which the settlers would have found with perhaps more justice on other big farms, and they accounted for a considerable part of the dissatisfaction with Casa Grande. Another considerable part—for which the cooperative nature of the project was also blameless—was dissatisfaction which arose from the stresses and strains of poverty. Although they were better off than they had been and better off than they were likely to be in any other place they knew of, still, the settlers were poor—$52 a month in cash was hardly enough for a growing family. That the cooperative had eased their poverty somewhat they were not likely to take into account; the anxieties and frustrations of poverty were naturally expressed and rationalized in terms of the immediate environment, which was that of the cooperative, rather than in the abstract. In the same way some of their dissatisfaction could be attributed to the fact that they were farm laborers. The cooperative had improved their status as farm laborers; it had given them a guaranteed annual wage, vacations with pay, sick leave, some slight share in management with the promise of more, and unlimited freedom to criticize—all privileges which were unheard of on private farms. But the settlers were still farm laborers (indeed the nature of the project had made them more than ever conscious of that status) and if there were anxieties, frustrations, and resentments inherent in the role of farm laborer, these too would be directed against the cooperative farm and its management.

Early in 1941 the Buntzes decided to go back to San Diego after all. Some of the stresses and strains of poverty and the manner in which they were turned against the management of the cooperative could be seen in the reasons for their decision.

"My husband left for Oklahoma last Tuesday because his father was dying," Mrs. Buntz explained to a visitor. "We didn't have any money, so he had to buy gas to run up to Mesa to borrow $40 from my father. We agreed to pay it back $10 a month starting this month—my father needs the money just as badly as we do.

"The $40 was just enough to cover the train fare and my husband didn't eat anything going or coming. He left me 28 cents and I still had two cents when he got back.

"This morning he got his semi-monthly pay check and it was for $14.78. They docked him for the week he was away.

"We have never been in debt. We always go without rather than get in debt. Now we have to pay my father, we have to get groceries for the next two weeks, and we have school lunches to pay for.

"It wouldn't be so bad if they didn't let other men take time off and pay them for it. They could at least have figured it as one week of his vacation. He's going to talk to Mr. Beatty this afternoon and then to the Board, and he'd better be paid. We don't want to leave, but we can and we will if he isn't paid."

Had Bell, the BAE researcher, interviewed the laborers on nearby private farms he would probably have found them discontented too. But their discontent would have rested on other grounds, at least ostensibly, and their hostility would have been directed against other objects. In all probability he would not have found laborers who held it against their employers that they could afford only one gallon of milk a day. And he certainly would not have found any who were angry, as Mrs. Buntz was, at being docked for taking time off without permission. On the private farm there were well established conventions of employer-employee relationships which would put such points beyond dispute. The anger, resentment, and frustration which the workers on the private farm might feel toward their lot might not be directed against the employer at all. Because of the discipline of habit, custom, and usage the worker might express his feelings in quite different ways—in drinking, wife-beating, knifing, gambling, racism, and crime, for example—which might not be recognized as "dissatisfaction" at all. But the disciplines of the private farm might also serve to check the growth of discontent, so that, although they had less security and independence, worse pay, and far worse housing, the workers on the private farms were perhaps better satisfied than the settlers, who had a considerable burden of freedom to bear.

If some of the settlers were dissatisfied because they were poor or because they were farm laborers there were others probably who were poor and who were farm laborers because they were dissatisfied. Most of the settlers—the "Okies" particularly—had had little or no opportunity to become anything but farm laborers. But there were some, like Mott, Olivier, and others of the "higher-status" whose opportunities had been reasonably good and whose presence at Casa Grande was probably due to some personal inadequacy or maladjustment. If it was some temperamental incapacity to get along in the world which brought these few relatively advantaged settlers to Casa Grande, the cooperative could not be charged with responsibility for their dissatisfaction, although, of course, it might accentuate it or give it new channels of expression.

However much of the settlers' discontent could be ascribed to the nature of industrial-type organization, the anxieties and resentments arising from poverty, and personal maladjustments, there was still some important remainder for which the project itself was responsible. Faul and Waldron sometimes thought that the government had spoiled the settlers by giving them too much. Others regarded the settlers as true frontiersmen whose inborn antipathy toward government was aroused by the presence of bureaucracy and by its continual interference in their affairs. By both these theories it was the too-helpful hand of the government which had withered the spirit of the cooperators and had set them against each other and it.

This theory could not be reconciled with the experience of FSA with its borrowers on individual farms. With these families FSA had relieved, not aggravated, the psychological stresses and strains of poverty. A summary of the annual reports of FSA farm and home supervisors in 11 widely separated counties where specially disadvantaged borrowers received intensive supervision rated improvement in the borrowers' attitudes one of the major accomplishments of FSA work.

"In the early stages of the program," the summary said, "the supervisors were aware of a feeling of inferiority and distrust of neighbors among the project families in all counties. Frustrations caused by their inability to satisfy their inherent craving 'to be,' 'to belong' and 'to create,' had destroyed their faith in themselves, their initiative and their hope for a brighter future. To several supervisors, who contact these families personally, the change in the mental attitude of these clients has been the most important and striking accomplishment effected during the year's work. The former defeated, whip-dog appearance and outlook on life has been replaced by improved facial expressions, strengthened faith and a friendlier and more cooperative spirit toward neighbors and supervisors. . . . Constant bickering and strained relationships between husbands and wives, caused to a great extent by the effort involved to obtain a bare existence, have been alleviated by frank discussions of problems and by improved living conditions."

Another study, this one made in 1946 by the Bureau of Agricultural Economics, showed that tenants who were buying farms with FSA loans were generally well pleased with that program. These loans were on generous terms; in fact a large proportion of them were for the full purchase price of the farms, yet the borrowers did not seem to be spoiled by the government's assistance. The borrowers were required to follow a written farm and home plan and in other ways FSA's relation to the individual families was much closer than at Casa Grande. But less than one in 25 of the tenant purchase borrowers expressed dissatisfaction with their purchases and only 1.5 percent disliked to have the supervisor visit them. If there was such a thing as a frontiersman's antipathy toward government, these farmers did not seem to share it.

The fact that the settlers had been presented with a ready-made opportunity by the government was probably not a cause of dissatisfaction in itself. Neither was the cooperative form of organization in itself responsible for the settlers' complaints. The fact that the farm's profits, if any, were to be distributed among the workers (which was what the cooperative form of organization signified chiefly at Casa Grande) was a business proposition which the settlers could readily understand and there was nothing troublesome about it.

While the peculiar character of the project—its cooperative nature and its relationship to the government—was not in itself unsettling, it did entail consequences which were exceedingly so. By its peculiar character, the project threw out of kilter the well-ordered system of conventional, taken-for-granted attitudes and behavior which Beatty and the settlers had always depended upon elsewhere. As a farm manager, or as an owner, tenant, sharecropper or laborer a man had always known where he stood, and so had his wife and his neighbors and the world at large. If he were a laborer, he knew without thinking how to place himself, his fellow-workers and his boss in the scheme of things—a scheme of things in which certain signs and symbols had agreed-upon, identifiable meanings. At Casa Grande some of the old signs were gone and others had ill-defined meanings. Habit and custom, the easiest of disciplines to bear, were no longer reliable guides. A foreman, for example, was no longer a symbol of authority. Instead, since he was a fellow settler, he was a competitor, and if he were a successful competitor he was certain to be an object of resentment. In the fluidity of the situation there was freedom—freedom to compete for status and power, and freedom to express dissatisfaction in new ways and discover it in new places. While some settlers welcomed the new opportunities to assert themselves, others felt uncertainty, anxiety, and insecurity because of them.

In the absence of conventions which would prescribe a 'right' way of looking at things, every man was forced to make up his own mind about the proprieties of almost every situation that arose. And of course a man had no appropriate standards to go by in making up his mind. Waldron, for example, once told the settlers, "If you don't like it here you can leave." It was a sensible piece of advice and, from Waldron's standpoint, perfectly fitting. But it gave such deep offense to the settlers that two-thirds of them remembered it with anger three years later. "It made this seem just like a job where we worked for a boss, instead of our own place," Telson said. "You expect that when you are working out for someone, but not here—this is supposed to be different." Yet if Telson's standards were different from Waldron's in one situation, they were like Beatty's (and very different from Mott's and Olivier's) in another. "I don't make suggestions to Beatty," Amos said on the same occasion. "When he asks my opinion, I tell it to him—that is as it should be."

An understanding of "what was supposed to be" and "what should be"—a set of conventions to fit the peculiar character of the project—was needed at Casa Grande. But it could not be obtained, as the lawyers and administrators seemed to suppose, merely from a set of by-laws and a work and occupancy agreement. It could not be fabricated in any logical way. It would have to be evolved by trial and error, by mutual accommodation and by friction in response to real situations as they arose. If they had possessed insight and flexibility and the gift of leadership, Waldron and Beatty could have facilitated the growth of the understanding that was needed. But Waldron was no better able to define the situation than were the settlers and so he met their questions and complaints with a stock reply: "This is an experiment." While it may have relieved some of his own doubts and uncertainties, the word "experiment" only aggravated the anxieties of the settlers.

Beatty, too, was confused, and his confusion also tended to increase the dissatisfaction of the settlers. He had come to Casa Grande expecting to manage the cooperative as he would any other farm, but somehow the rules of the farm management game no longer worked as they should. A farm manager should depend heavily on his foremen, but the more Beatty depended on his foremen the more ill-tempered and slack his workers became. Some of the fault, Beatty believed, lay with the foremen. He had observed the settlers for two months before making his appointments and he had relied heavily on Waldron's advice. He was confident that he had picked the best men—they were all hard workers, willing to spend nights and Sundays on the farm if necessary, and they were all doing the best they knew how. But even so, Beatty admitted privately, they were not the men he would choose if he were managing a private farm. Even Coker, whom he considered the best man on the place, was far from being an ideal general foreman. To be obliged to select foremen from among only 56 men, most of whom had no other qualification than poverty, was a serious handicap; the manager of a private farm would expect to search far and wide for a good foreman. Despite their limitations, the men he had appointed were the best available, Beatty felt, and he saw no reason why the men should not take orders from them as they would from any other foremen.

That the workers and foremen had equal status as members was something Beatty ignored. But it was this, and not any question of the competence or incompetence of the foremen, which was crucially important to the other settlers. They knew perfectly well that no foreman, however capable, could command respect if he were a fellow settler. "I could have had one of the better paying jobs," Martin King said one day. "But I turned it down because I'd rather have friends."

When the rules broke down and the men resisted the orders of their foremen, Beatty was at a loss to know how to handle the situation. "Some of the men can be told that a certain job needs to be done and that's all there is to it," he told a visitor early in 1941. "But most of them have to be pushed along or they are here every morning wanting to know what to do. If they don't know what they are supposed to do, I can't tell them again or bawl them out. I expect them to know why they are working and why they should do their jobs well."

Beatty was convinced that the settlers lacked the capacity to manage the farm and would never develop it. As a group they were not responsible. They would not accept discipline or restraint either from within their group or from without, and it seemed to Beatty that they had made no progress toward responsibility in the past three years. Two or three men were gradually learning. Forbes, for example, was almost in sole charge of cotton production and he was quite capable of going to the gin by himself. Hennesey, the livestock foreman, could be sent to Phoenix to handle sales. But except for these two men and Coker and Goody, none of the settlers were capable of managerial responsibility. Somehow they couldn't even learn to take orders from their own foremen.

Beatty was perplexed and confused, and this made him react in a way that increased his difficulties with the settlers. He never became angry; his manner, even with Mott and Olivier, was always mild and courteous. But he became more than ever inclined to insulate himself from the men—from workers who would not behave as workers were supposed to behave. For fear of appearing to yield to pressure from Mott and Olivier and as a means of keeping the settlers and their difficulties at a distance, he gradually gave the foremen more authority and stronger backing. At the same time he occupied himself more and more with the buying and selling of livestock. If he had given the men closer supervision he might have made up for some of the deficiencies of his foremen and he might have relieved some of the antagonism the settlers felt towards them. Instead, by retreating behind the foremen and the beef cattle, he made matters worse.

If the settlers' behavior puzzled Beatty, his puzzled them no less. No one knew for sure how the manager of a cooperative farm should behave; most of the settlers were inclined to agree with Mott and Olivier that the manager ought to take orders from the membership. But at the same time, they thought that a boss ought to boss, and this was a grievance that even his supporters held against Beatty. "Faul was more interested. He made us work harder," Dewey once said in criticism of Beatty. And Cecil Hopkins, a strong supporter of Beatty's, remembered Faul as, "good, very good—*he* really saw to things, everything." Probably all of the settlers would have agreed that the manager of a cooperative, particularly one who was a government employee, should give the workers more of his personal interest and attention than one would expect from a private employer. "I talked to Mr. Beatty once," Mrs. Goody said in 1941. "He wasn't interested. He's terribly interested in stock. People don't like that. He ought to be interested in them."

And Beatty, although he believed that a worker ought to behave like a worker, was disappointed and puzzled that, when he returned from Phoenix or Los Angeles after selling a load of livestock, only two or three foremen would come to him to ask what price the farm's cattle had brought. "The other men just don't seem to be interested," he complained in the same hurt tone Mrs. Goody had used.

Plainly it was impossible for the workers or the manager to think or act as they would on any other farm. The cows and the alfalfa, the tractors and the cotton, and all the other realities of daily life, including even the workers and the boss, were no different than might be found on another farm. Yet, because this was a government-sponsored cooperative, the familiar scene was thrown out of focus so that it was confusing, unsatisfying, and disturbing. Faul, the construction gang boss, had succeeded in ruling the project just as if it were another private farm and it was significant, perhaps, that the settlers remembered Faul's rule, a time when they knew where they stood, as the only happy and satisfying period in the life of the cooperative. Beatty, without quite intending it, had allowed the distinctive and confusing character of the cooperative farm to emerge. If now the project were to move further away from the familiar example of the private farm in the uncharted direction of 'true cooperation,' as Regional Director Hewes fully intended that it should, one might expect it to become more and more difficult for Beatty and the settlers to know "what should be" and "what was supposed to be." If Hewes should succeed in making a model, democratic community of Casa Grande, it would certainly mean that in place of habit and convention Beatty and the settlers had relied on intelligence and the moral faculty of goodwill.

8

Women and Children

For the women and children who lived there, life on the cooperative farm had its special trials. They lived in wonderful new houses—houses with electricity, flush toilets, screens, and modern appliances, and their men brought home wages every week. There was no reason to fear the end of the picking season and there need be no more wanderings from one ditch-bank shanty to another. It was for this, the comfort of the women and children, that many of the families had joined the cooperative, and it was for this that many of the men stayed at Casa Grande long after they had lost all patience with their jobs, their foreman, and themselves. "At least it's a place the kids can call home," they would say. But all the same, there were many things about the cooperative that made it hard for the kids and their mothers to call it home.

For one thing it was hard to learn to live in the clean, new, well-equipped homes. Things like flush toilets and electric refrigerators were a source of anxiety to people who had never used them before. One family left the project after a few weeks because the woman was afraid of electricity. No doubt there were others who felt the same kind of fear but managed to conceal it or at least to live with it. But it did not take long to overcome these fears, and by early 1941 most of the newness and strangeness was gone and the women had become very much attached to their homes. "When we first moved in we thought these were the ugliest walls," Mrs. Dewey said. "Yesterday the painters came. We told them to paint the walls the same color. We like it now. We've tried to feel that this is our home."

It was harder to learn to live with neighbors than with gadgets. Most families had lived a mile or two from their nearest neighbors before coming to Casa Grande. Now they lived in a compact community where on a quiet night one could hear the sounds of people talking on their porches up and down the street and where in the daytime, whether one wished it or not, one had to exchange words with half a dozen women while hanging out the wash. The children were a special problem now that the families lived together in a neighborhood. They had never learned how to play with other children and the parents did not know what to expect from children playing together. It may be that the tensions and conflicts which existed among the grown-ups were reflected in the behavior of the children. At any rate, the community was constantly upset by hoodlum acts and by fights, squabbles, and bickering among the children. Having very little experience with neighborhood life themselves, the parents were prone to take the children's difficulties very seriously, sometimes to make a family feud of a child's squabble. Even after three years experience at Casa Grande more than half the women felt that conflicts among the children were a very serious objection to community-type settlement—some said an insuperable objection.

Until sometime in 1940 there was a nursery school in the community and that helped. All but three or four of the small children were enrolled and they played together under supervision from 8:30 in the morning until early afternoon. Twice a month the mothers met with the nursery school supervisor, a woman with special training in child care whose salary was paid by WPA, for a discussion of practical matters like how to feed and clothe a child. But in 1940 WPA came to an end and the nursery school could be continued only if the women would support it by taking turns as supervisor or by sharing the expense of a paid supervisor. One of the settlers had a crippled daughter, a 'teenage girl who loved children, who offered to take over the school at very small pay. But some of the women, including the girl's mother, thought that it would cause jealousy if one family were to earn a few dollars a month more than the others in this way, so the nursery school was dropped. At about the same time the Sunday school which had been conducted in the community hall came to an end. The Sunday school had been popular with the children, but somehow it failed to get the support and interest of their parents.

The most difficult problems were with the school-age children. They ran wild whenever they were not in school because there was nothing to occupy them on the project. The association had set up no recreational fund from which playground equipment could be bought and Wildermuth believed that if the farm were to buy equipment the children would only break it. Beatty plowed up the ballpark to plant alfalfa because the men lingered there after lunch. The problem was serious enough so that

Mrs. Goody, for one, wished she lived on an individual farm where her children would be busy. Her boy had a rabbit project in connection with his 4-H club work at school, so he was better off than some. Most of the boys, Mrs. Goody said, didn't care especially for rabbits, and the farm gave them no opportunities to keep larger animals like hogs or calves. She thought Beatty ought to assign a plot where the boys could carry on 4-H projects under the supervision of a man appointed to that job.

It was probably true that Beatty, whose job was to run the farm profitably, was inclined to overlook the needs of the children. But he may have felt that the parents were too prone to call on him for things that they could do as well themselves. If a group of settlers had wished to build a playground of odds and ends in their spare time or if some of them had volunteered to serve as scoutmasters or 4-H leaders he would probably have helped. But to assign a man from the farm to look after the children was another thing. The settlers may have fallen into the habit of expecting too much to be given them, as Beatty and Waldron both thought, but other explanations could also be given for their failure to take the lead in meeting the children's needs. For one thing FSA's control of the project was so complete that they might easily have felt that no problem could be solved without an appeal to the management. Having had no experience with children's organized play, they may not have realized that the interest, encouragement, and help of parents is more important to the success of 4-H and other such projects than any amount of equipment or paid assistance. And of course the bitter factionalism of project life made it difficult or impossible for the adults to act together under any circumstances.

Factionalism was almost as strong among the women as among the men. There were a few exceptions (Mrs. Hall, for example, could never forget how nice Mrs. Olivier was to her during an illness), but generally the women divided along the same line as their husbands. Mott was not on speaking terms with Salter and so Mrs. Mott did not speak to Mrs. Salter, and with the others it was more or less the same. But while the alignment was the same, the relationship of the two factions to the government was very different in the case of the women.

The women's direct contact with the government was through Mrs. Hauge, the home management supervisor and family selection specialist. (Since they were not members of the association the women did not participate in its affairs, although some of them attended membership meetings with their husbands.) Mrs. Hauge had not even a nominal connection with the association and she did not participate in the management of the project. Her job was purely educational. She gave demonstrations and advice on cooking, canning, sewing, child care, handicrafts and other subjects which interested the women or which might help them to improve their standard of living. Since her time was divided among three other resettlement projects and a migratory labor camp she could usually spend only three or four hours a week at Casa Grande. Because she could use her time to best advantage by meeting the women as a group, Mrs. Hauge organized a Women's Club at the project during its first year.

Usually the club met once or twice a month in the community hall. Mrs. Hauge would give a demonstration or introduce a guest speaker or demonstrator from the Extension Service of the state college, there would be a discussion period during which the women could show off the dresses, rugs, and other things they had made, and then there would be refreshments and small talk. Often the club members would participate in the demonstrations. If the day's program happened to be on mattress making, for example, the women would make a mattress together. Sometimes there were group projects. One of the most popular of these was a recipe book to which each woman contributed the recipe for a favorite dish. Edited and arranged by Mrs. Hauge the book was a practical manual on diet and food selection. Usually the club meetings were attended by guest homemakers from the towns of Florence and Coolidge and on these occasions the project women had the opportunity to play the part of hostesses.

The Women's Club was something more than a vehicle for Mrs. Hauge to use in bringing her services to the homemakers. It was also a service organization and a center for the women's social life. By tacit agreement the community house was under the Club's auspices and the women used it for fund-raising affairs—to serve a monthly pie dinner to which the public was invited, to cater for the Lions and Rotarians who came from Coolidge and Florence, and for occasional parties and dances. The women used the proceeds from these affairs to buy materials for their homemaking classes and to buy equipment—a secondhand piano, for example—for the community house. In cooperation with the Casa Grande Women's Professional Club, to which Mrs. Hauge and several school teachers belonged, the Club operated a small library two afternoons a week in the community house. As Mrs. Hauge and some of the others conceived it, in the terms familiar to rural life, the community house was something like a Grange hall and the Club women were the "ladies' auxiliary."

But somehow the familiar terms did not quite fit at Casa Grande. During the project's first year the Women's Club was very active. As the women later recalled it, they had done lots of things together and had had lots of fun that first year. But in the second year interest waned and after that the club went steadily down hill until, early in 1941, neither the pie-dinners nor the demonstrations of cooking, canning, and sewing could be called popular. Some women never attended meetings. Others would not come in response to a bulletin-board notice but might be persuaded by a personal visit. Usually it was the same 10 or 15 women who attended every time. Some of the women believed that the change in spirit coincided with the wage-cut and most of them agreed that factionalism (which they blamed on the men) had something to do with it.

Whatever might be the cause, the women could not seem to do things together. Even those who attended the Club meetings regularly couldn't seem to cooperate. There were only five, Mrs. Coker once said, who would do any work (such as getting up a pie dinner, for example) and even these five would do nothing on their own initiative. It was up to her—Mrs. Coker—to plan everything, and she simply didn't have the time. When outsiders were present the women got along very well together, but when they were by themselves they argued constantly. Mrs. Graves said that was the reason why she quit going, and there were probably others who felt the same way.

The women who came from Oklahoma seldom attended. They were the ones who most needed help, Mrs. Hauge felt, yet they stayed home or, if they came to a meeting, refused to participate in the discussion or to bring along a sample of handiwork for display. "The women won't talk in meetings but they talk well enough in the cotton patch," Mrs. Dewey once told a visitor. "Oklahoma women resent these women from Tucson coming out to instruct. 'We know how to cook and can,' they say. They feel sensitive—afraid of educated people who come and always have an answer." Mrs. Dewey thought it strange that the Oklahoma women should take that attitude; she and the others who participated actively in the club work did not feel that Mrs. Hauge or the extension service agents were the least bit patronizing. Why, when the floor of the community house needed scrubbing the home economists would get down on their knees and scrub along with the project women.

But there was no doubt that the Oklahoma women were sensitive. Usually they showed it only by saying nothing or by staying home. But once one of them told the home demonstration agent fiercely, "I'm not going to look up to you. Some women do. But I won't."

It was the wives of the "higher-status" settlers who attended the Club meetings most often and were the most amenable to Mrs. Hauge's influence. In a way it was curious that this should be so, for the "higher-status" men (except those who were foremen) were bitterly antagonistic to Beatty, while the so-called "Okies," whose wives resisted Mrs. Hauge, cooperated with him very well. Yet this circumstance was not so strange as it seemed. Those who opposed Beatty did so because they were struggling for power, the symbol of status. Among the women status was to be had by exhibiting skill in the niceties that Mrs. Hauge taught, and so it was only natural that those who could display the most convincing evidences of refinement should attend most regularly. It was no coincidence that Mrs. Coker, who was Beatty's housekeeper and who took first prize in a canning exhibit at both the county and state fair, should be the most enthusiastic of the Club members or that the "Okie" women, who in all probability had never so much as embroidered a towel, should stay at home.

Although they showed clearly enough that they were acutely conscious of their neighbors' claims to superiority, the "Okie" women's reaction was of a kind that prevented them from learning the skills which would close the gap. After three years work Mrs. Hauge said flatly that she believed there had been no general improvement in home management. Those women who had been poor housekeepers were still poor housekeepers. Some houses were so dirty and disorderly that it was difficult for a visitor to step inside them. If the families' diets were better it was because they had more food and better food. There had been no improvement in the choice of food or in its preparation, although some of the families, Mrs. Hauge thought, may have learned something about canning. In 1940 all but six of the 48 families had vegetable gardens and all but one had flowers around their houses. But the value of the food produced at home and received from the community garden by the average family was trifling—it amounted to only $6 a year. The women were canning twice as much in 1940 as they had before coming to the project, but even so the amount canned was negligible—only 63 quarts for the average family.

Mrs. Hauge was liked and trusted by all of the settler families and so it was puzzling and discouraging that she should have so little effect among women who could have benefitted so greatly by her help and who were at the same time so acutely conscious of the social importance of her way of doing things. And it was discouraging too that the women could not enjoy each other or work together in harmony when it was so clearly to their advantage. If the community had been larger and if the women had been allowed to form themselves into several groups by their own natural process of selection, there would probably have been cooperation within the separate groups at least. But as it was the Women's Club had been organized by fiat of the government and, since all the women were encouraged to join, none could take a special pride in being part of the group.

In one matter—hot school lunches for the children—the settlers did cooperate, and although it was the men who took the lead the women must certainly have urged them on.

The children at the Kenilworth school paid ten cents for each hot lunch. This price seemed unnecessarily high to the school principal and he proposed to Beatty that the cooperative farm contribute a certain quantity of milk, eggs, and meat so that the children could have their lunches without cost. Beatty figured that the food which would be required was worth about $700. In the opinion of the San Francisco regional office this was a larger donation than the farm could afford, so Beatty was obliged to refuse.

When Martin King learned that FSA had refused to allow the contribution he went to the principal with a suggestion: if the settlers would take up a contribution of $60 a month by voluntary assessments, would he feed the children? The principal thought he could do it on that basis. After talking it over with some of the other settlers King invited the principal to state his proposition before a general meeting in the community house. All but two of those who attended favored the idea. Bowles, a Jehovah's Witness, was opposed on religious grounds. Olivier was also opposed.

"Why should I pay the same as everyone else when I've got only one kid and some have got four or five?," Olivier asked. "If I'm smart enough to have less kids why should I be penalized?"

The argument was hot when finally Harry Church proposed that he and King would make up the difference between what Olivier was asked to pay and what he was willing to pay. That suggestion made Olivier furious—he didn't need charity from anyone, he said, let alone those with big families. He would pay his own way. The motion was finally passed with only Bowles dissenting. The principal got the $60 regularly. Sometimes it was a few days late, but it always reached him.

Even more than the school children and the pre-school children, the older boys were a problem on the cooperative farm. There were nearly 30 'teen-age boys among the settler families in 1940 and there were eight who were in their early twenties. What these boys needed was not opportunity to play but opportunity to work—to add some share to their families' incomes and to get some useful training and experience in farming or in some trade. This was a need which the cooperative farm was poorly prepared to meet.

If the settlers had operated individual farms, the boys would have been no problem at all. A boy would work on his father's farm for his keep until someday the old man quit or died. Then he would inherit the farm and start out for himself as an owner. This at least was the settlers' idea of how things would have worked out on an individual farm. It was not a very realistic idea, perhaps, for very few of the settlers had ever owned farms or were likely to and furthermore a boy cannot always wait for his father to quit or die and he may have brothers and sisters who claim an equal share in a farm that is not large enough to support even one family adequately. But while the settlers could easily overlook the problems that would have existed on an individual farm, they could see those that faced them on the cooperative farm clearly enough. On the cooperative farm, if a boy were employed at all, he would have to work for cash wages and he would have nothing to look forward to except more cash wages. He could not even be sure of taking his father's place as a member of the cooperative. Most likely he would have to leave the farm someday as an ordinary laborer.

That work on the farm led to nothing better for the boys was a real objection. But the thing that was uppermost in the settlers' minds was that the boys were often given no work of any kind, so that there was nothing to keep them out of trouble, and that when they were employed the work was not fairly divided among them.

At first the cooperative employed none of the members' children. Out of regard for the Arizona child labor laws (which did not apply to family-type farms and were seldom enforced on other farms), because the government intended to set an example for other industrial-type farmers, and because it was clear that no one possessed enough wisdom to decide which children should have which jobs, Waldron and Garst decided that it would be simpler to avoid the problem altogether. But the problem was one which could not be avoided. The boys (some of whom were already men) needed something to do, and their families needed the money they could earn. At the cotton-picking season, especially, it seemed absurd not to let the children work, for many of the outside workers who were hired brought children into the fields with them. And, as the editor of the *Star* (who had visited Russia and found that on Soviet collectives the girls and boys worked and only the politicians loafed) observed, "children not taught to have reasonable duties to perform will become weak adults incapable of guiding the destinies of our great nation."

Early in 1939 the rule against employing members' children was lifted and the Board of Directors set their wage at $1.50 a day. Immediately there was trouble. The wage was more than some of the younger children were worth and it was not enough for some of the older boys. The new policy gave an advantage to the families with employable children and of course that made the families without children jealous. With some justice perhaps, Mott claimed that the children of the pro-government settlers were given more work than the others. In exasperation, Waldron recommended to the Board in June 1940 that it cease employing boys.

A month later, having changed his mind, Waldron wrote Beatty: "Since young people in these families are probably the largest asset they have it is only proper that they should be aided to realize on this asset. Also it would appear that we would be defeating some of the main purposes of the farm to deny the opportunity of these young people to get experience in farming and to earn a little money to meet the greater expenses of the larger families.

"Perhaps a different wage scale might well be established so that the younger boys would be paid less wages and the older ones more, thus arriving at an arrangement that is fair to the association and to the boys themselves. It is our opinion that the younger boys, especially those 14,

15, 16, and possibly 17 years of age might profitably work on what might be known as an apprenticeship basis at low wages but with the main objective to obtain experience. In this case they would want to be shifted from department to department in order to get as wide experience as possible."

Beatty continued to hire boys, but not on the apprenticeship basis Waldron proposed. He left it to Coker to assign jobs to the older boys according to his estimate of their capacities and he excluded the younger children from employment altogether except at the cotton-picking season, when a number of them stayed out of school to work on the farm. The wage-rate for those boys who were employed was still $1.50 a day early in 1941. There was one exception to this. Coker's son, who was older than most of the others, was employed steadily at $50 a month—a fact which many of the other settlers put near the top of their list of grievances.

Except for young Coker, who he said knew something about livestock and was willing to work 24 hours a day if necessary, Beatty believed the boys were nearly worthless on the farm. Coker agreed. Except for his own son, the Perry boy, one of the Hinton's and one of the Mott's, the boys were interested in nothing but driving tractors. His own boy never associated with any of the other boys on the project, which, in Coker's opinion, showed that the others were probably no good. "They are a different sort," Coker once said. "They have never learned how to work or to like work, and their fathers never learned either. They are lazy and dishonest. They'll steal anything in sight."

Beatty was surprised at how little the boys knew about farming, and he agreed with Coker that they had never learned to work. The boys' parents felt the same way for that matter; they were seriously disturbed to see their sons grow up without learning the discipline of work and without receiving any practical training. The fault lay not with the boys but with the cooperative farm, the parents felt, and they blamed Beatty for not arranging things differently.

The parents were disturbed too when the boys, having no opportunities at Casa Grande, went to work in the cities or joined the Army or Navy. Clinging as they did to the old ideal of the family farm, the settlers thought it was a misfortune that a boy should give up farming. Hinton, for example, had thought that his boys would get a chance to learn something at Casa Grande, but it didn't turn out that way. "What is there here for them at

$1.50 a day?," he once asked. "They go right on irrigating and they may be as old as I am without knowing anything. My oldest boy joined the Navy. We tried to talk him out of it, but I knew he was right. There he has a chance to learn a trade. My next boy loves farming. But what chance has he here?." Bill Forbes, the cotton foreman, had three sons. Early in 1941 he explained that the oldest, who was recently married, would have joined the association but for the fact that other boys had been refused membership. Instead he had gone to Tempe to work in the lettuce-packing sheds. The second boy, just out of high school, felt he could work on the project all his life and never have anything so he joined the Marines and was stationed in China, taking a course in Diesel engines. The third Forbes boy would soon join the Army because "that's all there is to do."

Hinton, Forbes, and others of the settlers felt that the project was some-how to blame for the fact that their sons were leaving them and leaving with what seemed to be a poor start in life. Of course the boys would have been no better off if their fathers had remained sharecroppers and farm laborers and, early in 1941, boys from all walks of life were going into the Army and Navy. But still, to the parents it meant failure that their sons were not to be independent farmers. Their own experience—the experi-ence of Forbes, for example, who had been driven by dust, drought, and tractors from three Oklahoma farms in a space of 12 years—might have shown them that to leave the farm for the city meant success, not failure for their kind. But the tradition that a farm boy takes over his father's farm or a neighboring farm was too strong, and since the cooperative could not fit into the tradition it was deemed in that respect a failure.

9

Pinal County Opinion

The little community at Casa Grande did not live in isolation. Coolidge and Florence, Pinal County's two chief towns, were only five miles away in either direction on the main highway and all but a few of the settlers had cars. The churches, schools, and stores were in the towns, so that contact between the cooperative farm and the larger community was close and frequent. The opinions of the men who played poker in the 21 Club in Coolidge, the opinions of the grocery clerks, gas station attendants, and schoolteachers, were all bound to have some effect on the opinions of the settlers.

At first Pinal County regarded the Casa Grande project with distrust and suspicion. The old-timers thought it was wrong and absurd to ready-make farms with WPA labor and, when they saw that the houses were grouped into a community and learned that the land was to be farmed cooperatively, they feared the political and economic influence that the compact settlement might have on the existing order of things in the county. But as the construction of the project went forward and the government's plans were made clear, Pinal County was reassured—this was simply another, although rather elaborate, relief project, and so there was nothing to be feared from it. There were of course leaders in the county—editors, big farmers, politicians—who were aware that the project was intended as a direct challenge to the evils of industrialized agriculture, but to most Pinal County people it was in the first year or two merely some new-fangled kind of work relief.

Regarding it so, the County was not unsympathetic. In the early stages of organization especially, when FSA was making a deliberate effort to select Arizona residents, the Pinal County people, a sizeable proportion of whom either were or had been on relief themselves, were friendly and warm toward the settlers. Later, as more and more cotton-pickers fresh from the Dust-Bowl joined the cooperative and its membership became predominantly "Okie," there was some change in the prevailing opinion.

Migrant cotton-pickers had long been regarded as an inferior species, a necessary evil to be tolerated only during the picking season and then sent packing down the road. To support them on relief or to encourage them to settle permanently in the community was something that Pinal County had never done, and it regretted to see the government do it now.

The townspeople's assumption that they were on relief was a sore point with the settlers, a number of whom had come to Casa Grande direct from WPA or FSA grant offices. Early in 1938 the *Star* reporter found that several of the settlers were sensitive and on the defensive:

"Harman (one of the settlers) said that some merchants had spoken bitterly about 'you folks out there spending the people's money.' His reply was: 'Maybe, but we're paying interest on it, working hard to protect it, same as if an individual owned it or had loaned us the money. Besides, show me a banker that isn't living on the people's money.'

"Another spoke in patient tones of some children visiting the farm from Florence or Coolidge. 'You know how kids talk? Well, the visitors said to our kids: "At least the government doesn't have to feed us." Now that's hardly fair, but you know kids.'"

At the end of the first year, when Faul resigned with a blast at the "basically communal" nature of the project and Waldron defended the project by recalling that the year before most of the settlers had been living in cotton-pickers' shacks, the reporters and photographers who swarmed over the project for a few days found the settlers inclined to ignore Faul's remarks but very much offended at Waldron's. "We didn't live in a shack before we came on this project," one of the settler's wife told a reporter with feeling. "Our home was comfortable, as nice as anyone's. We came on the project because it was painted rosy to us." The settlers were proud, another reporter found, "of the fact that they were carefully selected on a basis of character and ability from a mass of more than 1,000 applicants for places on the farm."

From the efforts put forth by several Pinal County leaders to soothe the settlers' ruffled feelings, and from the concern shown by FSA, which sent a publicity man from San Francisco to secure commendatory statements from these leaders, it is evident that Faul's remarks seriously disturbed the settlers and that the project had many well-wishers who were anxious to repair the damage of their morale. One of these well-wishers was the editor of the Casa Grande *Dispatch*. He visited the farm shortly after Faul's departure, then wrote, "The several men we met in our afternoon at the farm might well resent the slurs as to their character and ability if one may judge from appearances and conversation and from the well-kept look of the farm and the settlement. . . . Suffice it to say that the writer is convinced that the group is not made up of human derelicts who have lost the profit instinct and are glad merely to find shelter and a livelihood; but that there is as much enterprise and ambition and hope and general well-being per man as any we have ever seen collected in one spot."

W. C. Ketchersid, a member of the Chamber of Commerce and owner of the largest hardware store in Coolidge, seemed to think that he could remember when some of the settlers were rich men. In this he was mistaken, but his mistake helped to convey his point, which was that the settlers were respectable people. He gave the FSA publicity man permission to quote him as follows:

"I hope the experiment at Casa Grande succeeds financially, and if we get enough water in this part of the country I am sure it will. The people there are a fine lot. It happens that I know two of them personally. I knew them when they could each write a check for a hundred thousand dollars. This is a come-down for them, but they are working as hard as the others at Casa Grande and getting along with the other people in fine shape, even though they once owned their own places and had a lot of money.

"I knew some others out there too. They lost everything they had and were all broken up and downhearted; but I can see a big change in them since they went to Casa Grande. They've got their morale back now.

"All your people have paid their bills with us exceptionally well. Yes, without a single exception I consider them good credit risks.

"Maybe more water and better farm prices would keep our farmers on their feet, and then you wouldn't need a project like this. But right now Casa Grande is the next best thing to have, and I think the people there are wise to try that way of getting along."

E. G. Attway, operator of an 840-acre farm bordering on the project, was another who wished it well. He was quoted:

"Good farmers around here are having to get out and work at farm labor for $2 or $2.50 a day. They can't get anywhere that way. I hope the government can help keep more people on their own land, but if that can't be done the sort of project you have at Casa Grande is certainly the next best thing. Those are good, hardworking people out there, and I hope they will succeed."

The farm machinery dealer at Coolidge, C. A. Elquest, said he thought Casa Grande "one of the best solutions yet," and he added of the settlers: "I think they'll make a go of Casa Grande if anybody will around here."

Lee Hooper, the editor of the Coolidge *Examiner*, said that "the people down here (in Coolidge) were a little suspicious at first. They just didn't know what to expect. But I think they are all sold on the idea of this cooperative now, and I guess some of them wish they were up there themselves. We like the folks at Casa Grande, and hope they get along."

No doubt these friendly and encouraging words from some of Pinal County's leading citizens helped to reassure the settlers and restore their morale. But they did not entirely remove the settlers' hurt; the grocery clerks and the gas station attendants—and so the settlers themselves—would not entirely forget that the project families had been publicly and officially described as "cottonpickers" who had been living in "shacks." Some of the concern that the settlers later showed about status was surely attributable in part to this incident.

While Waldron's justification of the project had this effect within the Casa Grande community, Faul's charge against it had at first almost no effect. Then a curious thing happened. Pinal County learned that newspapers all over the country had carried news, pictures, and editorials about Communism at Casa Grande, and that made Pinal County laugh. The laughter—they called it kidding—never stopped and it had more effect on the settlers than all the serious words that were said by the hardware store proprietor, the machinery dealer and the others.

In the rash of editorial comment on Faul's resignation there was indeed a good deal to provoke amusement, although perhaps not at the expense of the project. The Eau Claire (Wis.) *Leader* said it was "just another of those things created by wastrel busybodies whose practical experience must be near zero." The Jackson (Mich.) *Citizen-Patriot* said Stalin would never tolerate the establishment of a democratic colony in Russia, and the Birmingham (Ala.) *Age-Herald* feared that such methods might degenerate into just another form of sharecropping. "What social implications do you see in that?," the Cleveland (Ohio) *News* asked of its readers. Confident of his readers' answers, the editor commented, "That makes you wrong, along with Mr. Faul and all the rest of us save FSA and FDR." The Baltimore (Md.) *Sun* was amused at the explanation, attributed to an unnamed FSA official, that the purpose of the project was to interest private capital in mechanized, large-scale cooperative farming. "It would be interesting indeed," the *Sun* said, "to learn what the FSA can tell these insurance companies about applying capital to large-scale farming that the companies don't already know." The Paterson (N. J.) *News* thought that for the government to try to interest private capital in cooperative farming was like encouraging an inventor to develop an improved guillotine with the idea of using it on the inventor if it worked. The Portland *Oregonian* said that it was not possible, under analysis, to find any weakness in Mr. Faul's argument. "This is a small thing," said the Spokane (Wash.) *Spokesman-Review*, "but it is significant of the thinking and planning that goes on under cover in Washington. It may be undertaken with the best intentions and the most generous of purpose, but it leads directly to what is set up on an all-embracing scale in Germany, Italy, and Russia."

Not all of the comment was adverse. The Communist *People's World* in San Francisco called the project, "a little Soviet which washed the windowpanes of life" for the settlers and gave them a clean view. The writer of "Topics of the Times" in the *New York Times* saw a difference between establishing sharecroppers in a community where their shares might eventually be worth more and forcing farm owners to choose between collectivization and Siberia. "Maybe it won't work, but it's worth trying," the *Times* writer said. In the opinion of the Richmond (Va.) *Times-Dispatch* Casa Grande was, "hardly a radical adventure." This editor believed that, "many more of them are needed in the South to provide both models for correct farming and employment for rural workers who have shown no signs whatever of ever being capable of operating farms of their own."

The strongest defense of the project and perhaps the most sensible came from close to home, where the editor of the Casa Grande *Dispatch* wrote: "In the experiment in Casa Grande Valley there is no confiscation of personal property or personal rights. The men on that farm are there voluntarily and from choice, and can enter upon any private ventures they see fit any time they wish. All that is required of them is that so long as they claim the right to share in the benefits and profits of the enterprise they contribute their share of work and claim only their fair share of benefits. We can see in this no essential difference from a thousand other business, economic, or community enterprises engaged in by the American people since time immemorial."

But despite the local editor's tolerant view, Faul's blast, when it was echoed by the big city press, had a decided and lasting effect on Pinal County opinion. The townspeople of Coolidge and Florence had no serious concern about the ideology the farm represented. They were merely amused. And so they named the project "Little Russia," called Beatty "Stalin," and kidded the settlers about being "Reds" when they met them in the gasoline stations, over the counters, and in the barber shops.

When they weren't kidding, the townspeople would look wise and understanding. "Sure would be a fine thing if it would work—but it won't. They can't make you Okies work together," they would say. Or, confidingly, "Well, now, I'll tell you. A thing like that just don't make sense."

The kidding and the shaking of heads had a cumulative effect on the settlers. An FSA official who observed them at close range said later that he believed the cooperative farm was kidded to death by the people of Coolidge and Florence. According to another opinion, the shaking of heads did even more to damage to the settlers' morale than the kidding. "You know how it feels when first one person then another asks you if you're sick and tells you you look pretty bad? After a while you begin to think you're sick as hell and maybe going to die. Well, that's what happened to Casa Grande."

Although the kidding and the shaking of heads did not stop, the settlers and the townspeople had come to terms by 1941—terms which, if not entirely satisfactory to the settlers, were at least a big improvement over the first year. The churches and schools in Florence and Coolidge provided the closest and most satisfactory points of contact between the project and the surrounding community. In the schools particularly the two groups were growing together. The project children who entered the Kenilworth school in the Fall of 1938 called all the other children "outsiders" and wanted to play their team against the outsiders. Then some of the farm owners' children began to call the project children "cotton-pickers." But it wasn't long before the sides were forgotten and the children chose their teams in the usual way by taking the best players first. Early in 1941 only about a dozen of the 140 pupils in the Florence High School were from project families but they nevertheless played a big part in school activities—seven were in the school band, four were in the school play, and several were on the football team. The school also brought the parents together; Mrs. Olivier for example, was one of several project women who took an active part in the local PTA chapter. Bill Forbes, the cotton foreman, served as one of three members of the school board and the principal of the school found him intelligent and easy to work with.

The settlers did not exercise a local political influence of the kind the leading citizens had at first feared, but their interest in civic and political affairs did increase. Only 20 of the family-heads had voted in local elections the year before coming to the project, but all but six voted in the 1940 election.

Most of the settlers—including practically all of those who came from Oklahoma—were members of fundamentalist religious sects such as Seventh Day Adventism. In Coolidge, where the underlying population were farm laborers of much the same background as the settlers themselves, they found plentiful opportunities to participate in religious services and "sings" which, as a rule, were all-day affairs at which several "crowds" would circulate in cars from one church to another. Sometimes the crowds came to the project. Often a Phoenix preacher would speak to his friends at Casa Grande over the radio and now and then a revivalist would conduct services in the community house. Some of the settlers achieved considerable local repute through their church activities; Cecil Hopkins, for example, preached regularly in Coolidge.

Among friends of their own class the settlers seldom needed to be on the defensive about the project. In fact many of their friends were envious. "They think it's an unusually nice place—grand," Mrs. Hopkins once said of her friends. But although they might be envious, they showed no awareness of the theoretic implications of cooperative farming. "It's a pretty good place," said one of them, a man who lived with his family in an old shack near the river bottom and was often employed by the project as a day laborer. "The men are good fellows to work with, and they're good to work for. I like to work and all they expect is a day's work so it's fine all around. The wages are nothing special—you can do just as well, and lots of times better, outside. But it's a permanent place, our kids can have steady schooling, and I don't have to go moving around looking for jobs even though they might pay more. All in all, it's better than you can get anywhere else." Once a visitor, a professor of economics, asked another of the project's neighbors, an old fellow who somehow managed to survive on a little patch of desert with no tools or stock, what he thought of the cooperative farm. "It's all right, I guess," he said. "But the thing I can't figure out is how a man tells his own chickens apart, runnin' them all together like they do there."

The settlers had a feeling of belonging in Pinal County by early 1941, but among the businessmen, farm owners, and professional people they were still ill at ease. "Coolidge people are less friendly. They are less genuine. They have an Associated Farmers' unit there and we don't like that," Mrs. Perry said. And Mrs. Smith complained to a visitor, "I don't like to go to Coolidge even to church. Those people dress better, act a little different, and they just speak a different language than we do here. We're farmers. They're lawyers, druggists, businessmen and so on. They're different from us. Oh, they're friendly enough. They're very nice—but, well, they just don't do a good enough job to make me feel at ease. I feel out of place there."

Some of the settlers felt that the people of Florence, the county seat, were easier to get along with—"perhaps because Florence is a political town," Mrs. Perry said. The underlying population of farm laborers there was "Mexican;" most of the Anglo-Saxons were county employees— teachers, prison guards, highway employees, and county office clerks. The presence of the "Mexicans" and the absence of other "Okies" made the settlers feel more comfortable in their relationships with the leaders of Florence. But because their friends were among the farm laborers of Coolidge, they went to church there and did most of their trading there.

In both towns the attitude of the leaders toward the project people was softening, Martin King thought early in 1941. "Those people in town thought we was getting everything—kinda ridin' the gravy train. Now they know different. They're friendly all right, but more so now." King's observation was probably correct, but even so it was doubtful if the settlers had achieved a status any higher than that of other "Okie" farm laborers in Pinal County. Sometimes they were sharply reminded not only that they were "Okies" but that they were "Okies" who lived at the taxpayers' expense. The Lions Club of Florence held one of its annual meetings in the community hall at the project. Several settlers were invited to attend the meeting, but only Beatty and Wildermuth were invited to join the club. "Our people think of the people out there as relief or transient people or maybe as small acreage farmers, not as better farmers," a member of the club later explained. And when one of the project children, whose father was Jehovah's Witness, refused to salute the flag in school the County Superintendent was outraged. After having everything given to them by the government, the Superintendent was quoted as saying, the least they could do was salute the flag.

10

The New Dispensation

When Regional Director Hewes, who was determined to make a democratic community and a true cooperative of the Casa Grande project, brought to Waldron's attention the fact that the community house was in a mess, Waldron replied that the inadequacies on the "social side," of which the condition of the community house was a symbol, were attributable to factionalism among the settlers and to the fact that Beatty "is not so interested in the social activities and the cooperative philosophy of living." His own efforts to develop community activities at Casa Grande had been badly diluted and—Waldron explained—"matters that do not seem to be quite so pressing are in the natural course of events delayed."

Hewes intended that there should be no further delay in educating the settlers to the real meaning of cooperation. He had in fact already decided to transfer Waldron from Arizona and to place Waldron's assistant, a young man named James Shelly, in charge of projects and certain other activities there. Shelly had demonstrated a knack for dealing with people and he was sympathetic to Hewes' idea of what a cooperative should be. He would be able to visit Casa Grande once or twice a week, and if he had the help of specialists he could carry on an active program of education on his own motion and by giving Beatty, Wildermuth, and Mrs. Hauge detailed instructions to follow. It would have suited Hewes better to employ a high-class educator as co-manager of the project, but this possibility had been foreclosed by the requirement that the choice be made from among Arizona residents.

To prepare the way for Shelly, Hewes dispatched a number of specialists from his staff to appraise the situation at Casa Grande and to formulate a program of action. The first of these was Russell Robinson, a farm management specialist who spent ten days on the farm early in 1941. (It was Robinson who had drawn up the original project proposal and the plan of operation for the typical year.) He had lengthy conferences with Beatty and Wildermuth, the Board of Directors, the committees of settlers who had been appointed to prepare budgets for the various enterprises, and, at one forum, with the entire membership. When he left for San Francisco to prepare his report, the settlers were satisfied that they had been heard fairly and in full by a man who knew his business thoroughly.

Robinson's report contained a good deal of aid and comfort for the Mott faction. It was imperative, Robinson said, that foremen be fully competent and reliable—a recommendation which seemed to imply that the incumbents were not. Wages should be raised to $60 a month at once, work assignments should be better organized, and—above all—the settlers should be given more responsibility in the management of the farm. "This will have to be done gradually," Robinson wrote, "but only in this way will the objectives of this project be accomplished. Errors of commission and omission will be made, but the membership should learn by doing. Unless the membership is made to feel that they have an active part in the conduct of the business and the responsibility for its success, there is a danger that the association will go to pieces."

Robinson proposed that all but two of the foremen be eliminated. One foreman should be in charge of livestock and the other in charge of crop farming, mechanical equipment, and irrigation. Both of these men should be selected by the manager. There should also be a head dairyman and a head irrigator and, when the men were working in the fields at scattered points, a leader for each gang. Robinson suggested that the men serve as gang leaders in rotation or that the Board submit a list of the entire membership, divided into groups by enterprises, leaving it to Beatty to select a leader from each group. Some such plan as this, Robinson felt, would give more of the settlers an opportunity to participate directly in management and might also cause Beatty to give closer personal supervision to the enterprise groups.

The report made it plain that the cooperative farm was paying dearly for the disaffection of its members. By working more conscientiously and by making a few minor economies, the settler could easily save the amount that would be needed for a wage increase.

"The labor is not at all efficient," Robinson said. "In many instances they are not diligent. The Board freely admits this. For example, in the dairy there are 274 man-hours of labor per cow and the normal is 130. Even though bottling and delivering is included in the figures for the dairy, it is obvious that the labor is excessive. The dairy crew says it can reduce the crew by two and one-half men, a matter of 27.7 percent. It is significant, however, that they add the proviso: 'if we get our wages increased.' The man-hours of labor in the poultry enterprise are 3.5 per bird. They should be 1.4. The reason the figure is high is that only 1,500 birds are being cared for. To be an economic unit the flock should be 2,000 to 3,000 birds. However, no additional use is being made of this man's extra time. Practically all enterprises reveal the same situation.

"If each member will diligently apply himself to his task and if there is good organization in the assignment of men to jobs the savings effected will be a substantial contribution to increased monthly wages.

"There is now an expenditure of $2,500 a year on a community garden. This is an average of over $50 per family. . . . Very few families said they received a benefit worth even half this amount. There is adequate land with each home for individual gardens and one family reported producing vegetables worth $100. If the community garden is not worthwhile it should be discontinued and the money now spent on it could be used toward an increase in wages."

Pointing out that it would take an additional $4,800 annually to raise the wages of 50 families from $52 to $60 a month, Robinson said he believed at least $2,000 of this could be saved by reducing the amount of paid labor on the community garden. A reduction of two and one-half men in the dairy crew would save another $1,560. The remaining $1,240 could easily be saved in other enterprises. The cost of machinery repair, for example, was 21 percent of the capital invested in machinery—at least twice the amount it should be with proper care and maintenance.

Robinson would probably have put less emphasis on the advantages of saving labor (for he knew that these were paper savings, since the farm had more labor than it could use and no way to eliminate the surplus) but for the fact that he expected his report to be used as the basis of an educational program among the settlers. In this expectation he was disappointed. Waldron's transfer was not accomplished immediately and Waldron withheld the report from the settlers, remarking privately to a visitor that the next time Robinson visited the project he would be asked to confine his discussion of management problems to the management.

A few days after Robinson's departure, Myer Cohen, another of the regional staff, appeared at Casa Grande. Cohen was an intelligent young liberal of urban background who had a degree in political science and some experience in relief administration. As a "specialist on social organization," he occupied an important position on the Regional Director's staff; problems like those at Casa Grande were not uncommon among some two score other projects and migratory labor camps administered from San Francisco, and Cohen was expected to bring the techniques of a social scientist to bear upon them.

Cohen began a five-day stay at Casa Grande by inviting the settlers and their wives to meet with him in the community hall for a discussion. Most of them came. He talked briefly on democracy and the desirability of a democratic community life, told of community activities being carried on at other projects and in migratory labor camps, and then asked for expressions of opinion. At first none of the settlers had anything to say, but when Cohen remarked that the Board of Directors could decide anything that came up someone said from his seat in the back of the hall that the management generally did the deciding. At that a group of men applauded.

Somebody recalled that they used to have regular Saturday night dances at the project. Nelson and some of the other boys had formed an orchestra, and it was pretty good. But then the dairy workers (whose day began at 2:30 a.m.) asked the orchestra to play until it was time for them to go to work. Playing from 8:00 p.m. until 2:30 a.m. was hard work, the more so since the dancers wouldn't let the musicians rest between numbers. Nelson and the boys consented to the long hours, but they decided to charge a quarter for admission. Nobody came to the dances after that. It was not that they were unwilling to spend a quarter for a night's fun, someone explained—they just didn't like the idea of paying money to other members of the cooperative. A couple of outsiders came to the project to play and the hall was crowded, even though the charge was a quarter. The outside musicians brought other outsiders with them and there was drunkenness and rowdyism. The settlers appointed a committee to police the dances, but the committee got drunker than anyone else and couldn't agree on who should be kicked out. So finally there were no more dances.

Cohen listened patiently while the settlers argued about who had done the drinking—project people or outsiders, young men or old? Then Olivier, who had so far said nothing, rose in the back of the hall.

"I came down here to farm on a big scale and work with a lot of people," Olivier said, "Otherwise I wouldn't be here. The people from San Francisco don't seem to care. We had a little store and a while back we decided to close it. The people were supposed to get their money out of that store, but the FSA collected it—about $200—and put it in the bank. If they had been for our interest, they'd have tried to get us some of that money back. But it's just laying there and nothing has been done with it.

"Come down here 30 days after this wage business is settled and I'll bet you'll get 100% cooperation—after we get our bellies full. How can you expect us to talk to you tonight when our bellies aren't full? Do you think that a family can be happy on about $45 a month? We are discouraged on that account. You can't have social activities when people are not satisfied."

There was general applause when Olivier finished.

Shelly, who was attending the meeting in Waldron's place, agreed with Olivier that the settlers' investment in the "little store" (a commissary which some of the settlers started in 1938 and which was closed by Beatty in 1939 when it ran up bills in the name of the association) should be returned to them. The trouble was that Washington had not been able to understand the situation. The money was still in the bank, and Shelly and others were trying to get it for them.

Before the meeting ended, Olivier made another demand for a wage increase. If they did not get one a lot of them were going to leave, he warned. "The old Board didn't try to get a wage increase. The new Board represents the people and has our confidence. They will vote an increase. Then it will be up to FSA to decide. Until we know whether we are going to stay or not, we can't get interested in talking about recreation and social activities. We came here to build our future, but we can't do that at our present wage. We'll have to leave if we don't get more."

Cohen was disturbed by the settlers' angry tone, but he did not consider the situation hopeless. "Discontent, grumbling, confusion, and misunderstanding," he wrote later, could all become "healthy aspects of a vital process—if properly channeled." He met with Beatty, Wildermuth, and

Mrs. Hauge to suggest activities which would channel the mis-directed energies of the settlers. These were his proposals:

1. Hold a general assembly or town meeting every two weeks or every month for discussion of community problems. The assembly would establish committees to look after sanitation, recreation, and education needs, and, as part of its educational program, would hold discussions on the reports of the various enterprise budget committees.

2. Enroll youth and if possible adults in the vocational agriculture classes of the Coolidge High School.

3. Arrange special activities for the ladies, including a reading room in the community house, consumer education, a buying club, supervised play for pre-school children, a well baby clinic, Red Cross courses, dances, and home management demonstrations.

4. Organize a young people's club and provide it with facilities for baseball, volley ball, basketball, tennis, and dancing.

Cohen's proposals came as an unpleasant surprise to Beatty. Up to that time the regional office had expected nothing more of him than a good job of farm management. Now it appeared that he was supposed to organize dances, tennis games, consumer education, and what not. It was more than he bargained for and, as he thought for a while, more than he would stand. "Maybe they need a different kind of manager here," he told a visitor to the project a few days after Cohen's departure. "Maybe they need a community man who can have meetings and make speeches and handle that sort of thing. I'm a farm manager. I told them that if the manager is supposed to do that other sort of thing then I am not the man for the job and they had better let me step out. I don't know anything about that sort of stuff, and I can't do it."

The settlers were puzzled that Cohen should see a relationship between pie dinners and democracy. Opinion was sharply divided as to whether more "get togethers" were desirable. Olivier, who was opposed to all FSA suggestions on principle, said he didn't care for that sort of thing. "On

Sundays five or six of us like to take our families, drive out into the hills and park, let the kids loose, take a rifle and go over the hills to see what we can find," Olivier said. "After work, during the week, this place is my recreation. I like to build it up and work around it." Mrs. Dewey said that the women did a great deal of visiting during the day and since the men saw each other all day they weren't interested in visiting at night. A few played dominoes at the 21 Club in Coolidge and a few sometimes got together for poker. But mostly the men weren't inclined to be sociable.

There were some settlers who agreed with Cohen, or at least with what they understood him to mean. Ernie Bates, who came from Oklahoma, was one. "Back there," he said, "we had sings and dances and services every night of the week. Here we have nothing." Salter was quite a hand at visiting. His family and others often ate together, and they had picnics and weenie roasts on Sundays and a good time generally. They went to town every other night. Sometimes they went to town in the afternoon to play pool after Salter had finished his work in the dairy. Saturday nights they went to the show. Allen, the night watchman, complained that his job prevented him from having any good times. Back home he had gone to church four nights a week and here he hadn't been able to go once. "People aren't friendly the way they are back home," Mrs. Allen complained. "When I was sick practically no one came to see me. At home that would have been done by everyone."

Mrs. Perry, who saw that FSA might only aggravate the settlers by pushing them into social activities, was in favor of letting community life develop naturally. In her opinion there was nothing abnormal about the social life of Casa Grande. "Mr. Cohen shouldn't be worried about that," she told an interviewer a few days after the meeting in the community hall. "We had lots of activity at first but it ebbs and flows. In summer it is too hot—people are away or working nights. But as it gets cooler things pick up. We have our sings and our suppers. We have enough. At first we were all getting acquainted and we had no electricity. Now that we have, we like to be at home in the evening a lot. We read and the family gets together as a whole to talk over the day. There is no need to worry about lack of community activities here.

"We need some facilities for the children—a ball field and a place set aside for them to play. Mr. Beatty doesn't seem to understand that. He fenced the ball field for a pasture. We need music for the children too. I don't care about the old folks—they're not worth much anyway; it's the young ones I'm interested in. They need opportunity to dance and play here. We are trying to get the Board to install a Victrola. Of course some parents disapprove, but the youngsters go to town and dance. I think they might as well do it here.

"We go to meetings of homemakers in Florence and they come here. At first they came to everything. So did people from surrounding farms. But somehow word got out that they weren't allowed. They quit, but now that mistaken impression has been removed and they come again. There is plenty of visiting back and forth with Florence."

If Cohen had not convinced Beatty or the settlers that community activities were the solution to the Casa Grande problem, he had at least convinced himself. "From a theoretical standpoint," he wrote on his return to San Francisco, "it is inconceivable that a cooperative farm can succeed in the absence of a carefully worked out plan of community organization not only based on a faith in democratic processes, but also implemented with the machinery for making these democratic processes effective. . . . And Casa Grande Valley Farms will be destroyed, so far as its cooperative side is concerned, unless positive and energetic steps, are taken to correct the existing situation. By positive and energetic steps, I of course recognize the need for proceeding at a pace and in a manner consistent with the psychology and habits of present residents."

Soon after his return to San Francisco, Cohen was appointed assistant regional director in charge of project management.

A week or ten days after Cohen's departure, Waldron came to Casa Grande to attend a membership meeting. The settlers had recently elected a Board of Directors from the Mott faction—a Board which was pledged to a wage increase, abolition of the wage differential, and election of foremen—and they were looking forward with relish to a show-down. But Waldron, whose transfer was now in process, proved unexpectedly and perhaps disappointingly pliable.

Waldron opened the membership meeting with a short talk on what he called philosophy. He quoted from a *Readers' Digest* article which reported on studies of workers' efficiency that had been made in a Western Electric Company plant. The workers' output, the article showed, depended on their attitudes as well as on working conditions.

"Indeed," the article said, "it was found that employees were more concerned about relations of their pay to that of fellow workers than about the actual amount of cash they got. Even if their wages were high, they were burned up if somebody whose position they considered inferior received more. Someday factory managers are going to realize that workers are *not* governed primarily by economic motives."

The feeling that they were appreciated by management was an important factor in the workers' rate of production, Waldron noted. "But you have to win appreciation and confidence," he commented. "Remember that the men guiding this cooperative farm, before they can place confidence in people, have to be sure that their confidence won't be misplaced. We've got to prove ourselves to the organization, just as if we were working for J. C. Penney or any other organization. We can't drive people. It's a matter of proper organization and conscientious effort by the men. If everyone does that, things will work."

Turning to the issues that were uppermost in the minds of the settlers, he was tantalizingly vague about a wage increase. "It looks as if we would be in a position to recommend a small wage increase. Remember now, we can only recommend." Later he returned to the wage question. "I am willing to recommend a $60 wage, or maybe $65—or at least $60 now retroactive to the first of the year and $65 from here on. You can decide what you want to do. It's up to your Board of Directors and you."

But if the men expected to get more money they would have to work harder, Waldron said. Revealing that the association had paid out $18,920 in wages to non-member employees as against $20,212 to members in 1940, he said it was plain from these figures that the men weren't working as hard as could be expected, and he added, "Lack of effort by the members means a money loss to the association."

Olivier jumped to his feet. The real trouble, he said, was not that the men didn't want to work; it was that the work was not properly organized. Sometimes it was 9 o'clock before they got their assignments down at the warehouse and sometimes they lost time coming home for lunch because they weren't told the night before whether or not to take lunch with them. Moreover some men were assigned to jobs where they were not needed.

"That's a lie," snapped Coker, getting to his feet. "You are around the warehouse because you are too lazy to work. You stand there until somebody makes you go to work."

Coker moved over toward Olivier. "You come outside and we'll settle this now," he said. "Come on."

But Olivier had taken his seat again. He looked up calmly and said that it was no lie but the truth.

Waldron interrupted to say that he hoped Coker would not take any of the discussion personally. And Beatty remarked from his seat that there was "a lot of laying down on the job."

"What are you going to do about differential wages?," someone asked Waldron.

"You can do anything you like," Waldron replied. He went on to say that the men should decide for themselves how the foremen were to be chosen. Mott and Olivier said promptly that the foremen should be chosen by vote of the settlers. Waldron countered by proposing that the settlers nominate five men for each of the important foremanships and let Beatty select one man from each panel. Mott and Olivier opposed this plan vigorously, but they finally agreed to a compromise under which the settlers would nominate panels of three men.

Mott proposed that they wait a day or two before the election. This brought snickers and smiles from the settlers, and a firm veto from Waldron. The voting went quickly by secret ballot with three of the settlers acting as tellers.

Despite their wish for a delay, the Mott faction was not altogether unprepared for the election. Olivier had circulated a slate of candidates a few days before and he had reason to believe that if a single Mottite were nominated for each panel that candidate would receive 20 votes. The unprepared pro-government faction would surely nominate more than one of its men for each panel, and so it would split its 16 votes. Thus the Mott candidate would stand far out in the lead in each panel and if Beatty passed over these high men in making his selections the affront would provide a burning issue for the opposition.

If it had not been for Bill Forbes, the plan would have worked. Forbes was a member of the pro-government group, but he had friends in the other faction who crossed the party line to vote for him. For the most important position, that of general foreman, the three nominees were Coker, Forbes and Thomas, the Mott lieutenant who had recently been elected president of the association. As Olivier expected, the pro-government faction split its vote, giving Coker and Forbes eight votes each. But Thomas did not get the 20 votes that Olivier had counted on; three of his faction voted for Forbes, and so Forbes became the middle man. It was obvious that Beatty would choose Forbes.

Only in the balloting for irrigation foreman did the lines hold. Mott received 20 votes and the pro-government faction's 16 votes were divided among five other candidates. In all other panels Forbes' name split the opposition vote. The bitterest disappointment was reserved for Olivier himself. One of the pro-government settlers shrewdly nominated Thomas as one of several to run against Olivier for the position of crop foreman. This move split the Mottites so badly that Olivier, who thought he was sure of winning, got only five votes.

When the votes had been counted and posted, Waldron said he expected there would be harmony now. But Mott and Olivier, as they moved toward the door, answered that the election settled nothing. Beatty was close to tears. This would mean losing several of the best families, he told Waldron—families who had stood by and worked without complaint for three years. Waldron said he would ask Mrs. Hauge to visit these families and ask them to stay for the good of the community. But Beatty shook his head. Like Mott and Olivier, he believed that the election had settled nothing.

Waldron's transfer was completed shortly after the membership meeting, and, with Shelly's appointment as Arizona Area Supervisor, the new dispensation at Casa Grande was fully established. The system of wage differentials was abolished immediately, and in April the Directors were permitted to vote a wage increase which brought the monthly allowance to $65 retroactive to January 1. In addition to the wage increase, Shelly allowed the Board to sell the farm's produce to members at less than market prices. Under a schedule of prices set by the Board, the settlers received the equivalent of another substantial wage increase. On the items which were most important in the family food budgets, the cuts amounted to about one-third:

		Non-Members	Members
Sirloin steaks	per lb.	.35	.20
Ham steaks	per lb.	.28	.18
Pork chops	per lb.	.30	.18
Milk	per gal.	.30	.20
Eggs	per doz.	.39	.22

The settlers' chief grievance was now fully satisfied. The increases in their incomes were a net gain, for at this time (the Spring of 1941) the cost of living was only slightly more than it had been in 1937 and 1938. The association's non-member employees were still receiving $2.00 a day (85 cents a hundred-weight for cotton picking), which was the prevailing wage in Pinal County. Taking into account the value of their housing, vacations and sick leave, and garden space, the settlers were now getting almost double the income of the average year-around worker. Compared to the migratory cotton-pickers, the members of the cooperative farm were almost wealthy.

Shelly believed that the wage increase had created an atmosphere in which it was possible to solve the underlying problems of the community, and he determined to press forward at once. One of the first questions that confronted him was whether to rid the project of Mott, Olivier, and the other troublemakers.

Waldron had at last concluded that some of the settlers would have to be forced from the project if harmony were ever to be achieved. In his final report he said that on his last visit to the ranch he sensed that a well-organized plan of sabotage was being carried out, and he recommended strongly that Mott, Olivier, and one or two others be fired. Myer Cohen, who was now in charge of projects, wrote at once to Shelly to ask if he agreed and, if so, what he proposed to do about it.

"I have felt for a year that this association would be a lot better off if about four members were expelled," Shelly replied, "and several times I have argued with Mr. Waldron that Mr. Beatty should be authorized to cancel the Work and Occupancy Agreements of these members. But now I am afraid that I have been to one conference too many, and so long as the sabotage is not physical or more clearly defined, and so long as Mr. Beatty is able to cope with it as well as he has been in the past, I am in favor of giving the members more time and the disconsolate leaders more rope. . . ."

Shelly planned to approach the problem in a quite different way. He would accept the recommendations of the Board of Directors whenever possible, even though he might disagree with them. This, he thought, would make the Board more responsible in its actions. While giving the Board more authority, he would carry on a vigorous educational campaign to prepare the settlers for greater participation in the management of the farm and for harmonious, democratic government of their community life. There would be two chief vehicles of education—the enterprise budget committees, which had been established in 1940 on advice from Washington and in which the settlers had so far shown little interest, and a forum or assembly along the lines Cohen had proposed on his visit to Casa Grande. The budget committees would be the medium of education on the "business side," while the assembly would serve the same purpose on the "social side."

On his return to San Francisco Cohen arranged for a University of California sociology student, Roy Giordano, to spend July and August at the farm as an "interne." Giordano found "confusion, dissatisfaction, lethargy and lack of loyalty." On the basis of his interviews and observations he made this tally of the strength of the opposing factions:

Communists	18–23
Technocrats	17–18
Non-classifiable	4–11
New Members	8

(The settlers did not use the terms Communist and Technocrat in their dictionary meanings, of course. They called members of the anti-government faction Technocrats because Mott and Olivier, the leaders of the faction, were believers in Technocracy. The Communists were so called because they had once naively signed a petition to allow the Communist Party to appear on the Arizona ballot. The petition had been circulated by plausible outsiders, and the settlers who signed it were surprised and horrified to learn later what it contained. Most of those who signed were members of the pro-government faction. This proved, Olivier jeered, that the pro-government settlers—Communists, as he and others began now to call them—were illiterate, or worse.)

Giordano, no doubt reflecting conversations he had had with Cohen before leaving California, believed that "the best way to aid in the adjustment of these individualistic families from an old environment to an entirely new one so as to make possible group thinking and action is by bringing them together through a comprehensive program of community activities." But the settlers, he soon found, were not at all inclined toward social activities of the kind that would make for "community integration."

"It's really too hot," some of them told him. (The temperature on the farm is usually between 100 and 120 during July and August.) Others said that the people "just didn't seem to be interested." But Giordano was not discouraged. The best way to overcome the settlers' inertia, he decided, was "to present them with the fait accompli." This he somehow managed, and the result was a busy social season: in two months there were three dances, a Fourth of July barbecue, a carnival, a wiener roast, an all-day swim and picnic at Phoenix, weekly community sings, a playground program for the children, Sunday school classes, Sunday night church services, a book exchange, and semi-monthly lectures with speakers supplied by the Coolidge and Florence American Legion, Rotary, and Lions clubs. On his return to Berkeley at the end of August, this energetic young man listed no less than twenty-seven additional activities which he believed should be undertaken to divert the settlers' attention from their problems—problems which he said "have become enormous due to incessant consideration."

A few days before Giordano left, another expert arrived from the regional office in San Francisco. Fred Ross, who had succeeded Cohen as "specialist in social organization," came to size up the situation at Casa Grande for himself and to launch the educational program by which Shelly hoped to prepare the way for real cooperation and democratic self-government. Since he was a specialist and since he came from the regional office where he was staff aide to the Regional Director, Ross was not expected to take instructions from Shelly, much less from Beatty.

Ross, like Cohen, stayed for five days. He found "hopelessness, defeatism, and apathy," all stemming from the management's lack of sympathy with the aspirations of the more aggressive settlers. Shelly was not able to be at the project while Ross was there, and Ross soon lost his patience with Beatty, who said that the purchasing and marketing phases of the farm business were too elusive to be taught to the settlers, and with Wilder-muth, who doubted that adults would turn out for educational meetings. Ignoring Beatty and Wildermuth, Ross met with the settlers in the community hall on three successive evenings. His purpose, he later explained, was to draw from the members a list of their more pressing grievances, discuss these with them, and formulate a plan of action. "Of the scores of complaints brought to light," he reported later, "all appeared to spring from a single source: failure on the part of the management to develop a satisfactory system for clearing with the members such things as government policies, project fiats, and serious problems arising on the farm."

At the second of the three meetings, the settlers elected a council of 12 members. With Ross' help, the council undertook to draft a constitution which was ratified by the membership the following evening. The constitution, which Ross conceived as an elementary lesson in democracy, began with a preamble couched in familiar style: "We, the people of the Casa Grande Valley Farms Cooperative Association (the correct name was "Casa Grande Valley Farms Inc.," a fact which Ross preferred to ignore for propaganda purposes) in order to develop a more successful cooperative farm, form a more perfect community, promote the general welfare, and insure domestic tranquility, do hereby establish this constitution. . . ." The constitution concluded with a bill of rights which assured the settlers of freedom of speech, of the press, and of assembly, and which secured them against unreasonable searches and seizures.

Between the preamble and the bill of rights certain "advisory powers" and "actual powers" of the council were enumerated. The advisory powers related to farm operations; they authorized the council to make studies of buying and selling, wage rates, machinery requirements, work techniques, and the like and to present recommendations to the Board of Directors and the Manager. The actual powers included regulation of community property (by which the community house was meant), the right to collect and disburse a community fund, to pass ordinances in the general welfare, to try violators of ordinances and refer decision reached in these cases to the Board and the Manager. The constitution also gave the council authority "to take whatever steps appear to be necessary, either by way of assuring that certain agreements reached have been acted upon, or that possible unsettled issues have been brought to the attention of the proper administrative officials within the district or region." This of course was a direct invitation to the settlers to appeal Beatty's decisions or Shelly's to the regional office, where Ross, Cohen and Hewes himself would make the final decisions.

Returning to San Francisco, Ross reported that there was now a rebirth of hope at Casa Grande. But the new hope was doomed, he warned, unless staff members gave it continual encouragement. If Beatty and Wildermuth could not, or would not provide the necessary encouragement they should be replaced.

Shelly, commenting on the organization of the community council in his regular report, remarked that the settlers seemed "enthusiastic about the possibility of getting some practical experience in group discussion and action." If he had any criticism to make, he said, it was that Ross "may have put too much emphasis on the use of the council to pressure management." To this Cohen replied, "We are in agreement with you that it should not be thought of as an instrument for bringing pressure on the management—although it may bring such pressure occasionally. The council should be seen as an instrument through which the management is kept informed of the wishes and desires of the people. It may be that in many cases the council will disagree with either the Board of Directors or the management. However, the emphasis of the council's approach should not be one of basic antagonism to the management."

In reference to Ross' suggestion that Beatty and Wildermuth be replaced, Cohen wrote to a colleague in the regional office, "I am not at all certain that we can succeed. We must recognize that the manager and assistant manager were selected with no consideration given to understanding of the non-economic side of rehabilitation. In my opinion, one of these two individuals should be competent along non-economic lines. A basic consideration is their understanding of and sympathy for the cooperative idea in all its implications. If this is not present it must be developed. If it cannot be developed, we must find personnel capable of supporting the social rehabilitation involved in the cooperative idea."

11

The Ills of Prosperity—1942

As 1941 drew toward a close it was evident that the cooperative farm
would end the year with a good profit. The cycle of drought which
had so drastically reduced the farm's production and income in its first
three years had ended with 1940, and with a plentiful supply of water in
the Coolidge Reservoir and farm prices rising steadily the new prosperity could be depended upon to continue and increase. Prosperity, which
brought with it the prospect of further wage increases and a surplus to
divide in labor bonuses, would be the most convincing evidence of the
advantages of cooperation, and—so it seemed—the settlers would at last
find the stimulus they needed to work with enthusiasm and with good will
toward each other and their benefactor, FSA.

Mott died suddenly late in 1941 and Olivier left the project immediately. Coker, having lost his position as general foreman to Forbes, was
known to be planning to leave soon. With the leaders of both factions
gone and with Waldron gone, the old wounds might quickly heal. There
was all the more reason to think so because the character of the membership as a whole had changed considerably during 1941. Eight of the
old members had left the project and 16 new members had joined, bringing the total membership to 53 at the end of the year. Most of the new
members were "Okies" recently arrived from the Dust Bowl. They were
the type of settlers who had proved most tractable in the past and, since
the memory of poverty was fresh in their minds and they had no share
of the old animosities and grievances of project life, their infusion might
have a healthy effect on the life of the community. Most of the newcomers had served six months probation as non-member laborers, so it could
be assumed that they and the old settlers were satisfied with each other
and with the trial they had made.

At the end of 1941 Cecil Hopkins, whom Beatty considered one of the
most capable of the settlers, became president of the association, and the
settlers learned that they had made a profit of $33,183 in the year past.

From the budget estimates then in preparation they could see that the next year's profits would probably be much larger.

The 1941 annual report showed that the crop enterprise made a profit of $20,257 and the livestock made $15,791. The poultry enterprise had made a few dollars profit for the first time and the dairy enterprise had again incurred a small loss. The assets of the association were now $285,811 and its liabilities $248,547, leaving a net worth of $37,264. In 1941 the association had for the first time paid FSA the maximum rent called for under the flexible lease—$22,847.

The record of the past year's operations was studied in detail by the enterprise budget committees and by the Board of Directors, for this was part of Shelly's plan for preparing the settlers to assume more managerial responsibility. The Board's comment on the annual report was brief and to the point; they were not uncritical of the management, but the criticism showed a restraint and a deliberation that Shelly found encouraging:

Dairy
Rapidity with which it is necessary to depreciate cows due to age accounts for major part of dairy loss, but will eventually reach sound financial condition. Think milking machines will help in decreasing cost and also help with labor trouble.

Poultry
Decline of cost of production and increase in prices accounted for small profit in poultry, instead of $1,000 loss as shown on 1941 budget estimates. We feel that a little more saving could be made on labor, and also some saving could be made in method of feeding by using more home-grown feed.

Livestock
1941 budget estimates showed a profit of $6,823.85—actual profit, $15,791. Gain was due to unexpected rise in prices. Handling and feeding were all that could be expected.

Crop farm

Alfalfa was some handicapped at start of the season from short-age of equipment. A baler was purchased. Seemingly an attempt was made to harvest more than could be taken care of at the proper time.

Some difficulty in planting cotton. Some tendency to plant too fast. If more care was exercised, a better stand could be procured. However, a profit was made. 1941 budget estimates showed net profit of $13,769.54. Actual profits were a little over $200 more.

Beatty, too, was encouraged. With his justification of the 1942 budget he wrote, "The study of operating plans for this year, estimated costs, and incomes has given the members a much deeper, clearer insight and understanding of the management and operation of this farm."

But while there was reason for encouragement at the beginning of 1942, there was still much that was disappointing and much to show that it would be a long, hard job to get the settlers to conform to FSA's present idea of what a cooperative farm should be. Bill Forbes, for example, had hardly taken up his duties as general foreman when the settlers, including some of those who had been his ardent supporters, made his life so miserable that he resigned. After Forbes' resignation, Beatty resumed his practice of appointing foremen and the settlers continued to resist them as before. The social life of the community continued unsatisfactory by FSA standards, although Miss Gay Elkins, a home management supervisor, was assigned to devote almost her full time to the project. Miss Elkins succeeded in reactivating the Women's Club, reviving the Sunday school and the nursery, and in organizing a spate of dances, games, and educational classes, but it was quite apparent that if her services were withdrawn the social season at Casa Grande would end abruptly. The project families were still unable to enjoy each other or to work together harmoniously.

Regional Director Hewes was encouraged but far from satisfied by the changes he had so far wrought. "We believe it can be safely said that we have demonstrated the economics of large-scale irrigated agriculture," he wrote the Administrator early in 1942. "I really believe that from the point of view of financial stability our tough years at Casa Grande are behind us. On the other hand, we are continually nagged by our own feeling of inadequacy on the social achievements of this project. In the first place, it has been very difficult to find Arizona people who are properly trained or who could be educated to a proper viewpoint in regard to this project. Since we could not take any chances with the economic side, it was necessary to get a high-type farm manager. This I think we have succeeded in doing, and Ralph Beatty has demonstrated his great usefulness in this regard. It seems to me that we should not have expected Beatty would develop on the social side since he had such a whale of a job on the farming and economic side. Therefore it seems clear that we underestimated the over-all management responsibilities of this undertaking."

Shelly was doing his best to help Beatty overcome his deficiencies on the social side, and Beatty was trying hard to learn. But neither the community council nor the enterprise budget committees, the two chief media of education in Shelly's plan, could be called successful. In fact there was now some reason to believe that education, like the election of foremen, might settle nothing. The experience of the dairy budget committee was a case in point.

When he visited the project early in 1941, Robinson, the farm management specialist, was told by the dairy crew that it could spare two and one-half men "if we get our wages raised." In April of that year the wages were raised, but still it was found not feasible to reduce the crew. The crew then decided that the only way to save labor in the dairy barn was to install milking machines. When the crew first proposed this idea, Shelly saw an opportunity for education of a very practical kind. He explained to the milkers, to the dairy budget committee (which consisted of three members of the crew), and to the Board of Directors that the association would be justified in installing milking machines only after an exhaustive study of the question. The dairy budget committee ought to investigate every phase of the subject, Shelly suggested, then present a written report to the Board of Directors. If the Board agreed with the Committee's findings, it could then present its recommendations to the Manager for discussion and decision.

The committee took its assignment in earnest. It interviewed distributors of milking machines and, with Wildermuth as a guide, visited the University of Arizona's dairy faculty, the University's demonstration dairy farm, and several leading privately-owned dairies. Then it submitted a report:

Reason for requesting purchase of milking machines.

1. Milking machine would save two men's labor at Five Dollars per day at present wages or One Hundred and Fifty Dollars per month. Beginning in September would save three men's wages, or $7.50 a day on account of fresh heifers coming in.

2. During past year we have broken in fifteen new men, at a loss of time and money to the dairy.

3. Good machine milking is better than indifferent hand milking which we have at present time.

4. Dr. Reddel of the University of Arizona recommends purchase of milking machine.

5. Mr. Wilson of the University farm said he would purchase milking machine just to milk heifers.

6. Cost of four unit machine installed $775.20 quoted by agent. Upkeep cost estimated less than $120 per year, this includes repair parts and electricity.

7. Total cost of labor without machine $11,956 per year. Total cost of labor plus cost of machine $9,731.20. Total saving in labor $2,224.20 per year.

8. Scarcity of labor. Use of machines would release two to three men to do other work on farm.

> by dairy budget committee
> (signed) C. S. Dewey
> Ebert Shepard
> Harry Church

P.S. At present we are using four milk hands and or wrangler. With machine we would use two milk hands, or machine man and one wrangler.

The committee's report was approved by the Board of Directors and by the entire membership at its annual meeting early in 1942. The matter was now clearly up to FSA, which would have to install the machines or overrule the whole body of settlers, thereby discrediting the educational program it was attempting to establish. Beatty somewhat doubtfully agreed to the settlers' recommendations and referred the question to Shelly for final decision.

Shelly was in an uncomfortable position. He had hoped that the settlers would convince themselves that milking machines were unnecessary. The main function of the dairy in the farm's economy was to provide work for the settlers, and while it seemed the part of good management to stress the importance of labor efficiency in discussions with the men, the truth was that there was little or nothing to be gained from mechanization. Moreover, unless the dairy crew handled the machines with more skill and care than seemed probable on the basis of past experience, the cows might be seriously injured. Robinson advised against installing the machines. Not wishing to act contrary to the farm management specialist's advice, Shelly deferred his decision until he could explain the circumstances to him.

The dairy crew took matters into its own hands while Shelly wavered. Five of the crew came to Beatty one morning after the milking.

"Mr. Beatty," one of them said, "as members of the dairy crew we are either going to have milking machines or we are going to strike."

"Did I hear what you said?" Beatty asked quietly. "Please repeat that statement."

The spokesman repeated what he had said, then Beatty asked each of the others if they agreed. They all said they did.

"You're fired!," Beatty said. "You are jeopardizing the loan of the United States Government, and it's my job to protect that loan. You're through, every one of you—get out!"

The crew was astounded. "We thought one of those German bombs dropped on us," one of them said later.

Two of the milkers returned to Beatty before the afternoon milking to say that they had acted in haste and wanted to apologize. Beatty restored these men to the crew at once. The others left the project.

Shelly immediately authorized installation of the machines, at the same time reporting sadly to the regional office, "The Committee did a swell job, but then couldn't wait for an answer."

Robinson took a dim view of the outcome. He wrote Shelly, "It is my opinion that Mr. Beatty will be compelled to insist that there be an actual reduction in the crew since they now have the machines. Mr. Wildermuth will have to exercise a considerable degree of supervision over the dairy operations. Otherwise there will not be a saving of labor to offset the machines, there will be spoiled quarters on the udders, reduced production, and a high bacterial count."

The history of the community council was only slightly more encouraging. One of the council's first acts, some three months after Ross' visit, was to pass a number of ordinances which, if the character of a people can be deduced from its laws, are noteworthy. The ordinances imposed fines of from fifty cents to five dollars for:

1. Breaking or destroying any windows, door or part of any dwelling or community building; or breaking or severing any property gate, fence, railing, trees, vines; or defacing or mutilating same.

2. Felonious stealing or carrying away property, such as light bulbs, books, literature, chairs, benches, lavatory fixtures, playground equipment or misuse or abuse of same.

3. Any unsanitary or filthy practice in Community Hall lavatory.

4. Disturbance of any religious, educational or recreational meeting or assembly by vulgar, lewd, or profane language or any drunken or disorderly conduct.

The ordinances were unenforceable because the community refused to take the council's police powers seriously. There were of course other matters of community interest which required administration such as the council was designed to give. But the council was either unwilling or unable to cope with these other matters of community importance. Its influence in fact was soon negative, as was evident from its handling of a series of proposals which the Women's Club, encouraged by the new home management supervisor, Miss Elkins, placed before it at the end of 1942. The women's proposals and the council's actions were as follows:

1. That the council supply four or five bales of cotton from which the women could make mattresses for the farm's hired cotton-pickers. ("No cotton until the 1942 crop.") 2. That the council permit the women to start a lunch program. ("Passed up because indefinite.") 3. That the council urge the Board to appoint a woman as its secretary. ("Passed up. Already have secretary.") 4. That a responsible person from each family be required to work in the community house one Saturday a year. ("Already taken care of by Wilks.") 5. That the Council supply seed for planting flowers around the community house. (Motion carried that seeds be furnished.) 6. That a hanger for coats and hats be provided in the community house. ("Passed up because indefinite.") 7. That a stove be provided for the women's club room. (Motion carried that a stove be furnished.) 8. That arrangements be made for community purchase of fruit. ("Suggest that members do their own buying of fruit.") 9. That arrangements be made for community sale of excess garden vegetables. (Deferred.) 10. That the Council assist in the organization of a nursery school. ("Let the women take care of it.")

Of course the administration of community affairs was only one of the Council's functions. In addition to its "actual powers," which related to the administration of community life, it had "advisory powers" in connection with the management of the farm. While it allowed its actual powers to go to seed, the Council assiduously cultivated its advisory powers so that it soon became a junior partner of the Board of Directors in the continuing struggle with management. Self-government, as the settlers still conceived it, was something to be wrested from FSA.

A glow of satisfaction had spread across the project in the Spring of 1941 when the settlers at last succeeded in getting their wages raised to $65 a month.

The news that they would also pay less than market prices for the farm's produce was slow in reaching Washington. When it finally penetrated, there was an immediate reaction. Shelly was ordered to rescind the Board's action on the grounds that it constituted an unauthorized wage increase which would complicate the association's bookkeeping and make it difficult to determine the amount of rent owed to FSA under the share-crop lease.

Shelly protested. "The Board of Director's approval of the differential," he wrote, "was a sincere attempt to partially stabilize income and expense on the part of its employees by fixing the resale price of certain commodities rather than by increasing the wage scale from time to time. Also it was an attempt to improve the living standards of its employees by encouraging consumption of farm-produced, health-giving foods.

"Insofar as possible, we encourage the Board of Directors to establish policies, and even though we may not completely agree with some of the so-established policies, we try to go along when the difference is not too great and the cost not likely to be excessive—even though it may occasion the FSA staff some additional labor and inconvenience."

Washington ignored Shelly's letter, and he had no alternative but to announce to the members at their annual meeting in January, 1942, that henceforth purchases from the farm would have to be at the full market price. Within a few days a petition bearing the names of all of the members was presented to the Board. Containing six "whereases," the petition called for an increase to $3.50 a day—$91 for a 26-day month, retroactive to the first of the year.

Shelly again saw opportunities for education, and the Board, acting on his advice although all of its members had signed the petition, determined to make a study of living costs and prevailing wages before taking action. Three days after the petition was presented, two of the Directors, Cecil Hopkins and Albert Jones, reported in writing to Beatty on the results of inquiries they had made from "a fair cross-section" of local employers. "We expressed ourselves very clearly as wanting only a fair deal and had no desire to set up a wage that would be above the average in the county," they wrote. North and west of Florence Jones and Hopkins "got the impression there was a desire to oppress wages regardless of living cost." South and east of Coolidge things were different. A. L. McCann was paying $3.00 and he thought the cost of living would soon force wages higher. Simmons, south of Coolidge, was paying $2.50 and furnishing cabins and utilities. "I'll frankly admit I'm going to get my work done as cheaply as possible for as long as possible," Simmons said. Jones and Hopkins noted of him, "A definite tendency to organize and prevent a rise in wages."

While the two directors were making their survey of wage rates, Miss Elkins was preparing a study of living costs at the Board's request. She found that the price of groceries and clothing in Coolidge stores had increased nearly 40 percent in the past year. Ten pounds of potatoes had been 25¢ in 1941 and were now 37¢. Flour, which had been 70¢ for 24 pounds, was now $1.05. Three pound cans of shortening had gone up from 58¢ to 75¢. Hercules shirts had gone up from 89¢ to $1.29, and ladies' print dresses from $1.00 to $3.00.

After examining several family record books (some of which had obviously been doctored to show the need for a wage increase), Miss Elkins drew this comparison between the 1941 and 1942 expenses of a family of four:

	Monthly Costs	
	1941	1942
Church	.20	.20
Movies	.75	.90
Milk (4 qts. daily)	5.60	5.60
Meat	8.00	8.00
Groceries	15.00	30.00
Rent (1 extra room)	2.00	2.00
Gas and lights	5.00	5.00
Car payments	15.00	15.00
Gasoline	8.00	8.00
Clothes	4.00	5.00
Medical care	3.00	3.00
Furniture rent	2.00	2.00
Total	$67.55	$74.70

Both Miss Elkins and Beatty recommended the wage increase. Beatty said he thought $3.50 a day was considerable, even taking into account the higher cost of living. But he said that the settlers had been accustomed to a higher standard of living than other farm laborers in the community, and he supposed the higher standard would probably have to be maintained.

A bulky collection of documents in support of the wage demand— the settlers' petition, resolutions from the Board and from the Community Council, the Hopkins-Jones report, the Elkins report, and Beatty's recommendation—were forwarded to the regional office on March 25 along with a letter of endorsement from Shelly who, the day before, had received this note from the Board of Directors: "The people are verry verry anxious to know sompthing about the Wage increase please give some explanation of same as we do not wish to be forced to take further action on this question."

Three weeks later nothing had been heard from the regional office. Beatty then wired that the directors had voted to give each member a gallon of milk daily and two dollars worth of meat weekly unless the wage increase were granted by April 21. "Please advise," Beatty urged. On the deadline day the Regional Office wired approval of the increase, adding, "This approval must be confirmed by Washington. Motion by Board regarding free distri- bution milk and meat exceeds Board's authority." In a letter following the wire, the regional office pointed out that the prices of groceries and clothing in Coolidge were so high as to suggest that the merchants there were over- charging. This being the case, San Francisco said, the settlers would do well to establish a consumers' cooperative on the project.

On May 7 Washington confirmed the wage increase, commenting, "Many cooperative associations find it much more practicable to furnish meat and milk and firewood and other farm products to members on an equitable basis as part of their wages, rather than pay the members an additional cash wage in order that they in turn may pay the cash back to the association for such subsistence."

The regional office did not pass this latest advice from Washington on to the settlers, whose sense of humor was not to be trusted.

As Hopkins and Jones had recognized in their conversations with neigh- boring farmers, the members of the cooperative were both farm laborers and employers of farm labor. In one role they might regret a tendency to oppress wages, while in the other they could assure their fellow employers that they had no desire to raise the prevailing wage. Such a situation was bound to be confusing, but there was some advantage in the confusion, for the settlers could step from one role to another almost at will and they could avoid the more onerous features of both. As farm laborers they could refuse to accept the discipline of management while driving a hard bargain for wages. And as employers they could heedlessly run up their wage bill while paying their workers at the lowest possible rate.

Although it was designed to level out seasonal peaks in employment and give the members steady work all year round, the preliminary farm plan drawn up before the association was organized made some small provision for the employment of non-member labor, chiefly at the cotton-picking season. The project planners included most of this expense for non-member labor as income in the settlers' family budgets, for they assumed that most of the cotton-picking would be done by the wives and children of the members. That was the way it worked out in the cooperative's first year, and the labor bill for that year was almost exactly what the planners had anticipated.

In 1939 however the bill for outside labor came to almost one-third the amount paid to the settlers themselves. In 1940 (as Waldron had pointed out, infuriating Olivier) the non-members earned almost as much as the members. In 1941 the non-members were paid about $20,000. This was more than the year before but because the settlers received a wage increase it was only about two-thirds of the amount paid to the members. In 1942 and 1943 the wage bill for both non-member and member labor continued to increase because of higher wage rates for both, but the cost of non-member labor remained about two-thirds that of the member labor. That the bill for outside labor should increase steadily to such a proportion could not be explained by changes in the farm management plan; on the contrary, the sharp reduction in cotton acreage during the first three years because of drought should have almost eliminated the need for outside labor.

A good share of the expense for outside labor went to the settlers' families or to their relatives, and that was probably one reason why the total was so large. About half a dozen of the older boys were employed almost steadily and several were employed intermittently. The wives and the younger children of some of the settlers picked cotton, but the number of these decreased steadily, for cotton-picking was associated with a class status which the settlers wished to escape. But while the number of family members decreased, there was a more than corresponding increase in the employment of other relatives. The "Okies" were accused by the other settlers of bringing their relatives to Arizona to get them on the farm's payroll. For a time there were several families of in-laws living in trailers on the home-lots of some of the settlers. This angered Olivier and some others because the trailers were attached to the community utility systems, which had common meters. ("The two-families-in-one-house argument is endless," Shelly wrote early in 1942. "The Board of Directors and the Community Council are working towards a definition of a family as well as a definition of when a relative ceases to be a visitor and becomes an occupant.") Finally the Board ruled that the farm would neither accept relatives as members nor employ them. After that relationships were concealed, so that it was impossible to tell what proportion of the expense for outside labor went to relatives.

But while the desire of the members to employ their relatives accounted in part for the farm's increasing dependence on outside labor, an even more important cause was the members' increasing reluctance to do hard work themselves. They used Indians, Mexicans and other "Okies" for low-caste jobs almost exclusively in 1942 and they were more and more inclined to use hired labor for "better" jobs like tractor driving.

The association's by-laws provided that non-member employees were to have wages, hours and conditions of employment not inferior to those that prevailed in the surrounding community. This was not a hard standard to meet, and Beatty had no fear that the settlers would be unduly generous with the outsiders, even though some of them were relatives. He left the Board of Directors free to fix the prevailing wage on which the non-members' pay was based.

In arriving at the prevailing wage for this purpose, the Board did not take into account the standard that prevailed among the settlers themselves; outsiders were consistently paid less than members. In 1938 the wage for outsiders was $1.50 a day. In 1939 cotton choppers were paid $2.00 a day, which was the rate on which the settlers' cash monthly allowance was based; the cotton choppers of course did not receive housing and other privileges as did the settlers. The outsiders' wage continued at $2.00 a day through 1941, while the members were receiving $2.50 a day and a discount on the price of milk, eggs, and meat from the farm. In the Spring of 1942, when the settlers got their own wages raised to $3.50, they paid their hired help $3.00. A year later the settlers paid themselves $5.00 for a day "or any part of a day, however small," and put the outsiders on a straight hourly basis at 40 cents an hour.

The housing which the association provided its cotton-pickers was also of the prevailing standard—a standard which the Resettlement

Administration had described as wretched. In fact the same shanties which stood on the land when the Resettlement Administration bought it were used without any repair or improvement to shelter the outsiders. Late in 1941 the FSA Administrator visited Casa Grande and was shocked to find that the very conditions his agency was crusading to correct were being tolerated on one of its best advertised projects. He ordered immediate improvement in the farm's housing. The matter was put before the Board of Directors by Shelly. The Board referred it to the Community Council and the Council referred it to the Women's Club. The Club proposed to turn the settlers' old mattresses over to the cotton-pickers and to make new mattresses for replacements if the farm would supply the cotton. The Council replied that no cotton would be available for another year, and there the matter was dropped, the cotton-pickers having finished their work and moved on long since.

In 1942, FSA recruited farm laborers and transported them to Western farmers as a war-time aid to employers who were short of labor for harvesting essential crops. As a condition to this assistance, FSA required that the employer pay the prevailing local wages, provide housing to meet minimum standards, and guarantee to employ the workers for at least 75 percent of the time they were available. Most big farm employers were easily reconciled to these requirements, but the Directors of the association, "after considering the terms of the contract," voted to decline the offer of help. Later the Board changed its mind, perhaps at Beatty's insistence. Since housing for the workers would have to be passed on by inspectors from FSA's labor branch, the Board gave some thought to demolishing the old shanties and building one-room (some Directors favored two-room) dwellings with outside privies. Instead, an old frame house which had been described as badly dilapidated in 1936 was screened and the cotton-pickers took up quarters there.

The settlers were not unaware that they might be expected to set a better standard than other employers, and some of them were embarrassed by the irony of the situation. "We invite cotton-pickers in, we're glad to have them during the season," Mott said in the Spring of 1941. "We urge them to come and to move into the shacks on the place. Then when the season is over we kick them out. I was kidding old man Forbes about that. He's one of those who believe if you can't get a decent wage you work for whatever you can get and like it. I asked him, 'How about that? We get moved out of those shacks by the FSA and then we turn around and invite a bunch of cotton-pickers to live in them, and in tents we provide, to pick our cotton at a measly wage they can't live on. How does that figure out?' He didn't know the answer, but he was a little embarrassed about kicking them out now that we don't need them any more."

12

The Ills of Prosperity—1943

That the farm's increasing prosperity, the turnover among the settlers, and FSA's more liberal policy of administration had brought about no radical or fundamental change in the underlying elements of the situation at Casa Grande was apparent at the beginning of 1943. The cooperative's net profit in the year just past was $36,803 and its assets now stood at $313,000, of which $74,000 was the settlers' equity. This was success beyond anyone's expectations and there was the promise of even greater success in the year ahead. Yet the membership dropped from 53 to 39 in the face of this unparalleled prosperity and factionalism was as keen among the settlers as ever before. Although Mott and Olivier were gone, the opposition faction continued under a new leader, more politely now, but uncompromising still in its drive for power.

The new leader of the opposition was John Sanford, who had joined the association in April 1941, served as the first secretary of the Community Council, and graduated to the Board of Directors at the beginning of 1942. In its essentials, Sanford's history was no different from that of many of the other settlers. Thirty-seven years old, a native of Bald Knob, Arkansas, he had completed nine grades of school, been a farm laborer in Oklahoma and southeast Missouri, cash-rented a 40-acre farm, and worked for two years in a machine shop in Canton, Ohio for $190 a month. In 1935 Sanford came to Arizona as a farm laborer and five years later, just before joining the cooperative farm, he and his family—a wife and four children—lived in a two-room shack without electricity, running water, an indoor toilet, or even a kitchen sink. Early in 1941 his assets were an old automobile worth $50 and household goods worth $25.

The memory of his one-time prosperity in Ohio was perhaps more real to Sanford's mind than the recollection of the very severe poverty he had just escaped. At any rate, he had no sooner moved to Casa Grande than he began to feel the itch for power. When Mott died, Sanford was ready to succeed him as the most energetically dissatisfied of the settlers. Early in 1943 he was elected president of the association. Meanwhile Ernest S. Perry, the only settler who had come to Casa Grande because he wanted to cooperate, emerged as leader of the pro-government faction, a position he shared with the retiring president, Cecil Hopkins.

The educational program by which Hewes hoped to make a model community of Casa Grande had been under way only two years by the beginning of 1943, and so it was perhaps too early to look for basic changes in the structure of the situation. Acknowledging that the effects of education are felt slowly, at first on the surface and then underneath, one might find some encouraging signs in the farm's recent history; on this and other grounds one might even explain away most of what was discouraging.

The drop in membership, for example, could be explained by the attraction of war industries; the cooperative farm could not be expected to retain all of its old members or to recruit new members in competition with the shipyards of San Francisco and the airplane factories of Los Angeles. That the settlers were still antagonistic to management and unreasonable in the demands they made upon it could be explained as the inevitable result of the restrictive policy followed by FSA in the cooperative's formative years, and there was some evidence that the new policy of education was having an effect. The dairy crew had almost, if not quite, mastered a lesson in the techniques of responsible participation in management, and Beatty had almost, if not quite, mastered a lesson in labor relations; perhaps the next time both the crew and Beatty would succeed. Although it had shown little or no interest in administering community affairs, the Community Council was at least alive and was making active use of its advisory powers. Blundering interference from Washington had precipitated a demand for a wage increase by denying the settlers the right to buy food from the farm at reduced prices, but the settlers had conducted the negotiations in a manner which, if it did not wholly conceal the threat of force, was at least a marked improvement over earlier occasions when Mott and others had threatened to denounce the project as a peon camp and go on strike.

Shelly and Beatty were both convinced that the settlers had learned a good deal about the business of the farm through participation in enterprise budget committees. But still the serious business of budget making could not be left to the settlers and Beatty, at least, remained convinced that they would never be capable of running the farm successfully. How far the process of education could go without bringing the settlers to the point where they could think as businessmen, rather than sharecroppers, was evident one day in 1943 when the Board of Directors met to approve the monthly bills. An FSA official, acting in Beatty's absence, read out the bills one at a time and the Directors voted approval of each item. One Director sat quietly in a corner taking notes, a worried expression growing deeper on his face as each bill was read. Finally this man broke out:

"Do you men realize, our expenses for this past month have run $1,000 a day?."

The others were appalled.

"$1,000 a day!"

They stared at each other and at the FSA man.

"There isn't any business," the note-taker went on with conviction, "that can stand expenses of $1,000 a day!"

The FSA man dashed to Beatty's office and returned with figures showing that the farm's income had been nearly $1,500 a day during the same period. The Directors relaxed when they saw these, but not without a good deal of shaking and scratching of heads.

Perhaps the greatest encouragement that Hewes and Cohen could find was in the changed manner of the opposition. Sanford never ranted. His tone was friendly and conciliatory and, in a letter to Cohen, he once mentioned his devotion to the ideal of democratic community life. Mott and Olivier were irreconcilables, but Sanford, it seemed, was reasonable, and this was certainly a cause for optimism and an evidence, perhaps, that Hewes' more enlightened policy was having an effect.

It was true, no doubt, that Hewes' policy accounted for the change in the opposition's manner. Dealing with Waldron (the palm of whose hand was harder than Faul's iron toe, someone once said) had required a toughness which was now wholly unnecessary. But, as Hewes and Cohen discovered during 1943, a change in the settlers' manner did not necessarily indicate a change in their motivation.

It was with Hewes and Cohen that the settlers dealt on major matters in 1943. Shelly resigned in 1942. Since there was no hope of finding a suitable replacement for him in wartime, the "social side" of the project was thereafter directed by Cohen from the regional office. This shifting of power from the scene of action at Casa Grande to San Francisco had begun with

Waldron's transfer and proceeded with the creation of the Community Council, which was given the right to carry its appeals beyond Beatty and Shelly to the regional office. Now there was no intermediary in contact with both Beatty and the settlers who could reconcile their differences and push forward a positive program of education. Beatty was left free to devote himself entirely to the "farm side," while Cohen, occupied as he was with many other matters, could only handle the "social side" by giving yes or no answers to questions that the settlers put before him by correspondence.

Cohen was inclined to answer "yes" to the settlers because in his innate liberalism he believed that a low-income farmer's leadership would take constructive directions—the logic of his situation, if not the essential goodness of his nature, dictated that the low-income farmer should eventually do what was good for him. Cohen did not regard Sanford as an antagonist, as Waldron had regarded Mott, and he was reluctant to oppose Sanford or the other aggressive settlers whom he considered natural leaders for fear of stifling the nascent democracy at Casa Grande. This being Cohen's view (which Hewes shared), Sanford found it possible to assault the strongholds of power pleasantly, politely and only now and then forcibly.

Cohen was to find during 1943 that it was the logic of Sanford's situation as the leader of an opposition party, rather than as a low-income farmer, which governed his actions. The opposition had to remain in opposition in order to preserve its power, and so when Cohen took a skip to get in step with the more aggressive settlers they at once took a skip to get out of step. It was the same with the pro-government faction. Finding itself out of step with FSA, the pro-government group would take a skip to get back in step. There were times when all sides became confused in their footwork, and the confusion tended to destroy the pro-government faction and add strength to the opposition.

Beatty, who now had more authority in the day-to-day operation of the farm than ever before, became the one point at which the opposition encountered real resistance. It was therefore inevitable that he should become the chief target of the opposition, which was exasperated to find that it could win a dispute with Cohen over an important matter like wages and at the same time be ignored by Beatty in a trivial matter like when to cut alfalfa. With the position of the pro-government faction (and therefore the position of the foremen) weakened by Cohen's collaboration with Sanford, and with the opposition centering its full attack upon him, Beatty's situation was becoming more difficult and hazardous day by day.

Early in 1943, when a special agent of FSA's investigation division (a kind of intra-agency FBI) made a routine report on the project, the settlers' complaints were directed exclusively against Beatty. Like Faul before him, Beatty was being called a dictator.

The grounds on which the charge of dictatorship rested must have seemed weak indeed to those who remembered Faul. For one thing, the Directors complained that they were not given adequate monthly reports of the association's business as the by-laws required. It was true that the Board often missed seeing the reports, the association bookkeeper explained, but the reason was that they were often held too long by the regional office. Why the reports were sent first to the regional office or why copies were not kept for the Board was not explained.

The by-laws authorized the Board to approve all purchases, and the Board had delegated this authority to one of its members. But this man rarely had an opportunity to approve purchases before they were made, the settlers told the special agent. Ordinarily Beatty would send the purchase order around for signature only after delivery had been made. Moreover, although the by-laws gave the Board authority to fix the amount of credit that might be given or taken, Beatty, early in 1943, had run up a feed bill of over $10,000 without consulting the Board.

The settlers blamed Beatty for the fact that they were not allowed to buy milk, meat, and eggs from the farm at less than market prices. This complaint was suggested to the settlers by Miss Elkins, the home management supervisor, who disliked Beatty. It was entirely untrue, for the ruling had come from Washington, but nevertheless this was one of the principal grievances held against Beatty.

When the special agent asked him to comment on the charge of dictatorship, Beatty said he was sorry the settlers felt that way. He had no intention of acting like a dictator—he was simply trying to run the farm the best he knew how. He might have pointed out, if he had wished, that as the government's supervisor or creditor's representative he had authority, which the settlers had until recently acknowledged, "to conduct the business of the borrower in all its branches." And he might have added that the difficulty was not that he had become more dictatorial but that the cooperative had become, after a fashion, more democratic.

Besides this question of their proper authorities, there was another issue on which the Board and the Manager differed. The Board accused Beatty of neglecting the crop enterprise, particularly the cotton, in favor of his specialty, livestock. In the Board's opinion cotton, not cattle, should be the farm's principal enterprise. Beatty freely admitted that he was placing the chief emphasis on livestock. He was fully convinced, he said, that the success or failure of the project would ultimately depend upon the success or failure of the livestock enterprise.

So far the cotton had done very poorly and the cattle very well. Beatty pointed to this as a justification of his policy. The Board, of course, pointed to the policy as the reason for the cotton's failure. The farm budget had anticipated a profit of $18,000 from crops in 1942, but there had actually been a loss of $15,000. As much as $10,000 of this loss could be accounted for, perhaps, by a too-conservative method of appraising the inventory on hand at the end of the year. But, even so, why wasn't the cotton crop profitable? Beatty said it was because of a crop failure and because of the inefficiency of inexperienced labor. The settlers said it was because the cotton was planted too late, and some of them hinted that Beatty had sabotaged the cotton in order to make the record of the cattle look better by comparison.

If not by this means then by some other, Beatty had certainly succeeded in making the record of the cattle look good. In its first year, 1939, the livestock enterprise had incurred a small loss. But in 1940 the profit was $12,000, in 1941 nearly $16,000, and in 1942 $52,000. Casa Grande livestock had consistently topped the market in Los Angeles and in some instances it brought record prices.

Thomas, who was then a director, confided to the special agent that he, Sanford, and some other settlers had discussed the advisability of liquidating the livestock enterprise, paying off the FSA loan with the proceeds of the livestock, "and then either farming or quitting." This was an entirely practical plan, if FSA could be brought to consent to it. The association had paid $14,453 principal and $18,807 interest on its $173,288 operating loan and on April 30, 1943 its net worth stood at $128,681. The livestock on hand at that time were worth $185,343 and of course they were an entirely liquid asset. There was no doubt that, if FSA agreed, the cooperative could pay off its loan, fire Beatty, and go its own way without interference. But before FSA could be expected to agree to such a plan, the members would have to agree to it themselves.

In its first three years the association had made no profit, or virtually none, so there could be no question of a dividend or "labor bonus." But toward the end of 1941, with a good profit from that year's operations assured, the settlers began to consider what might be done with the $6,597 which had accumulated from past years.

Half of that small sum represented "house rent credits." Since the summer of 1938 the association had carried on its books the extra rent, computed at two dollars a room, chargeable to the families occupying houses with extra bedrooms. Many families having moved away from the project without accumulating an equity from which these charges could be deducted, the Board of Directors decided that it would be unfair to collect in cash from those who remained. Accordingly the Board voted to cancel all house rent credits and require full rent in cash from all families in the future. FSA quickly approved the Board's decision.

That left $3,259 available for distribution. Thirty-four settlers promptly petitioned the Board of Directors to declare a labor bonus. For a time the Board hesitated. The association's by-laws required that a labor bonus be distributed to both member and non-member employees in proportion to the hours each employee had worked. The Board was reluctant to allow the non-member employees a share in the earnings, but on inquiry from the FSA regional attorney it found that this was one of the several provisions of the by-laws which could not be changed without the government's consent. After consultation with the Community Council, the Board decided to declare a bonus anyway.

The settlers' sudden and somewhat premature desire to distribute their small surplus was provoked by Sanford and others of the opposition faction, Shelly explained in a letter to the regional office. Sanford and his friends wanted to demonstrate their contention that FSA would never permit the settlers to take their earnings under any circumstances. Perry and others of the pro-government faction were equally sure that FSA would approve a labor bonus, and to prove their point they also signed the petition. Together the two factions were presenting a test case. "The most effective answer,"

Shelly wrote Hewes, "will be prompt approval of the Board's recommendation for a 50 percent labor bonus."

Hewes acted upon Shelly's advice. Early in 1942 he wired his approval, with three conditions attached:

1. Before declaring the dividend, the Directors must first set up a reserve fund for educational purposes and, particularly, for purchasing the equities of members who might withdraw.

2. The Board and the Manager must give assurance that payments due FSA will be made on schedule without impairing capital assets.

3. The dividend will have to be paid to non-member employees on the same basis as to members.

"No future dividend will be approved by me unless cash position of association fully justifies," Hewes added—a statement which might easily be interpreted to mean that he was capitulating in this instance against his better judgement.

When the Board received Hewes' telegram, it promptly rescinded its vote on the labor bonus. Sanford's manoeuvre had failed. He and his friends of the opposition now decided that the objectionable provision of the by-laws requiring payment to non-members should be removed before any of the earnings (now greatly swelled by the addition of the 1941 profit) were distributed. On this point the opposition felt it could rely on FSA to provide some real resistance. But before this issue could be put to the test there were other matters which required attention.

One of these matters, anticipated by Hewes in his telegram, concerned payment of equities to withdrawing members. Up to this time members who left the project had made no claim for their property interest in the association, but, shortly after the abortive move to distribute a bonus, Coker resigned and asked the Board of Directors to purchase his equity.

The Board went to a Florence attorney who pointed out that the by-laws permitted the association to buy equities only when it had reserves already established for that purpose. The Board had not established a reserve (since it had not availed itself of Hewes' permission to declare a bonus), and so it decided to table Coker's resignation until a reserve could be set up. Most of the settlers felt that it was unfair that former members should have no share of the farm's present prosperity; not only Coker, but Mott's widow was concerned, so the issue cut across factional lines. The Board proposed to establish a fund from which equities could be paid retroactively, but this proposal was vetoed both by the Florence attorney and by the FSA regional attorney. Finally Coker's resignation was accepted with no payment being made to him.

In July 1942, acting on the advice of the lawyers, the Board declared the equities of all former members forfeit and fixed the equities of the current members at $651.51. This was the amount to be paid to any member who might withdraw or die, and it was the amount that any new member would have to pay, either in cash or in deductions from earnings, in order to be admitted to membership. From time to time the Board would re-calculate the individual member's equity on the basis of the association's changing net worth. Although the Board could not pay out equities retroactively, it was able to rule, ex post facto, that all applicants who had been accepted for membership since April 27, 1942 would be considered "tentative members" until they had signed contracts agreeing to have the amount of the members' equity deducted from their earnings.

Another matter which troubled the settlers in their prosperity was wages. The association was now fat with profits, but the members could still fall readily into the role of mere laborers on a government farm— laborers who were grossly underpaid—whenever wages came up for discussion. This they did although their incomes and standard of living continued much higher than in the surrounding community.

In the Spring of 1942 the settlers had succeeded in getting their wages raised to $91 a month ($3.50 a day)—an amount which more than offset the value of the discount they had previously enjoyed on the purchase of the farm's products. Before the year was out, $91 a month was too little for many of them. In March 1943 the Community Council called for another increase, and the Board of Directors, which was under Sanford's control, followed immediately with a resolution favoring $5 a day. The Council canvassed nearby farms, as Hopkins and Jones had done the year before, to find the prevailing wage. But this time FSA sent one of its own men to make an independent investigation, and, while the Council reported that $5 was "not out of line," the FSA official found that the prevailing wage was between $3.50 and $4.00.

Cohen proposed that the settlers accept a wage of $4.00 retroactive to the beginning of the year (it was then April), with the understanding that the prevailing wage would be ascertained again on July 1 and a further increase made then if warranted. Having distributed none of its surplus, the association was well able to pay at the rate of $5, but it seemed to Cohen that the settlers ought to learn that there was a matter of policy involved. High wages could easily become a habit, and over the long run a dangerous habit; if the settlers made it a fixed policy to pay themselves no more than the prevailing wage and to distribute their surplus in bonuses they would be in a far better position to weather the lean years which might lie ahead.

Cohen's arguments were lost on the Sanford faction. The Board refused the proffered $4 and the opposition faction made preparations for a strike. Cohen countered with the suggestion that the settlers take a labor bonus instead of the disputed dollar. This would establish the principle and at the same time give the settlers the money they wanted. The labor bonus proposal was put before the Board, the Community Council, and the membership. A majority of each body voted to reject and to insist upon the $5 wage. Sanford explained the reasons for their preference somewhat vaguely in a letter to Hewes. "Various reasons are being offered," he wrote, "such as the difficulty the association might incur in the matter of ready cash to pay a labor bonus. Also it is pointed out that a labor bonus has never been paid and some doubt is expressed whether it would be wise to expect such a thing."

With this second sentence Sanford apparently meant to suggest that Hewes had vetoed the Board's previous move to distribute a bonus by attaching unacceptable conditions to his approval of it, and that the settlers suspected him of planning to do the same thing again. No doubt Sanford had persuaded his followers, and perhaps himself, that FSA was to blame for the fact that there had been no bonus, but this could hardly have been the settlers' reason for refusing the bonus again. For Sanford and the other opposition leaders the reason lay solely in the necessity of opposing FSA. For the rank and file of settlers, however, the reason was probably that a high wage rate meant high standing in the Pinal County community, whereas a labor bonus meant nothing at all.

While Cohen's proposal was under study, the opposition made ready to strike. The strike would not seriously interrupt the farm work, for the pro-government faction was still numerous enough and determined enough to keep things going on an emergency basis. But the opposition knew that a complete work stoppage would be wholly unnecessary. If only half or two-thirds of members struck, even that would be enough to bring a swarm of newspaper reporters and investigators from Washington and to damage FSA's prestige seriously. With this keg of dynamite at hand, the opposition made as if to strike a match. FSA surrendered unconditionally, and the $5 wage was established retroactive to January 1.

A few days later an FSA official who visited the project was surprised to find that a majority of the settlers regretted that their wage demand had been granted. "A large majority felt that FSA had lost interest in the project," he wrote later. "In fact, a majority felt that the wage advance would ultimately jeopardize the association. One of the members told me that although he had talked for $5 he never expected that FSA would allow it. If he had thought they would, he certainly never would have recommended it. I asked him why the members did not cut wages back to what they felt was a safe figure and I assured him they would have no trouble in getting FSA to approve such an action. 'It's harder to take candy away from a baby than to give it to one,' he said, and it was his opinion that it was going to be very difficult to get wages down when times are not so good."

While the wage issue boiled, Sanford and his friends were preparing another. They had long intended to force a change in the section of the by-laws which required that labor bonuses be distributed to non-member employees as well as to members, and they were not entirely satisfied with the arrangements that had been made the year before respecting the payment of equities to withdrawing members. As the association's surplus grew, these two issues became more and more important to the settlers and it was easy for Sanford to win followers by pointing out that no one—not even Coker—had so far received a penny from the cooperative except in wages, and that when and if a bonus was at last distributed, "outsiders" would get a big share of it.

Early in 1943 the Board asked its lawyer to draft some amendments to the by-laws to cover these points. The lawyer proposed that the association set up a revolving fund and issue "certificates of interest" against the fund. At the end of each fiscal year the Board would distribute the entire net earned surplus in the form of credits against the fund. Each member's credits would be in proportion to the hours he had worked during the year and would be evidenced by certificates of interest. Having distributed the entire surplus as credits, the Board would then decide how much of the surplus would be required for operating and other needs during the year ahead. Whatever was not needed for these purposes would be applied to the payment of credits outstanding from former years. The credits for any particular year would be pro-rated against the credits outstanding for that year.

Under this plan, the association's membership fee would be set at $300. A withdrawing member would have his $300 returned to him and in due order he would receive the value of his credits against the fund. Beyond this, he would have no property interest in the association. This plan of course gave the non-member laborers no claim at all on the association's earnings.

FSA agreed to the proposed amendments with two minor changes. Hewes had been concerned for some time at the steady decline in the number of members (there were only 36 in the summer of 1943) and at the settlers' reluctance to admit new members for fear of reducing their share of the profits. It seemed quite possible that the association might eventually have only half a dozen members, who would live a life of ease while employing non-member labor to do all of the work. He therefore insisted that the membership fee be set at $100 rather than $300 so that this would not be an obstacle to the recruitment of new members, and that the earnings be distributed among non-member employees as well as members if at any time the membership should fall below 30. These small, face-saving conditions Sanford readily accepted.

The new by-laws, as finally approved by the membership, provided, significantly, for "dissolution and liquidation" of the association—a possibility which the officials of the Resettlement Administration had overlooked when they drafted the first by-laws seven years before. In this now conceivable eventuality, the net assets of the association, after payment of outstanding credits, were to be distributed among the members in proportion to the credits each man held.

13

Liquidation

Tucked away in the voluminous Agricultural Appropriations Act of 1943 were a few words forbidding FSA to use any of the appropriated funds in connection with resettlement projects or cooperatives, except as might be necessary to bring about their liquidation as soon as possible. Congress had served notice the year before that the projects were to be liquidated as rapidly as consistent with the purposes for which they were established, and it had created a select committee under the chairmanship of Representative Harold Cooley of North Carolina to investigate the activities of FSA. In 1943 Cooley and others charged that FSA had ignored Congress' mandate to liquidate the projects. This time they intended to make it stick. The new appropriations act was drawn so as to give FSA no alternative but to begin the liquidation of Casa Grande and the other projects at once.

C. B. Baldwin, the FSA administrator, had not ignored Congress' order to dispose of the project. At the end of 1942 he decided to liquidate the Casa Grande project by selling it to the association. By selling the land and buildings to the membership on a "flexible" repayment plan extending over 40 years, he would put the cooperative farm out of the reach of Congress, for Congress itself could not break a legally executed contract of sale. The switch from a lease to a purchase contract would make little difference in the affairs of the association; under the flexible repayment plan amortization charges might even be less than the rent. Of course if FSA could not assist a cooperative in any way, Beatty's salary would have to be paid by the association henceforth, but that was not a serious drawback, for the farm was now well able to afford the cost of management.

There was nothing undercover about Baldwin's plan. He frankly told the Cooley Committee that he planned to sell the Casa Grande project to the association. While the appropriations bill was in the hands of the House and Senate conference committee, he telephoned Senator Carl Hayden of Arizona to ask if in the Senator's opinion the language of the bill would permit sale of the project to the association. Hayden said that he had gone before the conferees himself to ask about this point and had been assured that there was no objection to such a sale—the bill meant simply FSA could use none of the appropriated funds to assist a cooperative.

Baldwin had ordered an earning capacity appraisal of the project early in the year, and so, when the appropriation bill passed and his authority was clear, he was ready to proceed at once. On July 27 a letter from Hewes was handed to the president of the association, Sanford. The letter offered to sell the project to the association for $800,000, almost exactly the amount of the government's investment. Since its articles of incorporation limited the association's indebtedness to not more than $250,000, it would of course be necessary for the membership to act upon the offer. Sanford, who favored accepting it, said he would bring the proposal before the members at a special meeting.

Baldwin's intention to sell the farm had been a matter of public record for some time but the news had not reached Casa Grande. Some of the settlers were no doubt aware that FSA had been under fire because of the resettlement projects, but the few lines of news which had trickled through from Washington had made no impression. Other matters of much greater interest were occupying the settlers' attention early in 1943.

For one thing, Ralph Beatty resigned on June 1 to accept a position as manager of a movie magnate's stock farm. FSA informed the settlers that they were now sufficiently experienced and sufficiently prosperous to employ a manager who would be accountable only to the Board. FSA would assign a representative to the project to look after its creditor's interest, but he would be there only part-time and would exercise no more authority than was absolutely necessary to protect the government's investment.

When Robert G. Craig, an experienced Arizona farmer who for several years had been in close touch with the project in a variety of FSA positions, arrived at Casa Grande to take up his duties as creditor's representative, the settlers were delighted to hear him say that he had no intention of selecting a general foreman or enterprise foremen and that the day-to-day operation of the farm would be entirely in their hands. He wished to be consulted from time to time by the manager they employed, and he would like an opportunity to make suggestions now and then. After Craig had explained his position to a membership meeting in the Community Hall, the settlers crowded around him to offer congratulations and to give assurances that the hands-off policy would work wonders.

It was up to the Board of Directors to employ a manager, but the Board soon decided that it could not find a suitable man. Craig believed that the real reason was that the settlers were unwilling to pay a manager's salary. As far as he knew, the Board interviewed only one or two applicants for the job before asking Sanford to serve as manager at his regular pay until a final decision could be reached.

When he took over the management of the farm, Sanford was the acknowledged leader of the opposition faction, which at that time was the stronger of the two, and he was also president of the association. His position was already hazardous because of its prominence—at every past election the settlers had thrown out the faction and the leader in power. Now, as acting manager, it was even more perilous, for every settler who had so far assumed to be a foreman had brought the wrath of the others down upon his head and to play the part of manager was certainly a far greater incitement. Yet it was Sanford who, as president of the association, would put FSA's proposal of sale before the members.

Sanford had scarcely seated himself at Beatty's desk when he was visited by the fate which the settlers held in store for those who were set above them. It came first in the guise of fortuitous circumstance. Mrs. Martin King was rumored to have made certain allegations against her husband. The rumors stirred the community. King was one of Sanford's lieutenants and a member of the Board of Directors, but Sanford, aware of the popular feeling against him, joined with other settlers to force King's resignation from the Board, thereby incurring his enmity and that of several settlers who sided with him. By this incident Sanford lost a fragment of his support.

At the same time Sanford was leading the fight to amend the by-laws so that withdrawing members could more easily claim their equities. On the whole, the changes were popular. They were accepted by majority vote of the membership after due deliberation, though there were some who opposed them strongly. (Bill Forbes, a pro-government leader, asked, unanswerably, "If these ideas are good, why weren't they put into the by-laws in the first place?") But after the amendments were voted, there was a reaction. Sanford, some of the voters decided, had "railroaded" the changes for some private, selfish reason of his own.

Within a month of his appointment as manager it was plain that Sanford could not muster a majority among the settlers. In fact it seemed certain that they would quickly reject any proposal he might sponsor. This was the situation on July 27 when Hewes' letter offering to sell the project was handed to Sanford.

"In offering to sell Casa Grande Farms to your association," Hewes wrote, "the government is mindful of the values, both social and economic, which are inherent in continuing its present operation. Furthermore, the government is mindful of the urgent need of continuing production of foodstuffs needed for the war effort. Your association and the membership thereof can make no greater contribution to the war than to continue the present operation of the association. The volume of foodstuff flowing from your effort is vitally necessary. . . ."

FSA was extremely grateful for the great consideration and cooperative attitude demonstrated by the association through the years, the letter continued. "Although, of course, we shall have no direct interest in the management or supervision of the property if the sale is consumated, we shall continue to have an interest in conserving the government's equity until the ultimate payment is made and, further than that, the individual welfare of each family resident on the project will continue to be a matter of official interest to FSA. . . ."

All this was interesting, but the settlers' attention was no doubt drawn particularly to the first and last sentences of the letter:

"The Farm Security Administration has been directed by the Congress to sell the property as soon as possible," and,

"The Farm Security Administration is urgently under the necessity of consumating at the earliest possible date a formal transfer of the property outside of the government. . . ."

Plainly FSA was in a very poor position to bargain. That it should squirm and plead in this way was a matter of delight to many of the settlers (some of whom had broken machinery just to show their spite for the government) and they determined to make the most of the occasion. This determination was strengthened, a week before the membership meeting at which Sanford was to present the offer of sale formally, when the Cooley Committee, then on a Western junket, visited the project briefly. The Congressmen questioned the Directors, foremen, and office staff, and they let it be known that FSA was on the carpet because of Casa Grande and other alleged transgressions. Some settlers may have concluded from what the Congressmen said that the association could not continue as a cooperative under any circumstances. Others decided that since this was to be a forced sale they ought to be able to buy the project for a lot less than $800,000.

When at last the membership met to vote on Hewes' offer, the positions of the two factions were curiously reversed. Having attained power, Sanford was now siding with FSA by endorsing the offer of sale. But Sanford was now a leader almost without a following. Ernest S. Perry, the one settler who came to Casa Grande because he wanted to cooperate and a man who led the pro-government faction from the start, now was chief of the opposition. Perry fought strenuously against Sanford's recommendation that the offer be accepted and he was supported not only by his own "pro-government" faction but by many of Sanford's former friends as well. The vote was 21 to 11 to reject the offer.

A week after this vote was taken, the members met again. Fearing that FSA might now make a forced sale to some other buyer at a figure so low as to endanger their equity, the settlers voted to ask FSA's permission to sell enough of their assets to pay off the operating loan. This time the vote was unanimous with a few not voting. A day or two later 21 members petitioned for the resignation of Sanford and his entire Board of Directors, giving notice at the same time of a membership meeting at which they would recall the Board by vote if it did not resign. It was Perry who circulated the petition, and he did so because he believed that Sanford, who still favored purchasing the farm, would not insist that FSA allow the association to sell its assets.

Hewes realized that he had made a blunder. He now wrote Craig, "FSA is not 'compelled' to liquidate—there is no particular time limit . . . and therefore no need of haste on the part of the association." At the same time he rejected the members' request for permission to sell the association's assets, declaring in a letter to Sanford, "that all farming operations should proceed with due regard to the principle of maximum production, that FSA has always been interested in the welfare of low-income farm people and will continue to be interested in the welfare of this group, and that FSA intends to protect these principles and will therefore execute its full rights to insist on the continued operation of the project."

It was easier to insist on the principle of maximum production than to enforce it. Sanford was still technically the manager of the farm but neither he nor his foremen could get the work done because Perry and the majority he represented were intent on forcing liquidation.

Faced with the petition for his recall, Sanford resigned both as president and manager. He and the other director sincerely regretted that a continuance of the present arrangement could not be looked forward to, he now wrote Hewes. "We realize," he went on, "that many of the fine principles of the FSA with respect to the welfare of our people will be lost. It was our desire to preserve these principles. However, we were in the minority."

When the settlers met at the call of the petitioners, they elected Martin King, the man Sanford had helped to force off the Board, president. This election was the first not attended by an FSA official; Craig made a point of staying away from it because he wanted to show the settlers that they were now free to act without interference. But when Craig learned (from Sanford) that three more votes were cast than there were members present, he promptly ordered a new election, which he attended. Running against King, Perry received 22 of the 37 votes cast. All of the places on the Board went to members of the Perry faction.

Now a thing happened which, out of its context, would seem startling indeed. Perry was no sooner elected president of the association than he swung strongly in support of the proposal to buy the farm. Within a few hours of the election, the new Board chose Cecil Hopkins manager and instructed Perry and Hopkins to do everything possible to maintain full production and to effect the purchase.

Sanford reacted violently to this change of face. These same men had bucked him at every turn while he was trying to negotiate the purchase, he told Craig, "and he for one was not going to leave a stone unturned until he had busted the association." Sanford now joined forces with Martin King, his former ally. King of course still smarted from the defeat he had suffered from Perry in the second, and honest, election. Thus the Sanford faction was again united, again in the opposition—and again in a majority.

On October 25, 1943, the association held its regular quarterly membership meeting. The treasurer's report was the most favorable in the history of the association—the excess of income over expenses for the quarter was

$29,212 and for the year thus far $60,236. But unfortunately most of the settlers were not present to hear the report. Twenty-four of the 35 were occupied elsewhere. They were meeting with a Coolidge attorney, Charles Reed, whom they had engaged to force liquidation of the association.

Among those absent were some who had been stalwarts in the pro-government faction. Bill Forbes, who had been cotton foreman and later general foreman, was one. Hennesey, the livestock foreman under Beatty, was another. Having lost their places of power, these men had drifted into the opposition even before Beatty's departure. Now, along with several others who had held and lost lesser positions, they had joined with Sanford to bring the association to an end.

When Hewes learned of this development he sent his chief assistant, Ralph Hollenberg, (Cohen had recently quit FSA and was preparing to become an administrator of UNRRA in Germany) to Casa Grande at once. Hollenberg met separately with the leaders of both factions. Both sides, he found, were willing to continue the association and buy the farm, but only on one condition—that the government put a man in charge of the project, and tell the members that this man was boss and that they were to do as he said. It didn't matter whom the government might select to be their boss, the settlers said—they would be glad to have Faul, the first manager, who still farmed nearby. Hollenberg assured them that if they wished to hire Faul as their manager FSA would willingly approve the choice, and he urged them to do so. But neither side would agree to this suggestion. A boss who could be fired by the group in power would be no boss at all, the settlers said, and this would be true even of Faul, who, some of them remembered, had been a very high-handed one.

The language of the Appropriations Act made it impossible for FSA to employ a manager for the association. Reluctantly Hewes notified the association that its lease would not be renewed.

"Evidently Americans do not like to be collectivized even under the most bountiful kind of circumstances such as were provided in the case of this farm," the *Star*, which had watched the beginnings of the experiment with sympathetic interest, now concluded, "Americans like to be their own bosses, and they apparently get tired of being wet-nursed by the government. In spite of the fact that the members found 'security' in the collective farm, they apparently cannot eradicate from their American character a belief that there is something more in life than security, and that freedom to act and do as they choose are still more precious than security."

Attorney Reed advised Sanford and the other settlers who engaged him that a two-thirds majority of the membership would be necessary to force liquidation of the association. When the settlers handed him a petition bearing the names of 25 of the 35 members, Reed filed a lawsuit in Pinal County Superior Court, of which Reed's brother-in-law, William C. Truman, was judge, to require the directors to appear in answer to 13 charges of mismanagement brought by the complainants, and to compel liquidation.

After the suit was filed, it was discovered that three of the names on the petition had been forged. Lacking these three signatures, the Sanford faction lacked the two-thirds majority necessary to force liquidation. Meanwhile Perry and his fellow directors engaged a local lawyer on behalf of the association.

When he learned that the court had been asked to appoint a receiver to liquidate the association, FSA's regional attorney rushed from San Francisco to Phoenix by plane and immediately telephoned the association's lawyer to arrange an appointment in Coolidge later that day. The FSA lawyer was anxious to protect the government's interest as creditor, but this was not his only reason for concerning himself in the matter. The association had made good profits; its assets stood at $326,150 on September 30, and of this $134,620 was net worth belonging to the settlers. Liquidation of such a business by a receiver might be very expensive, but if it were done voluntarily under FSA auspices the liquidation could be accomplished quickly with no expense whatever to the members. The FSA lawyer was therefore anxious to forestall receivership; since the Sanford faction lacked the necessary two-thirds majority it seemed quite feasible to do so.

But unfortunately the lawyer Perry had hired for the association's defense was too busy to see the Regional Attorney that afternoon. Not until 10 o'clock the next morning would he have a moment to spare.

When he arrived at Casa Grande the next morning, the FSA attorney discovered that the local lawyer had indeed been busy. He had spent the afternoon at the farm with Perry and the other directors and had persuaded them to agree to the receivership. A few moments before the courthouse closed for the day, he had filed an amended petition which bore the signatures of the Directors. These of course were more than enough to make up the necessary two-thirds majority.

Judge Truman now appointed Leon Nowell, a farmer with large holdings in both Arizona and California, as receiver. Nowell's brother, as it happened, was a brother-in-law of both the Judge and of Reed, the attorney Sanford hired. (The lawyer Perry hired for the association was soon removed from the case by death.) In appointing Nowell receiver, Judge Truman did not consult the association's one important creditor—FSA, as another judge might have done in similar circumstances.

The Regional Attorney now made ready to ask a Federal court to take jurisdiction on the grounds that the government's interest was involved. Anticipating this move, Attorney Reed began pulling political strings. He wired Arizona's Senator MacFarland, urging him to do "anything possible" to prevent the government from fighting liquidation of the association by resort to the Federal courts. The Senator did not see fit to interfere, however, and the case came before a Federal judge who, to the Regional Attorney's disappointment, said that if the government's loan were repaid promptly he would have no further interest in the matter. Over the protests of Bill Forbes and other settlers who wanted the livestock fattened with the farm's ensilage, Nowell promptly sold the feeder cattle and the ensilage, thereby reducing the debt to FSA by such an extent that the Federal court declined to take jurisdiction. There was now no further possibility of avoiding the receivership.

When FSA presented a bill for $22,000 for rent and minor repairs which it claimed were due under the lease, the receiver refused payment. The United States Attorney instituted suit in the Superior Court and Judge Truman, at the request of the United States Attorney, disqualified himself. These proceedings began in 1944 and were not concluded until late in 1946, when FSA was awarded $14,000. During this time Nowell, the receiver, and Reed, who was now attorney for the receiver, were of course obliged to give the association's affairs their attention from time to time. For their services, Nowell and Reed were each awarded $15,000.

While the liquidation was in progress, Perry, Thomas, Lewis and other long-time members became concerned for fear the association's net worth would be divided equally among the settlers, rather than in proportion to the hours each had worked. Sanford (who had been appointed as the receiver's representative at the project) was said to have suggested the likelihood of an equal division in order to persuade some of the more recent members to sign the petition for receivership. Perry and the others employed a Phoenix lawyer to protect their interests. His fee was $1,000.

Hennesey and Graves wanted to go to California after the association broke up, and they needed ready money. Both were among the first settlers to join the project, so their equities should have been as high as any. But they had no way of knowing even the approximate value of their equities—this information was available only to the receiver and his attorney. Rather than wait whatever time it might take before the equities were distributed, Graves and Hennesey—and possibly some other settlers—sold their equities to a local farmer named Lacy. According to some of the other settlers, Graves received $400 and Hennesey $700.

Late in 1946, when the liquidation was at last complete, 36 settlers had received $63,698.69. Twenty-six of these settlers had been members of the association since 1938, one had joined in 1941, and the remaining nine had joined in 1942. The earnings were distributed in proportion to the hours each man had worked since January 1, 1940, so the original settlers received more than did the late-comers. On the average the members who joined first probably received about $2,000, while the average for those who came later could not have exceeded $1,000. The cost of the liquidation, including the legal fees paid by individual settlers, was at least $35,000—an average of almost $1,000 for each member.

"We not only killed the goose that laid the golden egg," Charles McCormick, who had come to Casa Grande with a family of five and assets of $200, remarked disgustedly when it was all over,—"we even threw the goddam egg away!"

* * * *

Pending sale of the project property, FSA offered it for lease in 1944. The former settlers were given an opportunity to rent tracts of about 80 acres for individual operation, but only six chose to do so. After the needs of these six were met, the remainder of the land was offered for lease by public bid. The houses were also rented. About half of them were occupied by war workers, who were charged $36, $32, and $28 a month depending on the size of the house. Farm laborers—into which category the former settlers fell—were charged only half of this rental until, late in 1944, the war workers complained to their Congressman that they were being treated unfairly. Then FSA abolished the differential by charging the farm laborers the higher rate. Twenty-two of the former settlers were living on the project at that time, and when the rent was raised several were forced to leave because they were unable to pay the increase. FSA's rental receipts for the land and buildings totalled $178,078 for the years 1945 through 1948.

For a time FSA attempted to work out a plan whereby the farm could be subdivided into family-sized units suitable for sale to low-income farmers, including the former settlers, under the generous terms of the Bankhead-Jones Farm Tenant Act. But there were many obstacles in the way of sub-division—much of the land would have to be re-leveled and re-ditched for irrigation in small units and some of it was so far from the houses that it would be necessary to build additional dwellings, so that finally the Farmers Home Administration (a new agency into which FSA was merged in 1946) concluded that it would be practicable to subdivide only the 2,400-acre Coolidge tract. Twenty-one family-type farms (all but one with accompanying houses in the community center) were sold in 1948, five of them to former settlers and the others to veterans. The farms were planned as "economic management units;" they ranged in size from 80 to 160 acres, and sold (with the houses) for an average of $11,587. This was only a very little more than the Resettlement Administration had paid for the land alone in 1936. In order to make it possible for family-type farmers to pay for the farms from "normal" earning capacity, the Farmers Home Administration was selling them for much less—perhaps only about half—what it could get on the open market.

The remainder of the project property—41 houses, the community house, four irrigation wells, the utility systems and about 2,500 acres of land—was offered for sale to the highest bidder.

The land sold readily for an average of $65 per acre, which was almost exactly twice what the Resettlement Administration paid for it. The sale of the land in this manner restored the old tenure pattern (the 2,500 acres went to six buyers, one of whom was the Clements Cattle Company, which bought 560 acres of the same land it had sold to the Resettlement Administration in 1936) so that, on this portion of the property at least, there remained no trace of this last endeavor to establish the working farmer on his own land.

In 1950 the last of the property was sold. All told the government received $518,920—$243,340 for the family-type farms, $161,165 for the remaining land, $92,165 for the remaining houses and ten vacant lots, $3,250 for the community house, $9,000 for the utilities, and $10,000 for the irrigation wells. The government's loss on its capital investment was therefore about $280,000. Offsetting this loss in part were the rentals it had received. These totalled $361,066, but half of this would be needed to equal interest charges (figured at two percent on the investment). It can be said, therefore, that the net cost of the project to the government, exclusive of the cost of administration, was about $100,000. But if the government had chosen to sell the Coolidge tract on the open market rather than to family-type farmers at earning capacity values, it is not unlikely that it would have made a profit of $100,000. The loss, therefore, is chargeable to the existing family-type farms rather than to the defunct cooperative.

Most of the former settlers were still in the vicinity of Casa Grande early in 1947. A few rented project homes, but most lived in Coolidge and other nearby towns. Several were farming rented tracts of the project. Young Mott, who had married one of Ernie Bates' daughters, leased 620 acres, not all of which was irrigable. Tom Wilkins, who was married to a Bates, leased from the government, and so did Ernie Bates himself until his death. One T. S. Jones (there were two T. S.'s) rented a piece of project land, as did Jake Lewis and the Dewey family (although Charley Dewey, discouraged by ill health, shot himself dead after the association broke up.)

Most of the others who remained in the community were now day laborers. Perry bought a small house in Coolidge and supported his family by driving the school bus until he died of a heart attack in 1947; Topton was a section hand on the railroad; Hakes was a laborer for a gravel company; Thomas and Hill drove road-blades for the county; H. J. Bowles was a fireman at a deserted prisoner of war camp nearby; Sanford worked in a Coolidge feedstore; Dunn was a lettuce-picker; Collier was caretaker at the project for FHA; Gifford was a service station attendant; Telson was a cab driver; old Nelson was a pool-hall loafer in Coolidge; young Nelson had been killed in action.

Some of the former settlers had gone back to farming in other states. Williams, for example, was known to be sharecropping in Oklahoma. Vincent was applying for an FHA farm purchase loan in Oregon and Malcolm was once more a laborer in southeast Missouri. Martin King and Tom Goody had both gone to Texas to buy farms when they received their equities from the association, but a few weeks later they were back in Coolidge, admitting sheepishly that they had lost their shirts. King went to work as a house-painter in Coolidge and Goody found a job as a laborer for an irrigation district. Although some of her friends had gone back to Oklahoma, Mrs. Bates flatly refused to go. "We never had anything there," she said, "and we always had something here—so we'll stay."

Although it might still be better than Oklahoma, the Casa Grande Valley was not a very good place without the cooperative farm. Laborers' wages were from $5 to $6 a day early in 1947, but rents were high. Only a few of the former settlers could afford to live in the project houses and the housing which laborers could afford in Coolidge and Florence and other nearby towns was almost uniformly bad. McCormick, for example, was now a tractor driver on a farm near Mesa and the only housing he could find was a chicken coop from which he had to remove the roosts to make room for his family.

Only Cecil Hopkins, who was the bookkeeper for a variety store in Coolidge, and the other T. S. Jones, who was the manager of a drug store in Coolidge, were known to be as well off as before. And only Hopkins and Jones could be reasonably confident about the future. The others could all expect unemployment should Pinal County settle back to its pre-war normal. The several who were farming project lands under lease might possibly find other land to rent when the project was sold, but, even so, they were in a hazardous position, for the cotton-ginning companies that financed them might call a halt whenever the price of cotton dropped.

Perry, whose soldier sons had written from opposite ends of the earth to protest when they learned that the cooperative farm was being liquidated, told Henry Morgenthau, a tourist from Washington who stopped by one day, that he was heartbroken at what had happened at Casa Grande. And Mrs. Perry, writing some time after her husband's death, said that all of the former settlers agreed that the cooperative "was far, far better than it is now, and they are so sorry it is destroyed."

At last the settlers could agree.

14

Experience Elsewhere

In many of its essentials the history of Casa Grande was like that of other resettlement projects. No detailed studies of life on other cooperative farms or on the "infiltration" type projects have been published and it is of course extremely hazardous to make comparisons on the basis of superficial evidence. But whatever may have been the dissimilarities lying beneath the surface, the experience of almost all of the projects showed something in common. For one thing, most of the project communities were torn by factionalism. For another, the attitude of the settlers toward the FSA officials was, in most cases, one of distrust and hostility. With perhaps one exception (a 1,720-acre farm in North Carolina the fifteen members of which are Indians) none of the project communities seems to have come reasonably close to the ideal of a harmonious, democratic, and integrated group. Judged against these others, Casa Grande was in fact an outstanding success. It was, the FSA administrator said in 1943, "one of the best examples of a cooperative farm, and certainly I would say the most successful cooperative farm we have."

Next to Casa Grande, the largest of the cooperative farms was that at Lake Dick, Arkansas. Between the histories of these two cooperatives there are many resemblances. While Bell, the Bureau of Agricultural Economics investigator, was finding that the Arizona project seethed with dissatisfaction in 1941, one of his colleagues was studying its Arkansas counterpart. "General dissatisfaction and unrest coupled with a high mobility have disorganized the life of the community," this man found. "'All that people do,'" he quoted one of the Lake Dick women as saying, "'is sit around and look sad and gripe.'" There was very little interest in church and Sunday School, he found, and the few organizations in the community were virtually inactive. Most of the persons who had been active in leadership roles had moved from the project. All but one of the settlers interviewed by the BAE man had ownership of an individual farm as his goal. The settlers' attitude toward the project was one of "getting by," the manager said. "That attitude," the manager went on, "not only includes doing as little work as possible in too many instances, with the time being turned in for the full ten hours a day, but also the matter of getting as much free as possible— such as commodities, excessive use of teams for personal use, together with the general feeling that it is a battle or a game of the members against or in opposition to Farm Security."

Lake Dick was always a financial failure. Planned for 80 families, it supported only 47 in 1941 and it supported them very poorly—the hourly wage for unskilled labor was then 10 cents and for skilled labor 12½ cents. Low earnings were chiefly responsible for the settlers' dissatisfaction, the BAE investigator believed. The Lake Dick settlers, like those at Casa Grande, were hostile toward FSA, but their hostility was not directed against the project management. The Lake Dick people were actually encouraged by the management to participate in the affairs of the association. Not many of them did participate, but the project management was nevertheless well regarded by the settler families. Hostility toward FSA was directed almost entirely toward the regional office officials whom the settlers blamed for what they considered arbitrary and unfair rulings in respect to earnings.

In 1943, while the Casa Grande association was being liquidated, the remaining members of the Lake Dick cooperative, all of whom were white, were replaced by Negroes. The ostensible reason for displacing the whites was that Negroes were less subject to the draft. The real reason, however, was probably somewhat different. It was no longer possible to maintain a semblance of order in a community of whites and therefore Lake Dick, pending the liquidation of the association and the sale of the project, was to become what a local newspaper called in a news story "just another sharecropping plantation."

Only in the case of the Indian cooperative farm in North Carolina was FSA able to sell a project to the settlers through their cooperative association. All of the other cooperative farms were liquidated more or less in the manner of Casa Grande.

Most observers have remarked upon the settlers' dissatisfaction, their factionalism, and their hostility toward the government. These attitudes seem to have characterized all types of projects, not merely the cooperative farms. In the mildest form they are described by Paul W. Wager in his account of the generally successful subsistence homestead projects in Jefferson and Walker counties, Alabama:

"Another major disappointment was the lack of community spirit. There is apparently pretty general attachment on the part of the homesteaders to their respective communities, but this is not translated into participation in community affairs. It is difficult to get a quorum to attend a meeting of the homestead association; some homesteaders are not even members. The civic clubs which at one time were active in promoting community development are all dead or dormant. In extenuation it should be explained that most of the homesteaders as well as many of the women were working long hours in war industries at the time of the survey and for this reason were probably less active in civic affairs than normally. Moreover, widespread participation in civic affairs is not a characteristic of American communities generally.

"Many families have become highly individualistic, some expressing an eagerness to finish paying for their place so they can be free from association control. This too is a characteristic American trait and not one to be wholly condemned, but it is distressing to find families which have been beneficiaries of a generous social program so self-centered. Of course, that attitude is not universal, and even those who exhibit it are willing to admit that the government put them on their feet."

Another resettlement project, Cumberland Homesteads in Tennessee, was sold by the government early in 1950. This one, like most or all of the others, had not succeeded in attracting private industry, and a number of cooperative projects—a sorghum plant, a coal mine, and a cannery—had all failed. "One manager after another was sent to struggle with the Cumberland project," the *Wall Street Journal* reported in its account of the sale. "One was an economist, one a sociologist and another a former Army officer. Each had different methods of management and each found a sizeable group of homesteaders ready to take exception to almost anything he suggested. The climax came when a band of dissatisfied tenants threatened the life of a manager accused of siding with the Federal Security Administration to their disadvantage."

Those who have written about the projects have generally ascribed their low morale to faults in FSA's manner of management. FSA made a decisive error, according to this view, by disregarding the "principles of cooperation," as the orthodoxy of the cooperative movement is often called. Before it made any attempt to organize a cooperative FSA should have conducted a long preparatory program of education; if this was not possible (and of course it was not), the defect should have been remedied so far as possible by educational efforts later. Nor, in this opinion, was FSA's management sufficiently democratic; failure to give the settlers more information and more opportunity to participate in the management of their affairs was a second decisive error.

Carl C. Taylor, a sociologist who as an assistant administrator of the Resettlement Administration had helped to plan Casa Grande and other projects, took this view. Taylor tried to draw some conclusions from the experience with cooperative farms that would be useful in planning rural settlement patterns for the Columbia Basin Reclamation Project. Investigation of the cooperative farms, he reported, "shows that they leave much to be desired, not because of the inherent impossibility of cooperation or the inadequacy of the sponsoring agencies, but because neither the settlers on such cooperatives nor the personnel assigned to administer them has adequate knowledge of cooperatives. Both material profits and settler morale were generally poor on the farms studied and this appears to be the result of an unawareness as to the aims of cooperatives and the nature of cooperation. Such unawareness will never result in a spontaneous or indigenous cooperative movement."

Charles P. Loomis, another sociologist, after a study of seven new resettlement communities (none of them cooperative farms, however), came to somewhat similar conclusions:

"(1) On all the new projects there were active forces which, on the one hand, tended toward community integration and, on the other hand, tended toward disintegration.

"(2) Indications are that in any community those families who are least mobile and participate most in the programs of the organized community agencies make the most stable type of settlers.

"(3) Uncertainty as to management policies vitally important to settlers and their families may lead to the circulation of misinformation and to unfounded dissatisfaction.

"(4) If the projects had discussion groups or other channels through which reliable information might be obtained and made part of the thought processes of the settlers, community integration would probably be furthered.

"(5) The more the local groups shoulder the responsibilities of administration, the less reason they have to find fault with the resettling agency.

"(6) In resettling families, it is important that the officials endeavor to avert situations that might result in powerful in-groups capable of destroying community integration."

In his generally uncritical account of the FSA cooperative farms, a third sociologist, Joseph W. Eaton, found "signs of weakness." "There are noticeable administrative difficulties on many projects," he wrote, "especially friction between FSA officials and the settlers. Many of the latter look upon their membership as a 'government job' and make little or no effort to transform their associations into genuine cooperatives. They often withdraw to take other farm-labor jobs which seem less promising, indicating that they do not understand the potential advantage of being members of a cooperative corporation." FSA had to take farm managers and make them social workers, Eaton said, and this was not made easier by the fact that some regional directors did not understand or were not in sympathy with the idea of developing genuine cooperatives. "Many managers operate more by issuing orders than by offering advice and information. They veto decisions of the Board of Directors indiscriminately, even if they are not of vital effect on the success of the project. They are more interested in getting their ideas accepted than in getting them understood. They take no pains to explain changes of policy, often made necessary by instructions from regional headquarters. These sudden policy changes result in insecurity on the part of the settlers. They often feel they are being treated 'like kids' instead of as responsible members of a cooperative project."

FSA administrators in Washington took much the same premises. In 1940 a committee of staff members evaluated the work being done with cooperatives. In its report the committee listed four "common errors" into which Resettlement and FSA had fallen. These were: 1. attempting to provide a cooperative before the members have the interest and knowledge to sustain it, 2. the tendency to give the directors responsibilities which they are unprepared to assume, 3. insufficient understanding of cooperative operation and purposes on part of FSA personnel, and 4. inclusion of members who do not use the cooperative. "It is apparent," the report said, "that cooperatives are notably democratic institutions. There is no doubt that the democratic features of the cooperatives have made a strong appeal to the FSA and that this is one of the factors that has led the Administration to support and develop their use. . . . They are possible safeguards against 'paternalistic' and 'bureaucratic' methods in the development of our program. We think we should point out that in practice these advantages have not always been realized. Not infrequently the democratic operation of the cooperatives has remained more of an appearance than a reality. These purposes are desirable none the less." The Committee acknowledged that FSA managers had tended to dominate the associations. "Where he (the manager) plays too strong a part in the development of a cooperative, there is a natural tendency for the members of the cooperative to view their association as simply another device for extending government control over their activities and their lives. This is, of course, the reverse of our intent in establishing cooperative associations and under the circumstances we can hardly wonder that misinterpretation of the Administration's motives arises. It not infrequently occurs that the Community Manager himself has a poor understanding of the purposes of the cooperative association or the spirit of cooperation action, and to this is sometimes joined a distrust of the settlers."

At the conclusion of their critical appraisal of subsistence homesteads, Lord and Johnstone addressed a number of questions to field workers who had participated in the study. "All the commentators agree that homesteaders' declarations of mistreatment by the Government are and may continue to be very common," they wrote, summarizing the replies to their questions. "They believe, however, that such declarations are only occasionally a compensation for a feeling of indebtedness. In fact, declarations of mistreatment represent many different reactions and may appear in a variety of situations. In some instances they result from the homesteader's feeling that the Government has not fulfilled what he took to be promises; his hopes have been disappointed. Sometimes they are evidence of a genuine conflict of interest between the Government and the homesteader. Often the Government manager is simply a convenient person upon whom to throw the responsibility for difficulties experienced by the homesteader. Sometimes these difficulties are the responsibility of the homesteader, sometimes they are the result of circumstances beyond anyone's control—the weather, for example.

"Several of the commentators say that in any type of situation there are always some adverse reactions to authority. This is true in any industrial or commercial organization, in any community organization, and in a subsistence-homesteads project. The greater the extent of the authority the more common will be adverse reactions, including declarations of mistreatment. When Government control of individual behavior goes beyond customary limits, as it has on some projects, it arouses resentment and resistance. It threatens the independent status of the homesteader in his own eyes and in the eyes of the community. Declarations of mistreatment then become more common and more frequent than in most situations."

Lord and Johnstone found the commentators emphatically agreed that the administrators of a project should leave the development of its social organization strictly in the hands of the homesteaders themselves. "The reasons given are that first, scientific knowledge of the development of social organization has not reached the point at which experts are qualified to direct the development of a community—in short, it cannot be done; and second, it is presumptuous as well as pretentious for administrators to tell any group of persons how they should live—in short, it should not be done."

* * * *

Lord and Johnstone did not conclude, however, that subsistence-homesteads were bound to fail. On the contrary, they were inclined to agree with FSA officials who claimed that they had discovered a formula for almost certain success:

"Just about the time this study was completed, an administrator who has had much to do with the subsistence-homesteads program told one of the editors of this publication: 'We could go out now and set up a thousand subsistence homesteads, and 999 would be successful.' Probably this administrator was being overoptimistic, but the essence of what he was saying was true. Experience, and experience alone, had taught him that certain things work, certain other things do not. 'Work,' of course, according to certain criteria upon which there might be no perfect theoretical agreement, yet which at least are clear, and known, and definable. All he would have to do would be to repeat, and go on repeating, the more suc-cessful formulas. More than that he would have a trained and unified and experienced organization knowing what was expected, and practiced in doing just that sort of thing. In a sense, all he would have to do to start a new subsistence-homesteads program—provided it were to follow certain models already working, and be subject to certain criteria already agreed upon administratively—would be to start giving orders. Then an adminis-trative machine would go into action, and in the end would produce, for better or for worse, more models of the kind of product that so far has, in the eyes of the administration, worked out best."

15

Why They Failed

Now that the record has been spread out it is possible to look at the Casa Grande experience as a whole and to come to some conclusions about it. Why did these people—Waldron, Mott, Olivier, Sanford, Beatty, Coker and all the rest—behave as they did? It would have taken only a little goodwill, self-discipline and mutual respect to have made the Casa Grande farm a success of a kind that would have assured security and opportunity for the settlers. Why, then, in the face of these inducements did they fail so perversely and so dismally? In this concluding chapter the interpretation that has already been placed upon the behavior of the Casa Grande people will be brought together and summarized; it will then be amplified and discussed in an effort to find answers to these questions.

The central fact in the history of Casa Grande is this: The settlers were unable to cooperate with each other and with the government because they were engaged in a ceaseless struggle for power. In part the struggle for power was "rational;" that is, certain conditions did factually exist which reasonable men would have acted to alter by changing the distribution and use of power. Assuming, for example, that a foreman was actually incompetent, it was "rational" for the settlers to seek to have him replaced. Similarly where a real conflict of interests existed (as, for example, over the issue of whether dividends were to be distributed to outsiders as well as to members) it was "rational" for the settlers to engage in a power struggle.

But the struggle for power was in part "irrational;" that is, there was sometimes no logical relation between the end sought and the means employed or, if there was such a relation, its significance was ostensible (it was "rationalization") rather than real and decisive. If, for example, a foreman was actually competent but was called incompetent because the settlers were distressed by low wages and uncertainty, the attempt to unseat him was irrational.

It is impossible to say with confidence what part was irrational. This is true because, for one thing, there would be a good deal of disagreement among reasonable men as to what constitutes grounds for struggle. Some readers, for example, may feel that the settlers would have been unreasonable *not* to have opposed certain FSA policies, while other readers may agree with Regional Director Garst that in a producers' cooperative it is reasonable for the members to give up their right to self-management. But aside from the very real difficulty of determining what is reasonable, there is the added difficulty of discovering and evaluating the true motives of the settlers. It is not safe to infer from behavior whether the motive was rational or irrational; it may be that in some instances the settlers, while acting upon grounds which were reasonable, did so not because of the reasonableness of the grounds but rather because of some irrational factors. If both elements are involved—and it may well be that both usually were involved—how is one to determine which was decisive?

In the author's opinion there existed rational grounds for power struggles at Casa Grande, but the decisive cause of the continuous struggle that took place was nevertheless irrational. Some of the settlers, including those who had the greatest experience of urban life and who, perhaps because of this experience, felt that the resettlement project was a "come down" and evidence that they had failed in life, had strong feelings of guilt which they expressed in hostility toward fellow settlers and government officials who were placed over them. Some were aggressive personalities of a type not uncommon in American life. A few may have been neurotic. These settlers (and many of the others as well) felt, or from association with others of the group came to feel, an acute need to assert claims to status. The chief avenue to status in the project situation was power in the management of the farm. This power could be secured in one of two ways: it could be had by joining forces with the government and serving as a foreman, or, informally, as a supporter of the management or it could be had by leading or participating in an anti-government faction. The settlers' need to seek status and power was accentuated by the undefined and fluid nature of the project situation, a situation which increased their opportunities to engage in power struggles.

It was impossible for the project to satisfy all the claims to status and power that were made upon it. Its inability to satisfy these claims was inherent in its nature as a government project; it was the very fact that this was a government project that made the settlers more acutely aware of their need for status. But aside from this, there were, especially in the first years of the project, limitations imposed by the farm's low earnings; without going into the red, the farm could not provide what the settlers had come to consider a respectable wage. Finally, the farm could never have satisfied the settlers' claims to status and power because none of the settlers, even if they had had undisputed mastery of the farm, could have managed it successfully; settler control and business success were mutually exclusive possibilities.

Probably the project could not have succeeded so long as this disproportion existed between the claims of the settlers and the ability of the project to satisfy them. In any case, the FSA officials made matters worse by their consistent failure to understand the psychology of the settlers. Except for Faul (an interesting exception in that he was not a professional bureaucrat), the government officials made the mistake of supposing that the settlers would act rationally in the manner of economic men—that is, they thought of the settlers as having one goal, to increase their level of living, and as logical enough to accept all the necessary means implied by this end. Thus, for example, group operation of the farm, community-type settlement, and lease tenure, all of which were severe psychological hazards for the settlers, were regarded by FSA as "safeguards" which would insure the financial success of the project. Packard, Garst and Waldron all believed that the financial success of the project would automatically lead to the satisfaction of the settlers; it did not occur to them, apparently, that only the satisfaction of the settlers could lead to the financial success of the project. Hewes, Cohen, and Ross based their efforts at remaking the social side of the project not on an understanding of the dynamics of the situation but on a value judgment (that a democratic style of community life ought to be achieved) and on the supposition that if the conditions justifying rational struggle with the management were removed and if social organization for rational decision-making were provided, the settlers would behave like reasonable men, that is, they would behave as their economic interest obviously dictated. Just as Garst supposed that economic organization could be provided through the exercise of technical skill, so Hewes supposed that social organization (which was thought of as being something different from economic organization) could be fashioned technically. Only Faul regarded the life of the project as a struggle for power. His understanding was doubtless intuitive rather than reasonable but during Faul's administration, when everyone knew who was boss and that there was no possibility of a settler's gaining power in the management of the farm, the settlers were, according to their later accounts and according to the more reliable evidence of their behavior, happier than at any other time.

None of the government official's errors seems to have been as important as this one of construing all behavior as rational and economic. The error is very widespread and characteristic in the thought of our day. According to Chester I. Barnard, a business executive of long experience, "non-economic motives, interests, and processes, as well as the economic, are fundamental in behavior from the boards of directors to the last man." Nevertheless, Barnard continues, "The contrary is almost always implicit and frequently explicit in the statements not only of business men but of labor men, politicians, statesmen, professional men, educators, and even church ministers. As one result, effective leadership has to be based on intuitions that are correct, notwithstanding doctrines that deny their correctness. Very often, I think, we attempt social integration by methods imposed by a false logic to the very limit that commonsense and hard experience will permit."

The same false logic that characterized the management of the projects characterizes much of the criticism that has been made of them. The contention of the critics that more education (particularly education in "the principles of cooperation"), information, and discussion would have made the settlers more reasonable in their behavior is entirely in harmony with the view taken by the FSA leaders from the start. It is true that Garst and Waldron did not think it advisable to encourage the participation of the settlers in the affairs of the project in its early years; nevertheless they did think of the settlers as reasonable men—indeed, so long as he could get a hearing Waldron explained in reasonable terms why reasonable men should not insist on participating in the management of the farm. Hewes and Cohen, of course, agreed fully with such criticisms as have been quoted from the sociologists Taylor, Loomis and Eaton. They differed from Garst and Waldron chiefly in believing that the reasonable men *should* manage their association.

There is a very extensive literature on "community organization" which exhibits this false logic and which may have had some direct influence on the thinking of Cohen, Ross and Giordano, the three young men who undertook to reorganize the "social side" of the project. One of the most characteristic features of the literature on community organization is that it views the community as if it were a formal organization having well-defined goals which it rationally tries to achieve. "The real community," according to a representative authority, "is one that has organized its population, invented social machinery, and has trained effective social engineers to make effective use of all available resources." Thus the community is a rational organism; it has central agency which "can direct the thinking, ascertain the purposes, and carry out the will of the community." The Social Engineer is typically the focal point in this process of the community organization. He (or she) gets the process underway by making a Community Survey which reveals Community Needs. The Social Engineer then places these needs before Community Leaders who represent Community Interests. The leaders then determine to federate their interests through the agency of a Community Council which will Coordinate a process called Community Action. The unit of community action is the Project or Activity. Successful coordination results in Community Organization and Community Integration. This imagery, which reflects the social worker's view of community life, is perhaps appropriate in thinking about the formal organization of social work agencies in a fairly large city. It purports to have a much wider application, however; in fact it draws no line at all between formal and informal organization—a community, one writer says, is a "social unit composed of a population center . . . and having the latent capacity of being organized for cooperative action."

Cohen, Ross and Giordano on their visits to Casa Grande acted precisely as if they were following the directions in one of the many manuals on how to organize a community. Their role, in fact, was that of "social engineers" engaged in "one of the newest branches of applied social science" and when Cohen reported that the settlers' discontent could become a healthy aspect of a vital process "if properly channeled" he reflected the social engineer's confidence in the possibility of fashioning institutions through which men would act rationally. "Community organization," one authority with whom he may have been familiar has written, "does not propose to eliminate social conflict but rather to rationalize it. . . ."

If the literature on community organization included more material of a descriptive rather than a normative nature, it might reveal both that conflict is characteristic of the life of small groups and that the techniques of the social workers have been signally unsuccessful in "rationalizing" it. Unfortunately there are few studies that tell very much about these matters. One of the first and best descriptions of community life pictures a New York state hop-growing community in the early 1800's as characteristically torn by factional conflict. James M. Williams in *An American Town* called the people of Blankton "choleric" and wrote of "continuing wrangling among church members, resulting in factional feuds. . . ." N. L. Sims described the people of *A Hoosier Village* as "jealous and suspicious of one another and 'afraid somebody has an axe to grind.'" Until about 1900, Sims wrote, a public fight could be seen almost any day on the public square of the Hoosier village, dances usually ended in a free-for-all, and political discussions were settled by fist-fights. J. F. Steiner has brought together twenty case studies of community life in the early 1920's. In these studies conflict and factionalism appear as normal features of community life. "Perhaps," Steiner comments, "it is the very lack of permanent status of social classes that intensifies the factional spirit and jealousies so detrimental to unity of action in community affairs."

In his autobiography Joseph A. Cocannouer gives an account of the jealousies, suspicions, and bitter discontents that marked the life of one Oklahoma farming community—just such a community as most of the Casa Grande settlers came from—and of his difficulties in trying to help the people with their problems. As a rural teacher Cocannouer set out to demonstrate scientific farming practices, using for illustrative material the successes of some of the farm people of the neighborhood. This approach he soon found to be unworkable because the community bitterly resented anyone who seemed to be getting ahead. If Grandma Ellis did well as a poultry raiser, why, it was only because she stole her chicken feed from the neighbors. The poorer farmers, Cocannouer found, "did not try to understand their situation; they felt only a blind resentment at the poor harvests they were now getting from soil that was becoming more and more depleted. This bitterness was constantly reflected in the scholars at school. Many farmers went about with chips on their shoulders—luck and the world against them. I often heard this wail of hard luck at school, a cry that could not have originated in the mind of a child."

The settlers' craving for higher status and the government officials' inability to understand them except as rational, economic men may be taken as two principal elements in the dynamic of the situation. There were other elements, however, which came into play in association with these and which were also important. One was the settlers' belief, partly true and partly false, that there were "two kinds of people" among them. That some of the stresses and strains of project life were caused by these feelings of difference can hardly be doubted; indeed the settlers' need to gain higher status was probably heightened by their belief that there should be—but was lacking—some "just" and formal recognition of these differences. Very likely there were some settlers who felt themselves "inferiors;" these as well as others like Mott and Olivier who were sure of their "superiority," wanted the differences marked with signs and symbols that would confirm and authorize the differing roles of "inferior" and "superior." It was this need for a social definition of the inferior-superior relationships, perhaps, which accounted for the attitude of many settlers toward Beatty. For some a government employee was clearly defined as a superior. Others, including Mott, Olivier and Sanford, regarded a government employee as a "bureaucrat" whose status was essentially servile. Only if Beatty could have been defined as their superior (and probably only success in private business would have so defined him for them) could these men have believed in his competence and in his right to direct their affairs.

Another fundamental cause of the tension and dissatisfaction at Casa Grande was the newness of the situation. It was new in two senses. The project was a new physical and human environment and this aspect of its newness created difficult problems for those families who had never before had near neighbors. The squabbles over the children's play are an example of this kind of difficulty, although perhaps not the most important one that could be found. The project situation was new in a second and more important sense, however: it was undefined. No one, perhaps least of all Waldron and Beatty—knew how one was supposed to act on a government project which was also a cooperative farm. The uncertainty about status was only one (although a very important) aspect of the general uncertainty. The settlers and the management had no habits and customs that would prescribe a right way of acting in the new situation and they had no group morality—no code—to provide and help enforce a common definition of right and wrong.

There was nothing abnormal or even unusual in the settlers' situation or in their behavior. This point needs some stress because, in the author's opinion, it is impossible to interpret their behavior correctly or usefully if it is viewed as pathological.

It may perhaps be argued that the settlers were afflicted by that condition called *anomie*. Durkheim used the term to describe the disturbed mental state of people who do not feel the restraint and discipline of socially-defined rules. In a state of rulelessness (*anomie*) the individual's ends are indeterminate; in other words, unless society provides the individual with goals, he is without any. Having no definition of ends a spirit of restlessness and discontent which is latent in the individual breaks forth, for it is only the rules of society which check these impulsive tendencies. The release of his restless discontent in a search for new satisfactions brings the individual the ever-repeated agony of an unquenchable thirst because, having no defined ends, his search must be an endless one: only if society reimposes its discipline upon him will he find ease.

It will be recognized that the situation at Casa Grande was in many ways one of "rulelessness." It is by no means certain, however, that it was exactly what Durkheim had in mind as the cause of *anomie* and neither is it certain that the settlers did in fact suffer from *anomie*. The situation at Casa Grande was undefined, to be sure, but only in the sense that no patterns of belief or conduct quite fitted it and none that were satisfactory arose out of the life of the community itself. But this is not to say that life at Casa Grande broke down *all* stable systems of belief and expectation, leaving individual ends quite indeterminate. The fact is that the settlers were held by a tight mesh of belief to the larger society that transcended project and state boundaries, and it was, perhaps, the very clarity of the definition supplied by this larger society that prevented them from adapting to the local situation. In a sense, then, the trouble was not that they were without a stable system of beliefs and expectations but, on the contrary, that the pattern that they brought with them to Casa Grande was altogether too stable to permit successful adjustment to the new situation. Similarly the trouble was not that the settlers lacked a sense of solidarity with their group, but that some of them (perhaps most of them) identified themselves with and felt solidarity with a group which was not their fellow-settlers but which was rather the larger, abstract society—the "outside world." It was largely because they felt a sense of solidarity with this larger world—because they took the role of the abstract outside group, a group which they believed to be hostile to or contemptuous of such undertakings as that in which they were engaged—that they were unable to cohere.

Having pointed out what may be said against the use of the concept *anomie* to describe the settlers' mental state, something may now be said in favor of it. It may be that, in their different manners, both the larger society and the smaller group were characterized by "rulelessness" and that, even though some matters which were left undefined by the local group were clearly defined by the larger society, other aspects of life were defined neither by the larger society nor the local group. In other words, it may be that the settlers suffered from *anomie* before they came to Casa Grande and that this *anomie* was reinforced and intensified by the different and in some ways more pronounced rulelessness of the life they found there.

That the elements which have been treated here as decisive in the Casa Grande experience are really normal features of experience in all organized activity may be conveniently illustrated by further reference to Barnard's *The Functions of the Executive*. ". . . successful cooperation in or by formal organization is the abnormal, not the normal condition," Barnard says. "What are observed from day to day are the successful survivors among innumerable failures." Non-economic motives and interests are fundamental in behavior from boards of directors to the last man, Barnard points out in a passage already quoted. "There is unlimited experience," he goes on, "to show that among many men, and especially among women, the real value of differences of money rewards lies in the recognition or distinction assumed to be conferred thereby, or to be procured therewith. . . ." It is common for men to refuse to work well when, as Olivier put it, "there are two kinds of people." Personal aversions based on race or class differences, Barnard says, may be pernicious but they are nevertheless based on a sound feeling for organizational necessities, for lack of compatibility makes communication difficult or impossible. He notes also the great importance of "customary working conditions and conformity to habitual practices and attitudes." "It is taken for granted," he says, "that men will not or cannot do well by strange methods or under strange conditions. What is not so obvious is that men will frequently not attempt to cooperate if they recognize that such methods or conditions are to be accepted."

It is, in fact, because organizations are invariably characterized by a chaos of conflicting motives and interests which must somehow be reconciled and brought into harmony with rational goals that executives are needed. The unique function of the executive, Barnard writes, is "to facilitate the synthesis in concrete action of contradictory forces, to reconcile conflicting forces, instincts, interests, conditions, positions and ideals." It is normal, too, for the members of the organization to need to have their situation defined and to need to share in an organizational code or group morality, and so it is one of the executive's peculiar functions to define the situation and to produce a code. To quote Barnard once more, "The distinguishing mark of executive responsibility is that it requires not merely conformance to a complex code of morals but also the creation of moral codes for others. The most generally recognized aspect of this function is called securing, creating, inspiring of 'morale' in an organization. This is the process of inculcating points of view, fundamental attitudes, loyalties, to the organization or cooperative system, and to the system of objective authority, that will result in subordinating individual interest and the minor dictates of personal codes to the good of the cooperative whole. This includes (also important) the establishment of the morality of standards of workmanship."

The ability to perform these functions (and not necessarily any other functions of an executive) will be termed here for convenience the art of "leadership."

Leadership was decisively lacking at Casa Grande. There was nothing in the FSA procedure manual to tell Beatty how to inspire the settlers with purpose and discipline. The leader's art is not something that can be written down in the form of rules and precepts. It rests on intuition and the "feel" of the situation; it includes (but is not limited to) a gift for handling non-logical elements in an intuitive way. Beatty did not possess this gift. Few people do. Because it is so rare, the skill of the leader brings high money rewards in our society; for FSA to have been able to hire a gifted leader for $2,300 a year, the amount of Beatty's salary, was out of the question. That there are only a few thousand farms in the United States as large as the one at Casa Grande and that even the largest farms are small by the standards that prevail in industry are circumstances that result in part from the high degree of leadership skill required for the successful management of a large farm, from the scarcity of this skill, and from the fact that a man who has the gift that will enable him to manage a large industrial farm can ordinarily manage a much larger enterprise (at a higher salary) in industry.

There is, it seems, a fundamental difference of kind between the skill of the bureaucrat and the art of the leader. The bureaucrat as a type is adept at managing a situation after it has been rationalized; he does his business, as Weber pointed out, according to calculable rules and "without regard for persons." When he makes a decision he takes the role of a procedure manual or of some such logical model as the "economic man" rather than that of living, interacting and therefore aberrant human beings. (It should not be supposed, of course, that the ideal or unalloyed type is often met with or that it is more often met with in government than in business. It should be recognized, too, that there are both bureaucrats and leaders in all organizations, government and private.) The mentality and skill of the bureaucrat are essential to the functioning of our highly rationalized society. But the very fact that he operates according to the rules of logic and "without regard to persons" incapacitates him for leadership. He is, in fact, specialized in the wrong direction to function successfully where the art of the leader is needed. The leader must be able to take the role of all elements within the organization and, at the same time, the role of the organization as a whole. His art is like that of the politician who, George H. Mead wrote, "is able to enter into the attitudes of the group and to mediate between them by making his own experience universal, so that others can enter into this form of communication through him." If he is the head of a large organization the executive must have a gift for entering into the attitudes of *abstract* groups and for mediating between them. This may be a radically different faculty than that of the leader who exercises his leadership largely through face-to-face contacts with members of his organization. It is no part of the intention here to explore the nature of this difference, if it is a difference. For the present purpose it is enough to observe that the government project was a small organization and that the gifts of leadership that were needed there were those that could be effective on a face-to-face basis. The words "leader" and "leadership" will be used hereafter to refer only to groups in which leadership is exercised mainly in face-to-face contacts; these groups will be called for convenience "primary organizations." Even in this restricted sense, leadership is a gift that is rare.

It will be seen that an important function of the leader is to aid communication; by his gift for role-taking the leader becomes a medium of communication. To a large extent the failure at Casa Grande was a failure of communication. Beatty was temperamentally incapable of entering emotionally into the situation of the settlers and so he could not make himself understood by them or help them to understand themselves or each other. But there were other elements in the situation which also contributed to the failure of communication. One was the newness, the lack of definition of the situation. Had he been a leader, Beatty might have done much to overcome this difficulty; he might, for example, have helped to fashion a code or group morality which in itself would have been a medium of communication. But no matter what qualities of leadership he had brought to Casa Grande, the newness of the situation would nevertheless have been a great, perhaps an insuperable, barrier to effective communication. So, too, would have been the real and fancied differences that divided the settlers into "two kinds of people;" it might be that no amount of leadership could have brought the two groups to understand each other. Surely more than "information" (including even information about "the principles of cooperation") was needed in order for the group to communicate sufficiently to maintain itself as a group; to suggest an educational program or a community council as a way of meeting this need was certainly an error of false logic, for the most important meanings would have to be conveyed in more delicate and subtle ways than by words and the medium of communication would necessarily be the situation in its wholeness.

Important as these failures of communication were at Casa Grande, it does not follow that all would have been well if communication had been good. Waldron and Mott, for example, might have understood each other very well without agreeing or without ceasing to struggle for power in the management of the project. Indeed it would seem that unless its content were radically changed by the very facility of communication, the effect would have been to accelerate the process of interaction and of conflict.

The analysis so far has suggested that it was the art of the leader that was decisively lacking at Casa Grande; perhaps not even a gifted leader could have overcome the difficulties that were inherent in the situation, but without a certain level of leadership ability, a level that was not attained, success was impossible. Without wishing to lessen the importance so far ascribed to leadership, it is intended now to describe how the level of leadership required for success might have been lowered. To say that if at Casa Grande there had been a person with a sufficient gift for leadership, that person would have led the settlers to cooperate is to solve the problem by definition or at least by a *deus ex machina*. As a practical matter it may be assumed that FSA could not have employed a sufficiently talented leader as manager of the association; what, then, could have been done to offset this lack and to make the success of the project more likely?

The level of leadership required for the success of an organization is not a function of the size of the organization as measured in numbers of employees or in dollars. It is, rather, a function of the demands that are put upon the creative ability of the leader—his ability to "facilitate the synthesis in concrete action of contradictory forces, to reconcile conflicting forces, instincts, interests, conditions, positions, and ideals." It is not so much the number of demands as it is their nature that tests the leader's capacity. Clearly the function of the leader is most difficult to perform when there is strong and sharp conflict, when definitions of the situation are lacking, and when an associational code must be fashioned from diverse and unlikely materials. At Casa Grande everything conspired to place extraordinary demands on leadership. If the circumstances had been different, the demands might have been less.

If, for example, Casa Grande had been called "a government poor farm—like a county farm only Federal" instead of "a cooperative" the situation would have been defined in such a way as to greatly reduce its inherent stress. The word "cooperative" introduced a whole complex of freedoms and accompanying uncertainties; the expression "poor farm" on the other hand, would have told Beatty and the settlers precisely where they stood. The settlers and the officials might have had some difficulty in getting used to the novelty of able-bodied men and their families being supported on a poor farm, but in the Depression when millions of able-bodied people were on relief this difficulty would probably not have been hard to overcome. The state farm would have served as well as the cooperative farm as an organizational device through which to provide management and capital and a basis for the distribution of earnings to the workers—and these of course were the considerations that led the Resettlement Administration to adopt the cooperative form of organization in the first place. The practical objection to the state farm idea, it may be supposed, was that public opinion—at least Congressional opinion—would not permit the government to own and operate farms for the avowed purpose of benefiting the farm workers. This was a point of view that the workers themselves would doubtless have shared after their worst sufferings had been eased.

Another way of defining the situation to reduce its demands on leadership skill would have been to call the project "a training farm" at which disadvantaged farm people and especially young people would learn new skills to fit themselves for employment on industrial farms or to manage their own enterprises. The projects were in fact defined in this very way by some FSA administrators, but the definition was not so much for the benefit of the settlers (whose uncertainty and insecurity was actually increased by it because they had always been led to expect something different) as it was a public relations line intended to explain and justify the very evident failure of the projects to develop the kind of community life that had been anticipated and promised.

A third way of defining the situation would have been to carry on what is called "education" in the doctrines of the cooperative movement. This, if it had succeeded, would have provided the settlers with a code, thus reducing the leader's responsibility for fashioning one. This is an approach which probably could not have succeeded however; the orthodoxy of the cooperative movement was radically foreign to the native ways of the settlers and to have converted them to it would have required a greater exercise of skill (if, indeed, it could have been done at all) than to fashion a code *de novo* from the morality they brought with them to Casa Grande. Moreover, even if the code of the cooperative movement was not distasteful to the settlers, the fashioning of a group morality of a kind to meet the unique and peculiar requirements of life at Casa Grande would still have remained as a problem for the settlers and officials to solve in their own way. This would be the case also if the project were called a state farm or a training farm, but not to the same degree; in these cases the definition would have been much more inclusive and practically useful in the small problems of day to day life.

If the settlers had come to Casa Grande bound together by a religious creed or by cultural or racial ties and with the feeling that they were set apart from the rest of mankind by these differences, and, especially, if they had found it necessary to struggle against a hostile world, they would probably have achieved a cohesion which would depend very little upon the harmonizing, organizing, and morale-building functions of leadership. Had FSA selected the settlers from among a religious or racial minority or had it been able and willing to present cooperation as a revolutionary creed to settlers who were devout radicals, it might thus have reduced the demands that would be placed on leadership. These possibilities were, of course, pretty much out of the question for (with the exception of Negroes) a minority which FSA could have assisted with the loan of a million dollars would not have been facing a hostile world.

The same principle would have been at work if FSA, instead of employing the services of a family selection specialist, had allowed the settlers to select themselves in the natural, informal manner by which people ordinarily form themselves into groups. The workings of natural selection, while it would not have produced a group having a bond of such strength as is sometimes found in religious association, would nevertheless have tended to bring together settlers who felt they had something in common and who, consequently, would have been able to communicate with each other. This, indeed, is the conclusion to which Waldron came even before the full quota of Casa Grande settlers had been selected.

Short of such a radical recasting of the nature of the project as is implied by these suggestions, a number of steps might have been taken to reduce the frictions and tensions at Casa Grande. One such move would have been to "fire" the dissatisfied settlers. By eliminating those whom Waldron called "strongheaded" personalities, it would have been possible to put a stop to some of the conflict that they continually generated. If, as Barnard maintains, cooperation exists only when there is an equilibrium between the burdens and satisfactions it entails, one way to secure cooperation (in fact the only way when circumstances are such that burdens cannot be reduced and the capacity to provide satisfactions, in this case chiefly those of status and power, cannot be increased) is by establishing the equilibrium at a lower level—that is, by selecting settlers who will endure more and demand less. There was no way of knowing which applicants would make good settlers and which would not. Under these circumstances the rule of trial and error offered the best, indeed the only reliance; by continually weeding out those settlers who would not work in harmony with the management and the other settlers, it would have been possible eventually to have collected a group who would cooperate and who would reach an equilibrium at the level of burdens and satisfactions actually afforded by the project. Some will say that such a policy would have resulted in an equilibrium at a woefully low level—in a membership composed of spineless wards of the government ruled by an autocrat. This may be true. But the experience at Casa Grande suggests that the establishment of conditions under which people will work together is a necessary although not a sufficient condition for attaining all other goals. The fact that the project was critically limited in the kinds and amounts of satisfactions that it could afford was a fact which could not be dodged and which necessitated the choice of settlers whose demands upon it would not be too great; not to recognize this real limit because it was distasteful would have availed nothing.

There were other moves by which conflict could have been reduced or by which the synthesis of conflicting forces could have been made easier to secure. If Beatty had been given authority by the regional and Washington offices to deal fully in his own way with all issues (and especially with the wage issue) he would probably have prevented certain disputes from arising which, once they had arisen, overtaxed his ability as an executive. (As a practical matter this course of action was impossible because of the great risks, especially to FSA's public relations, that would have been incurred by giving Beatty such wide authority.)

If the settlers had received higher wages during the first three years of the project, their morale during this important formative stage would probably have been much better—nothing, perhaps, would have done more to assure the settlers on the score of status than to receive in this period what their friends in Coolidge and Florence considered a high cash wage. (A businessman would have expected to pay the wages necessary to maintain morale even if doing so meant running in the red. But FSA, as a practical matter, had to consider how it could defend such a policy to the press and to Congressional committees.) If none of the settlers had been placed in positions of authority as foremen, some of the occasion for conflict—and conflict of a kind which was most destructive to the successful operation of the farm—could have been avoided. (But this, of course, would have necessitated the employment of at least two or three "outsiders" at wages which in the early years would have been more than the association could afford.)

If the project had not included a community—if the workers had found their own housing in Coolidge and Florence and had commuted to the farm in the usual fashion of the locality, even Beatty might have made the farm succeed. For one thing, the settlers would then have had an opportunity to select their friends from among a wider group and, each in his own way, to discover sources of status and power the enjoyment of which in no way endangered the success of the farm. For another thing, without the pastel-colored adobes and the community house the farm would have lost much of its distinctively "project" character and the settlers would have been less self-conscious and less in need of assurances as to their position in society. Finally, if there had been no community settlement, a much less comprehensive code or group morality would have been required— the situation would have been easier to define. It was one thing to create a cooperative farm. It was another and much more difficult thing to create a cooperative farm *and* a new community. (But to create only a farm would have been to sacrifice a part of the intention, which was to restore the social values associated with the family-farm pattern of tenure and to raise the settlers' standard of living as well as their incomes.)

No doubt this listing of ways in which matters could have been arranged to reduce the demands on leadership could be much extended. Only one more suggestion will be made here however. If the project had been given an identity apart from the government so that the complex of attitudes, beliefs, and expectations entertained by the settlers, the officials, the newspapers, the Congressmen and the public generally toward the government had not attached to the project, the possibility of appropriate and effective action by both settlers and management would have been greatly increased. The prevailing notions of how a government ought to act proved inappropriate as a basis for managing a large industrial-type farm; both the settlers and the officials were confused by their relation to government. (When, for example, the milkers served their ultimatum to Beatty he fired them on the inappropriate ground that they were jeopardizing the government's loan.) It was bad enough that the settlers and the officials should be confused in this way, but the identification of the project with the government had the further effect of forcing public relations considerations into a position of decisive importance in matters where public opinion could not play a constructive role. Whether or not to pay high wages or to risk a strike, for example, was a question which ought to have been decided on the basis of the realities of the project situation rather than in view of the probable effects of newspaper stories on the House Appropriations Committee. It is true, of course, that all management, not merely that associated with government, must take public opinion into account; the decisive differences, however, are that government business is much more a matter of public knowledge and the limitations placed upon government by public opinion are much more exacting.

If the public corporation has any unique advantage as a form of organization it is that it may afford a means of carrying on public business without having to conform to all the expectations that ordinarily attach to government. The other advantages that are claimed for public corporations—flexibility in the management of accounts, for example— could as well be shared by all agencies if Congress wished. It may be that a hybrid form of organization, one to which there attach only some of the expectations that ordinarily attach to government, will have valuable uses. But where, as in the case of the Casa Grande project, it is essential that people think and be thought about according to the flexible standards that are applied to private affairs, it seems improbable that the public corporation will be of very great value. If, for example, the FSA had been the Farm Security Corporation, Casa Grande would probably have been no less of a government project. If the object is to make use of a form of organization which is not thought of as government, the simple and direct approach is to use private corporations rather than to create public ones. Thus FSA might have contracted with a Phoenix bank to create a cooperative farm according to its specifications.

Of course to remove from such undertakings as Casa Grande the handicap of being thought of as government is also to put them out of the reach of detailed political discussion and so, one may fear, out of the reach of political discussion altogether. Since it is experimental and controversial undertakings that are most likely to require such protection, this consideration is a fairly important one. Moreover the use of corporations, public or private, implies lateral rather than scalar organization. There are many important advantages in the use of independent, decentralized organizations, but when something new is being undertaken—and especially when something unpopular is being undertaken—it may be essential that the chain of command extend directly to it.

The preceding analysis has stressed the reasons why the settlers behaved as they did, and, to a lesser extent, the ways in which FSA might have acted to change their behavior. That FSA was by no means free to act as the situation demanded has already been made clear; its inability to employ a gifted leader to manage the project and its constant need to take public and Congressional relations into account in conducting the affairs of the project have already been cited as important limitations. It is intended now to summarize briefly some of the other limiting factors which were inherent in the situation and which acted as checks on the FSA administrators.

The newness of the situation was a trial for FSA as well as for the settlers. What should be the goals and objectives of a "cooperative" farm project? No one knew for sure, and as long as people were going hungry there was no time for thoroughgoing analysis of such questions. Tugwell and his associates had no interest in promoting the cooperative ideology; their objective, they said, was simply to improve levels of living. But even this objective was not as unambiguous as it sounded; had the intent been merely to raise income (as contrasted to levels or standards of living) the settlers might better have been allowed to live in town and to commute to the farm. It was because the manner of life of the settlers, not simply the value of their consumption, was to be changed that the community form of organization and all that it entailed was made necessary. What, then, was the desirable way of living for these families? The Resettlement Administration did not pursue this question. Neither did FSA. Instead, FSA, being a good deal less determinedly "practical" than its predecessor, gave more and more weight to the largely undefined values which were supposed to inhere in the "social side" of a cooperative farm project. Even late in the life of the Project, after Cohen, Ross and Giordano had visited it, there was no effort to formulate these objectives in operational terms.

Some of the purposes of the project were in conflict with each other and since there was no explicit formulation and ranking of ends these conflicts were a source of confusion. One ineradicable conflict was between the goal of efficiency and that of service. FSA wanted the farm to be as profitable as possible, that is, to produce the greatest value of output with the least cost in input. But at the same time it wanted the project to assist as many families as possible—it wanted to use as much as possible of a certain input (labor) and to use it at as high a cost as possible. The result was an uneasy compromise: the farm employed more labor than it needed and per capita earnings were therefore lower than necessary. The situation had an adverse effect on the morale of both the settlers and officials, all of whom felt the incongruity of a situation in which a saving in the use of labor (e.g., the use of milking machines) yielded no economy. There was nothing that could be done to resolve the conflict, however, short of declaring that other considerations would be subordinated to that of profit. Of course if profit had been made the only consideration, the government project would have been run exactly like any well-managed corporate farm. It would, for example, have paid its manager perhaps $20,000 or $30,000 a year (which was two or three times what the FSA administrator in Washington earned) and it would have hired labor from day to day or month to month at the lowest possible rate. Only in the distribution of profit at the end of the year would it have differed from other farms.

Another conflict, while not logically inescapable, was nevertheless persistent. This was the conflict between the goals of democratic self-management (vaguely defined by Hewes and Cohen) and that of financial success. Should the government intervene in the affairs of the association to prevent the settlers from taking steps that were foolish and wasteful? Intervention would mean a sacrifice in terms of one goal, but failure to intervene would mean a sacrifice in terms of the other (and perhaps in terms of a third goal, that of protecting the government's loan). It was hard to decide how to order the conflicting goals; it was hard, for example, for Shelly to decide whether the settlers' experience in responsible decision-making would be worth the cost of a wrong decision in the matter of the new milking machines. Sometimes (the difficulties of communication within a large organization being what they are) no one person had all the information that was needed in order to weigh the ends against each other in a given situation. This was the case, for instance, when Washington ordered Shelly to rescind the Board's decision to sell produce from the farm to settlers at less than market prices. Shelly felt that any possible advantage to be had from rescinding the order would be more than outweighed by the loss of confidence it would engender in the settlers. Washington felt otherwise. But of course Shelly had no way of taking into account the considerations that seemed weighty in Washington and Washington could not appreciate those which seemed so crucial at Casa Grande.

There was, perhaps, a fatal disproportion between the goals of the project as they were finally formulated by Hewes, Cohen and Ross and the way of life of the settlers. It was morally desirable, no doubt, to bring about democratic cooperation and self-management among a group of ignorant sharecroppers whose struggle for existence had been bitter and cruel. But was it reasonable to attempt such a thing? No one would expect a hospital, for example, to provide its patients with new opportunities for democratic self-government; why, then, judge a rehabilitation project by such a standard? And, anyway, was it reasonable to make the experiment with such an unlikely group as this? In our society there are very few economic enterprises which are run by their employees. A college faculty is, perhaps, the only common example of such a body and, as everyone who has had contact with one knows, the capacity of a faculty for self-management is sharply limited. Why should a group of sharecroppers be expected to act in a more civilized fashion than a group of college professors?

There were other questions that more or less turned on the problem of goals. The question of what kind of people should be recruited for life on a cooperative farm was one. Mrs. Hauge, the family selection specialist, had almost nothing to go on in making her choices, and it must be admitted that if she were to do it all over again, this time with the advantage of full knowledge of how things actually turned out at Casa Grande, she could hardly be expected to do better. If she were able to identify types like Olivier and Mott (which is not improbable but not certain either), would she be well-advised to turn them down, noting on her forms, perhaps, "this man too intelligent, aggressive, articulate and anxious to get ahead?" Unless the goals of the project were defined clearly enough to indicate an operational principle of selection she would be without a basis for reasonable choice.

Other reasons than vagueness and inconsistency of goals prevented FSA from carrying on an educational program of the kind that is commonly recommended by the cooperative movement. It was quite impossible to educate the settlers in the principles of cooperation (assuming, indeed, that there are any such principles) before organizing the farm; the settlers could not be recruited months or years in advance and then kept conveniently on hand until the farm was ready to yield an income. Neither could FSA have passed over the hungry people who were in nearby ditch-banks and on the State House lawn in Phoenix in order to search out families, who, regardless of other qualifications, had some experience in what the cooperative movement chooses to call "cooperation." Even if such a procedure had been possible, there is no reason to believe it would have resulted in a group of settlers who would have been able to get along better with each other or with the government than did those who were actually selected. It is, in fact, quite possible that a group of experienced "cooperators," if such could have been found among the low-income farm people, would have included a very high proportion of urbanized, articulate, status-hungry misfits like Olivier and Mott and that these people would have exhibited a "trained incapacity" to cooperate.

The difficulties in the way of conducting an elaborate educational program *after* the project got underway were hardly less great. It was, as Faul and the settlers who voted to oust him even before the cooperative got underway clearly recognized, quite impossible to carry on an educational program that would at one moment assure the settlers that a cooperative was a notably democratic institution and at the next moment warn them that they could not expect to make decisions until some time in the indefinite future. It may be that reasonable men would have accepted the necessity of postponing the exercise of their rights until they had gained sufficient experience to use them wisely. But the settlers were not reasonable men. They believed that they already knew how to manage the farm and, as Shelly discovered, they were much more interested in challenging the management in a power struggle than in undertaking the onerous task of learning to manage for themselves. To suppose, as did Hewes, Cohen and Ross, that education could be conducted on the "social side" without interfering with the farm work was clearly a mistake. If Hewes had succeeded in hiring a "high-class educator" to take charge of the social side of the project, the man would have found himself forced either to supersede Beatty as manager of the farm (in which case he would soon have ceased to be an educator) or to engage in futile conversation or, worse, agitation among such of the settlers as had time to listen to him. There was no place on the project for a man whose business was to lead discussion groups. Unless he and his educational program had a close functional relation to the management of the farm, he could not possibly have had the respect or interest of the settlers. Education was not a function that could be separated from management, but, at the same time, no manager could have talked to his workers in the vocabulary of the cooperative movement and still have had their respect. It would have been possible, in the author's opinion, for a manager with the gift of leadership to have inspired the group to cohere and even to take a real interest in their work (this after all is what must be meant by education in this context), but such a manager would probably not have used methods which the cooperative movement accepts as "education" in "cooperation."

The history of the Casa Grande project, as it has been interpreted here, brings to attention the role of conflict within organization and of various elements of organization, particularly leadership, in reconciling conflict and in bringing about unified action directed toward a goal. At the risk of conveying the impression that social problems are merely or chiefly problems of organization or that all organizational problems are to be understood in terms of the presence or absence of leadership (which, after all, is only one factor of organization, although the one particularly brought into focus by the events at Casa Grande), it is intended now to draw chiefly some of the wider and more general implications of this analysis for social policy.

Our society may be thought of as consisting of millions of organizations; indeed it is more and more coming to be a society of organizations rather than of individuals. Most of these organizations are what has been called here "primary organizations," that is, the members are in fairly frequent face-to-face contact with the leadership of the organization. Many of the activities that we consider most important—especially that of making a living—are generally carried on within or in association with such organizations. It seems clear that organizations play an important part in containing and restraining the tensions, unrests and dissatisfactions which normally well up within us or, to put the same matter in its positive aspect, they help to engender morale. If this is true, the aggregative effect of organizations on the behavior of the whole society must be very great; if, for example, all of the hundreds of thousands of primary organizations in the United States were no more successful in building and maintaining morale than was the government project at Casa Grande, it seems likely that the result would be not only a great loss of productive efficiency but also social disorganization and unrest of a kind to generate sweeping social movements.

The role of organization and especially of leadership is made all the more important by the fact that our society is characteristically in flux; it is subject to ceaseless and rapid change of a kind that makes it constantly necessary for us to define new situations and redefine old ones. In this respect the newness of the situation at Casa Grande was simply an extreme example of a very common phenomenon of modern life. The process by which old ways of thinking and behaving are broken down and new ones are constituted operates largely through organizations; organizations, and especially the leaders of organizations, thus come to act as mediators between the requirements of the larger society and the ways of living and thinking of the individual. In this process leadership serves a unique and creative function by assisting the group to transcend or refashion its code to meet the requirements of the new situation. Any change involving the reconstruction of the code of the group thus puts heavy demands on leadership, and if the change is toward a more complex and exacting morality, a morality which restrains and redirects tensions and impulses into more intricate patterns—if it is what is called progress, these demands on leadership are at their heaviest.

It seems clear enough that leadership performs a vital function by preventing conflict from destroying organization and, what is very much the same thing, by preserving and renewing the code which binds the group to orderly internal and external relations. What may be less clear is that leadership performs an equally vital function by making conflict possible. There can exist within an organization "conflicting forces, instincts, interests, conditions, positions, and ideals" only as there is somewhere the capacity to reconcile and harmonize them so that activity may go on. It seems safe to say that the greater the capacity of leadership, the greater the freedom that can exist to express tension, unrest and conflict without destroying organization. The only ways in which the Casa Grande project could possibly have survived in the absence of gifted leadership, it should be noted, would have involved changing the situation (for example, by defining the situation as a "poor farm" or by firing the "strongheaded" settlers) so that the settlers would have had fewer demands to make or would have been less free to make them. The situation could have been changed to conform to the morality of the settlers fairly easily; the difficult thing—and the thing which would have required a high order of leadership—was to change the morality of the settlers to conform to the requirements of the new situation, a situation in which greater freedom was possible. The unique function of leadership in this context, then, is that it establishes an equilibrium (expressed in a code) between the necessities of the situation and the conflicting tendencies and impulses of individuals and, to the degree that it is gifted leadership, it establishes the equilibrium at a higher level (one which allows fuller expression of these conflicting tendencies and impulses). Thus leadership helps to realize the widely-held social values associated with the words "freedom" and "the dignity of the individual" by at once restraining and permitting the release of the individual's tensions, unrests, and impulses.

It seems evident that we ought to be very much concerned to increase our supply of leadership and to make the most effective use of it. We ought to increase the supply of leadership by education (but probably not by those techniques that are called "formal" education), we ought to remove the hindrances that prevent leaders from leading, and we ought to encourage the distribution of leadership into those social roles where it will be most serviceable. In the allocation of leadership we ought to take account of those uses where efficiency of organized effort is of importance, but we ought also to consider those situations where exceptional freedom (and consequently conflict) is necessary or desirable and those situations where change is at a pace and of a kind that puts a special strain on organization. On the negative side, we ought to discourage persons who are not leaders from occupying positions of leadership; especially we ought not to place bureaucrats in such positions or expect leadership as a function of bureaucracy as such. Wherever possible we ought to economize on leadership by making use of existing codes where to do so does not entail an undue sacrifice of other values. (In the author's opinion to convert all the large farms of the United States to cooperatives on the order of Casa Grande would involve an investment of leadership far in excess of any possible return.) This means that we should make use of existing institutions and organizational forms wherever possible and should expect to make progress by changing these old structures rather than by inventing new ones. As Rexford G. Tugwell wrote in 1925, more than a decade before Casa Grande got underway, "It would seem that if producers' cooperation is to develop it will go slowly and will probably develop out of the present tentative rearrangements being made in the world of production to allow the individuals who actually operate industry more and more voice in the management of affairs."

Notes and References to Sources

Except as otherwise noted, citations are to correspondence and related materials which were in the files of the Farm Security Administration in San Francisco, Washington, and at the Project. When the regional office of FSA was abolished, the project liquidated and FSA merged into the Farmers Home Administration these files were in part destroyed and in part reorganized in other places. Some documents have been preserved by the author in the records of the Program of Education and Research in Planning at the University of Chicago; in the notes below these documents are identified by the letter "C." Bernard Bell's notes, as well as an unfinished manuscript report by him, are in the files of the Division of Farm Population and Rural Welfare of the Bureau of Agricultural Economics.

Introduction

pp. 2–3, Charles H. Cooley, *Sociological Theory and Social Research*, Henry Holt and Company, New York: 1930, p. 335; pp. 3–4, the discussion of the ancestors of the cooperative farm is based on Russell Lord and Paul H. Johnstone, eds., *A Place On Earth*, Bureau of Agricultural Economics, Washington: 1942 (processed); pp. 4–5, Rexford G. Tugwell, "Cooperation and Resettlement," *Current History*, Feb. 1937, pp. 71–76; pp. 5–6, "Resettlement Administration," *First Annual Report*, Washington: 1936, pp. 36–37; pp. 5–6, *Senate Hearings on Agriculture Department Appropriations Bill*, 1944, p. 629.

Chapter 1

p. 8, the quoted characterizations of the project are from the *Christian Science Monitor*, Aug. 18, 1941; the San Francisco *People's World*, reprinted in the Salem, Oregon, *Capital-Press*, Jan. 27, 1939; Mott in an interview with Bernard Bell; the Arizona *Producer*, Feb. 15, 1938; F. N. Mortensen in a paper read before the Utah Academy of Sciences, Arts and Letters, May 3, 1941; and the Los Angeles *Herald-Express*, Jan. 1939; pp. 8–9, Philip Greisinger and George W. Barr, "Agricultural Land Ownership and Operating Tenure in the Casa Grande Valley," University of Arizona, *Experiment*

Station Bulletin No. 175, 1941, p. 282; pp. 8–9, FSA, "Casa Grande Valley Farms," Information leaflet, mimeographed, March 10, 1941; pp. 9–10, testimony of Walter F. Packard, Hearings Before Subcommittee on Education and Labor, (La Follette Committee), "Violations of Free Speech and the Rights of Labor," 1940, part 59, p. 21813; p. 13, the total authorization is broken down in *Senate Hearings on the First Deficiency Appropriations Bill for 1936*, p. 204, as follows: houses $200,000, land $240,000, farm buildings and out buildings $36,800, utilities $31,200, land improvement $28,800, operating goods $176,000, other costs $178,200, cost per family $11,140; pp. 14–15, this section is based on R. T. Robinson, "Narrative Covering Casa Grande Farm Management Plan," C, and the Dockets Suggestion No. X-Az6 and Farm Management Plan, dated Sept. 14 and 22, 1936; C; p. 18, The *Arizona Producer* of June 1, 1936, is authority for the statement that the bricks were made by hand; for the estimate of necessary waste see the testimony of C. B. Baldwin, *Senate Hearings on Agriculture Department Appropriations Bill, 1944*, p. 626; pp. 18–19, *Arizona Producer*, Sept. 1, 1936; p. 19, letter from Packard to Thum, Sept. 15, 1936; p. 21, the breakdown of costs is based on figures supplied the author by the Information Division, FHA, C; adding to the total given in the text $28,060 which was later paid for an additional 828 acres of land the eventual total cost of the project was $795,550 according to FHA. But testimony by FSA put the total at $810,860. See 78th Cong. 1st Sess, *Hearings Before Select Committee of House Committee on Agriculture to Investigate the FSA*, Part 2, p. 588; Walter Packard estimated savings resulting from community grouping at more than $100,000, exclusive of savings on roads. Cf. his La Follette Committee testimony, *loc. cit*, p. 21817. His figures cannot be reconciled with those of FSA and FHA however; pp. 24–25, memo Garst to Alexander, June 18, 1937, C.

Chapter 2

p. 27, Articles of Incorporation executed in Maricopa County June 18, 1937; p. 29, Garst's views were put forward in a letter from his assistant, R. W. Hollenberg, to Alexander dated Nov. 11, 1937; the quotes attributed to the Regional Director are from this letter; p. 34, interview with Robert Craig by the author; pp. 34–35, letter to the author from Mrs. "Ernest S. Perry," Oct. 7, 1947; pp. 35–36, memo Waldron to Garst, Feb. 11, 1938; p. 37, memo Hollenberg to Baldwin, Dec. 12, 1940.

Chapter 3

p. 38, Two studies of family selection methods and criteria, made especially for the Resettlement Administration, were published while Mrs. Hauge was choosing the families for Casa Grande, but, if she saw them, neither could have helped her much. John B. Holt in *Social Research Report No. I*, "An Analysis of Methods and Criteria Used in Selecting Families for Colonization Projects," U.S. Department of Agriculture, Washington, September 1937, reviewed the literature and concluded that settlers ought to have eleven qualifications, including for example: "a rudimentary educa-tion and as much additional education as is in harmony with a favorable attitude toward farm life;" "cooperative and harmonious family life;" "intelligence, alertness, resourcefulness, and judgment;" "community cooperative ability;" and "religiosity or loyalty to an idealistic group, if it tends to sanctify the above agricultural virtues." (pp. 4–5). Marie Jasny in *Social Research Report No. V*, "Family Selection on a Fed-eral Reclamation Project," U.S. Department of Agriculture, Washington, June 1938, concluded that "family selection is a worthwhile undertaking" (p. 62) but her rec-ommendations were by no means unequivocal. ". . . farming experience," she wrote (p. 65) "measured not in years but in years weighed by ability to utilize experience, is a highly important but not indispensable qualification. . . . In a relatively new area where there is much experimentation as to choice of crops and farm practices, it is replaceable for the most part by general education, intelligence, business ability, and willingness to read and observe."

A more recent discussion of the same subject is that by Henrik F. Infield and Ernest Dichter, "Who is Fit for Cooperative Farming?", *Applied Anthropology*, 2:2, January–March 1943, pp. 10–17. These authors propose a "psychotechnical test" in four parts: 1. The applicant would be asked to submit a complete narrative life his-tory, 2. the applicant would take a self-scoring personality test (do you ever speak at large meetings?); 3. an interview with a psychologist would be held "to establish the degree of dissatisfaction with the present life and the applicant's desire to change it"; and 4. a "farm ability" test would be administered. The farm ability test is too elabo-rate to be described in detail, but some notion of it may be conveyed by the following (p. 17): "The setting is a chicken-coop, presented either in a photograph, a film, or in reality. The candidate is told to observe the chickens and to indicate which among them are of an inferior quality, sick, non-laying, aggressive, etc. Or a cow barn might be the place. . . ." pp. 38–39, RA Administration Order 105 (Revision 3), Sept. 25, 1936, C; p. 39 the *Arizona Producer* of Nov. 13, 1937 had carried a column-length govern-ment press release on the Project. But that the *Producer* should treat the material as new suggests that the cooperative nature of the Project was not widely understood; pp. 39–40, telegram RP Az6-911-045; memo Garst to Alexander, Aug. 17, 1937, replying to RP-3-WFT, July 22, 1937; telegram Garst to Alexander, Dec. 17, 1937; telegram Garst to Alexander, Dec. 21, 1937; p. 40, Mrs. Hauge's and Faul's Selection techniques are described by Bernard Bell and have been characterized by Robert Craig in conver-sations with the author; p. 42, for an account of the forces that set the migrants in motion, see Paul S. Taylor, "Power Farming and Labor Displacement in the Cotton Belt," 1937, *Monthly Labor Review*, Bureau of Labor Statistics, March and April, 1935; the situation of the migrants in Arizona in 1937 is described by Malcolm Brown and Orrin Cassmore, *Migratory Cotton Pickers in Arizona*, WPA Division of Research, 1939; p. 44, Casa Grande *Dispatch*, Feb. 3, 1939; p. 44, Special Selection Criteria, RR-Az-6, May 1938, C; p. 46, information on the settlers' backgrounds was obtained from the family selection schedules taken by Mrs. Hauge (C) and from Bernard Bell's inter-view notes; p. 50, Arizona *Producer*, Feb. 15, 1938.

Chapter 4

p. 51, Tucson *Star*, Aug. 21–23, 1938; pp. 52–53, the characterization of Faul's manner of management is based on Bell's interviews with the settlers, on information supplied in interviews by Craig, and on the *Star* articles cited above; pp. 53–54, Olivier gave this account to Bell; pp. 56–57, memo Waldron to Faul, Aug. 27, 1938; p. 58, Garst to Alexander, Jan. 17, 1939, C; pp. 60–61, F. N. Mortensen, "Casa Grande Valley Farms, Problems and Progress," paper presented before the Utah Academy of Sciences, Arts and Letters, May 3, 1941; p. 61, Tucson *Star*, Jan. 5, 1939.

Chapter 5

p. 63, Richard L. Strout, *Christian Science Monitor*, Aug. 18, 1941; pp. 65–66, the figures on the farm enterprises are from a report (R9-RP-RR) made by Beatty on Sept. 17, 1940, C; p. 68, the data on family progress is from the paper By F. N. Mortensen cited above; pp. 69–71, Hewes' testimony was given Sept. 25, 1940 before the Special (House) Committee Investigating Interstate Migration of Destitute Citizens (the Tolan Committee); p. 72, the account of Hewes' views is based on discussions the author had with him in 1943 and 1944; pp. 73–74, memo Waldron to Coverley, Dec. 19, 1940, C; p. 74, the questionnaire was filed in Feb. 1941 under the designation Az6-935, C.

Chapter 6

p. 76, memo Waldron to Hewes, June 3, 1940; C; pp. 78–79, letter from Mrs. Huston to Mrs. Roosevelt dated June 6, 1940, copy in FSA files; pp. 79–80, information on the backgrounds of Mott and Olivier is taken from family selection records kept by Mrs. Hauge, C; pp. 80–86 quotations from Mott, Olivier and others are from Bell's interview notes; pp. 86–87, the 1940 survey was reported by Packard in his La Follette Committee testimony, *loc. cit.*, p. 21822; the 1941 study was by Bell.

Chapter 7

p. 92, the direct quotations in this chapter are taken from Bell's interviews; p. 99, the summary of FSA supervisors' reports is Conrad Taeuber and Rachel Rowe, "Five Hundred Families Rehabilitate Themselves," U.S. Department of Agriculture, multilith, Feb. 1941, pp. 18–19. The FSA supervisors were probably biased, but the author's observations over many years of close contact have convinced him that FSA's dealings with families on individual farms seldom aggravated psychological stresses and very often relieved them; p. 99, Bureau of Agricultural Economics, "Attitudes Toward FSA Tenant Purchase Program, Study 122," dittoed, Jan. 1946.

Chapter 8

p. 105, much of the detail in this chapter is drawn from Bell's notes and from Roy Giordano, "A Report on the Community and Farm Problems of the Casa Grande Valley Farms Inc., Pinal County, Arizona," undated typescript, 23 pp., in the files of Professor Paul S. Taylor, Economics Department, University of California, Berkeley; p. 113, Tucson *Star*, August 25, 1938; pp. 113–14, memo Waldron to Beatty, July 19, 1940.

Chapter 9

p. 117, Tucson *Star*, Aug. 21, 1938 and *Casa Grande Dispatch*, Jan. 6, 1939; p. 118, *Casa Grande Dispatch*, Jan. 6, 1939; pp. 118–19, the quotations from Ketchersid and others are from a mimeographed FSA press release originated in San Francisco; pp. 119–21, the editorials quoted appeared on the following dates, all in 1939: *Leader*, Feb. 18; *Citizen-Patriot*, Jan. 9; *Age-Herald*, Jan. 4; *News*, Jan. 5; *Sun*, Jan. 4; *News*, Jan. 12; *Oregonian*, Jan. 10; *Spokesman-Review*, Jan. 8; *People's World*, reprinted in the Salem (Oregon) *Capital-Press*, Jan. 27; *Times*, Jan. 4; *Times-Dispatch*, Jan. 9; *Dispatch*, reprinted in the Holbrook (Arizona) *Tribune-News*, Jan. 13; p. 121, for much of this account of local opinion the author is indebted to Robert Craig; p. 122, the statement regarding the settlers' voting is based on information in F. N. Mortensen, *op. cit.*; p. 123 the visiting professor of economics was Paul S. Taylor of the University of California; p. 123, Perry's statement was made to Bell.

Chapter 10

pp. 126–27, memo Robinson to Coverley, March 22, 1941, C; pp. 128–29, the account of the meeting is based on Bell's notes; p. 129, Cohen's report was an attachment to a memo from Hardie to Coverley, March 6, 1941, C; p. 130, Beatty's statement was to Bell; pp. 131–32 the views attributed to the settlers were reported by Bell; p. 133, Stuart Chase, "What Makes the Worker Like to Work?," *Readers' Digest*, Feb. 1941; p. 132, the account of the meeting is based on Bell's notes; pp. 134–35, the analysis of the voting is based on the minutes of the meeting, C; p. 136, memo Shelly to Coverley, July 14, 1941, C; pp. 137–38, Giordano's paper has been cited above; pp. 138–39, Ross to Coverley, July 7, 1941 and Ross to Cohen, April 21, 1941; the constitution was attached to a memo from Cohen to Shelly, Aug. 29, 1941, C; p. 140, memo Shelly to Cohen, Aug. 29, 1941, C; Cohen to Coverley, undated.

Chapter 11

pp. 142–43, the Board's comments were attached to a memo from Craig to Cohen, April 6, 1942, C; pp. 143–44, memo Hewes to Baldwin, date unknown; p. 144, memo and attachment, Shelly to Coverley, March 3, 1942, C; p. 146, the account of the firing of the dairy crew is as told to the author by Robert Craig; p. 147, Council minutes, Nov. 11, 1941, C; p. 148, Council minutes, Oct. 1942; p. 149, Shelly to Hewes, date unknown; pp. 150–51, the petition was dated Feb. 10, 1941; pp. 152–53, the author was not able to examine the Association's books; this account of labor expense is based on estimates and on a report on settlers' earnings which was forwarded from the Regional Director to Mr. Milton Siegal, Special Assistant to the Administrator, June 24, 1943, C; pp. 154–55, Mott's comment was in an interview with Bell.

Chapter 12

p. 156 the information on Sandford's background was obtained from a family selection schedule, C; p. 158, the incident of the Directors' meeting was described to the author by Craig; p. 160, First Inspection of Casa Grande Valley Farms Project, March 31, 1943; pp. 161–62, minutes of the Board of Directors, Nov. 12, 1941; pp. 162–63, memo Shelly to Hewes, date unknown; telegram Hewes to Shelly, Jan. 15, 1942; pp. 163–64 minutes of the Board of Directors Jan. 15 and July 11, 1942.

Chapter 13

p. 168, Evidence that Baldwin had not ignored the order to dispose of the projects is to be found in House *Hearings on Agriculture Department Appropriations Bill, 1943*, p. 223. However both Baldwin and Secretary Wickard took the position that the projects should not be liquidated with undue haste. See Wickard's statement, *ibid.*, p. 741; p. 168, Baldwin's statement to the Cooley Committee appears in *Hearings Before Select Committee of the House Committee on Agriculture to Investigate the Activities of the Farm Security Administration*, 78th Cong. 1st Sess., Part 2, p. 597. See also Baldwin's earlier (January 1942) statement to the subcommittee on agriculture of the House Appropriations committee in *House Hearings on the Agriculture Department Appropriations Bill, 1943*, p. 268; pp. 169–70, this account was given to the author by Craig in an interview; p. 171, letter Hewes to Kilman, July 27, 1943; p. 172, minutes of directors' meeting Aug. 16 and 27, 1943; p. 172, memo Hewes to Craig, Sept. 1, 1943; p. 173, letter Kilman to Hewes quoted in memo Hollenberg to Decant, Nov. 25, 1943; p. 174, the account of Hollenberg's conferences with the settlers is based on interviews with him; pp. 174–75, Tucson *Star*, Nov. 17, 1943; p. 176, Reed's telegram to Senator MacFarland, dated Dec. 7, 1943, is in the Washington office files of FSA;

p. 176, J. F. Aldridge et al. vs. Casa Grande Valley Farms Inc., Order No. 7194, April 18, 1946 and Order No. 7194, Dec. 18, 1946, Superior Court, Pinal County, Arizona; p. 177, the account of the liquidation of the government's holdings is based on information supplied by R. W. Hollenberg, state director, FHA; pp. 179–80, information regarding the whereabouts of the settlers was supplied by Craig; p. 180, the statement quoted from Mrs. Perry is in a letter to the author, C.

Chapter 14

p. 181, The statement by the Administrator appears in his testimony, *Senate Hearings on Agriculture Department Appropriations Bill, 1944*, p. 625; pp. 181–82, the account of the Lake Dick farm is based on a typewritten report (undated) by Waller Wynne of the Bureau of Agriculture Economics, C; p. 182, Memphis (Tenn.) *Commercial-Appeal*, April, 1947; p. 183, Paul W. Wager, *One Foot on the Soil*, Bureau of Public Administration, University of Alabama, 1945, p. 207; p. 183, Warner Ogden in the *Wall Street Journal*, Feb. 15, 1950; p. 184, Bureau of Reclamation, *Columbia Basin Joint Investigations*, "Pattern of Rural Settlement, Problem 10," Washington, 1947, p. 19; pp. 184–85, Charles P. Loomis, "Social Relationship and Institutions in Seven New Rural Communities," *Social Research Report No. XVIII*, U.S. Department of Agriculture, Washington, Jan. 1940. processed, p. 19; p. 185, Joseph W. Eaton, *Exploring Tomorrow's Agriculture*, Harper & Brothers, 1943, p. 187 and p. 117; pp. 185–86, the chairman of the FSA committee was Leonard Outhwaite; its mimeographed, undated report is in the files of FHA; pp. 186–87, Russell Lord and Paul H. Johnstone, eds., *A Place on Earth*, Bureau of Agricultural Economics, processed, pp. 196–7, 195, and 2.

Chapter 15

p. 189, It must be acknowledged that an attempt to make an interpretation that will fit the facts is not a logically satisfactory procedure in itself. As Robert K. Merton has pointed out *"post-factum* explanations remain at the level of *plausibility*. . . ." (The basis for 'plausibility' rests in the consistency between the interpretation and the data; the absence of compelling evidence stems from the failure to provide distinctive tests of the interpretations apart from their consistency with the initial observations. The analysis is fitted to the facts, and there is no indication of just which data would be taken to contravene the interpretations. As a consequence the documentary evidence merely illustrates rather than tests the theory.") Robert K. Merton *Social Theory and Social Structure*, The Free Press, Glencoe, Ill.: 1949, pp. 90 and 91; pp. 190–91, This assumes the existing state of public opinion. The author is indebted to Margie Meyerson for the thought: What would have been the case if the government had been able to send movie actresses out to Casa Grande to pin "the Order of Lincoln" on certain settlers?

p. 191, Walter Packard listed these "safeguards" in his testimony before the La Follette Committee. Explaining the advantages of lease tenure he said: "An objection sometimes made to this leasing arrangement is that it does not provide a depository for savings, which capital payments on land normally represent. Practically speaking, however, the settlers can invest savings in government securities, which in addition to their safety, yield about as much as the interest normally earned on land equities by farmers." Packard's observation was true enough, but it was dangerously irrelevant because what the settlers wanted was not "a depository for savings" but the *feeling* of being land owners which for them was the feeling of success. Thus this and Packard's two other safeguards at all, but hazards—obstacles that could be surmounted only if some extraordinary motivation could be called into play. For Packard's testimony see 76th Cong. 3rd Sess., Subcommittee of the Committee on Education and Labor (Senate), *Hearings on Violations of Free Speech and Rights of Labor*, Part 59, "California Agricultural Background," pp. 21814 and 21816.

p. 192, Chester I. Barnard, *The Functions of the Executive*, Harvard University Press: 1938, p. xi. Frank H. Knight has described business as a "game" which arises out of men's "intrinsic interest in action" and which is motivated not so much by mere cupidity as by the desire to keep the game interesting. *Ethics and Competition*, Harper and Brothers, New York: 1935, pp. 60–61. Knight's analysis here and elsewhere is entirely consistent with that of Barnard, who also stresses the tendency of men to engage in activity for the sake of activity.

p. 192, This literature emanates from what may be called a community organization "movement" which began somewhat before the First World War. The main elements of the movement have been social workers, particularly of the Red Cross and the Agricultural Extension Services, the recreation "movement," and rural sociologists. The best description of the backgrounds of the movement is to be found in J. F. Steiner, *Community Organization*, the Appleton-Century Co., New York: 1930. A characteristic example of this literature is A. E. Morgan, The Small Community, Harper & Brothers, New York: 1942.

p. 193, R. E. Diffendorfer, quoted in B. A. McClenahan, *Organizing the Community*, New York: 1925, p. 4; Dwight Sanderson, quoted ibid, pp. 40 and 7; Edward C. Lindeman, *The Community*, Association Press, New York: 1921, pp. 185 and 175; p. 194, James M. Williams, *An American Town*, New York: 1906, p. 54; N. L.; Sims, *A Hoosier Village*, New York: 1912, p. 78, J. F. Steiner, Case Studies of American Communities *The American Community in Action*, New York: 1928, p. 32; a somewhat similar collection of case studies is Walter Pettit, *Case Studies in Community Organization*, New York: 1928; pp. 194–95, Joseph A. Cocannouer, *Trampling out the Vintage*, University of Oklahoma Press. Norman: 1945, p. 84; p. 196, In this analysis I have found helpful Chester I. Barnard's essay on "Functions and Pathology of Status Systems in Formal Organizations" which appears as Chapter IX in his book, *Organization and Management*, Harvard University Press, Cambridge: 1948.

pp. 197–98, Barnard, Op. cit., p. 5, 145, 147; p. 198, Barnard, Op. cit, p. 279; p. 199, The word 'bureaucrat' is of course not used here in its pejorative sense; p. 199, Max Weber, Essays in Sociology, Translated and edited by H. H. Gerth and C. Wright Mills, (Oxford University Press, New York: 1946), p. 215. Weber here (p. 216) says that the specific nature and special virtue of bureaucracy is that it eliminates from official business "love, hatred, and all purely personal, irrational, and emotional elements which escape calculation." For purposes of contrast with executive as described above, the bureaucrat may be thought of as eliminating also the gift for operating intuitively according to the 'feel' of the situation and the gift of arousing strong loyalties to himself or to an organizational code, i.e. the gift of leadership. These qualities are more likely to be associated with another ideal type which Weber placed in contrast to the bureaucrat, namely the "charismatic leader."

p. 199, George H. Mead, *Mind, Self and Society*, (University of Chicago Press: 1934), p. 257. See also Mead's statement (p. 256), "Occasionally a person arises who is able to take in more than others of an act in process, who can put himself in relation with whole groups in the community whose attitudes have not entered into the lives of others in the community. He becomes a leader."; p. 199, "We may think of employees as mechanics, clerks, laborers, or as members of an organization, but to lead requires to *feel* them as embodying a thousand emotions and relationships with others and with the physical environment, of which for the most part we can have no knowledge." Chester I. Barnard, *Organization and Management*, p. 104.

p. 199, It is not suggested, of course, that the two types of leadership are entirely separable, except conceptually. The leader of a far-flung organization has to get along with the people with whom he is in face-to-face contact, although his special gift is for leading abstract groups such as "the market" or "the general public." If the distinction seems arbitrary and strained, it must be remembered that the alternative is to imply that Casa Grande and, say, General Motors are significantly comparable because both are "organizations" requiring leadership; pp. 201–03, See Joseph W. Eaton, op. cit., pp. 82–83; p. 203, Barnard's discussion of equilibrium is to be found in his *The Function of the Executive*, Chapter 5;

p. 207, It must be recognized, that there is a significant sense in which *all* social situations are new. In a defined situation one knows how people are *supposed* to act; strictly speaking a new (unprecedented) situation may or may not be defined but, in any case, one does not know how people will *actually* act. Thus, for example, even if Waldron had managed government projects like that at Casa Grande all his life (i.e., if the situation had been defined) he would not have known—although he might have made a shrewder guess—what would be the effect of his decision to use wage differentials as incentives or, again, how the settlers would react if he fired some of the "troublemakers." The newness, in this sense, of all social situations must be the bane both of the administrator and the social scientist.

p. 212, It must be noted again that the words "leadership" and "organization" as used here refer only to what occurs in primary organizations. If this caution is not enough, two unwarranted extensions of the argument made here are explicitly disavowed: 1. those organizations which are political in the narrow sense of the word may be considered a special category outside of the framework of this analysis because to the extent that they are sovereign they draw on inexhaustible reservoirs of power, a fact which raises special problems in connection with the social role of political leadership; 2. it is not argued that the equilibrium resulting from successful organization and able leadership will relieve the conditions which cause strikes; such disputes, in the author's opinion, are only incidentally affected by the tensions and impulses, satisfied or unsatisfied, of the individual worker.

p. 214, R. G. Tugwell, H. Munro, and Roy Stryker, *American Economic Life, and the Means of its Improvement*, Harcourt Brace and Co. Third Edition, 1930, p. 674.

Some Names Prominent in the Story

Officials

Jonathan Garst, Regional Director, 1936–40	San Francisco
Laurence I. Hewes, Jr., Regional Director, 1940–43	"
Russell Robinson, Regional Farm Management Specialist, 1936–41	"
Meyer Cohen, Specialist on Social Organization and later Assistant Regional Director in charge of projects, 1941–43	"
Fred Ross, Specialist on Social Organization succeeding Cohen	"
James Waldron, Area Supervisor for Arizona, 1937–41	Phoenix
James L. Shelly, Area Supervisor succeeding Waldron	"
Mrs. Theone Hauge, Family Selection Specialist and Home Economist, 1936–41	"
Miss Gay Elkins, Home Economist succeeding Mrs. Hauge	"
Robert A. Faul, Project Manager, 1937–38	Project
Ralph E. Beatty, Project Manager, 1939–43	"
Edward Wildermuth, Project Clerk and Beatty's assistant	"

Settlers

Usually Pro-Government	Usually Anti-Government
Harry Coker	Julius S. Mott
Ernest S. Perry	Harry Olivier
Cecil Hopkins	John Sanford
Bill Forbes	Harvey Thomas
S. O. Hennesey	Martin King

About the Author

Edward C. Banfield (1916–99) was a professor at the University of Chicago, Harvard University, and the University of Pennsylvania. He authored more than a dozen books on urban politics, political cooperation, and American governance.

The American Enterprise Institute for Public Policy Research

AEI is a nonpartisan, nonprofit research and educational organization. The work of our scholars and staff advances ideas rooted in our commitment to expanding individual liberty, increasing opportunity, and strengthening freedom.

The Institute engages in research; publishes books, papers, studies, and short-form commentary; and conducts seminars and conferences. AEI's research activities are carried out under four major departments: Domestic Policy Studies, Economic Policy Studies, Foreign and Defense Policy Studies, and Social, Cultural, and Constitutional Studies. The resident scholars and fellows listed in these pages are part of a network that also includes nonresident scholars at top universities.

The views expressed in AEI publications are those of the authors; AEI does not take institutional positions on any issues.

BOARD OF TRUSTEES

DANIEL A. D'ANIELLO, *Chairman*
Cofounder and Chairman Emeritus
The Carlyle Group

CLIFFORD S. ASNESS
Managing and Founding Principal
AQR Capital Management LLC

THE HONORABLE
RICHARD B. CHENEY

PETER H. COORS
Chairman of the Board
Molson Coors Brewing Company

HARLAN CROW
Chairman
Crow Holdings

RAVENEL B. CURRY III
Chief Investment Officer
Eagle Capital Management LLC

KIMBERLY O. DENNIS
President and CEO
Searle Freedom Trust

DICK DEVOS
President
The Windquest Group

ROBERT DOAR
President
American Enterprise Institute

BEHDAD EGHBALI
Managing Partner and Cofounder
Clearlake Capital Group LP

MARTIN C. ELTRICH III
Partner
AEA Investors LP

TULLY M. FRIEDMAN
Managing Director, Retired
FFL Partners LLC

CHRISTOPHER B. GALVIN
Chairman
Harrison Street Capital LLC

HARVEY GOLUB
Chairman and CEO, Retired
 American Express Company
Chairman, Miller Buckfire

ROBERT F. GREENHILL
Founder and Chairman
Greenhill & Co. Inc.

FRANK J. HANNA
CEO
Hanna Capital LLC

JOHN K. HURLEY
Founder and Managing Partner
Cavalry Asset Management

DEEPA JAVERI
Chief Financial Officer
XRHealth

JOANNA F. JONSSON
Partner
Capital Group

MARC S. LIPSCHULTZ
Cofounder and President
Owl Rock Capital Partners

JOHN A. LUKE JR.
Chairman
WestRock Company

PAT NEAL
Chairman of the Executive Committee
Neal Communities

ROSS PEROT JR.
Chairman
Hillwood Development Company

GEOFFREY S. REHNERT
Co-CEO
Audax Group

KEVIN B. ROLLINS
CEO, Retired
Dell Inc.

MATTHEW K. ROSE
Retired CEO/Chairman
BNSF Railway

EDWARD B. RUST JR.
Chairman Emeritus
State Farm Insurance Companies

WILSON H. TAYLOR
Chairman Emeritus
Cigna Corporation

WILLIAM H. WALTON
Managing Member
Rockpoint Group LLC

WILL WEATHERFORD
Managing Partner
Weatherford Capital

EMERITUS TRUSTEES

JOHN FARACI

BRUCE KOVNER

PAUL F. OREFFICE

D. GIDEON SEARLE

HENRY WENDT

OFFICERS

ROBERT DOAR
President

JASON BERTSCH
Executive Vice President

SUZANNE GERSHOWITZ
Senior Vice President and Chief Operating Officer

JOHN CUSEY
Senior Vice President for External Relations

KAZUKI KO
Chief Financial Officer

MATTHEW CONTINETTI
Senior Fellow; Director of Domestic Policy Studies; Patrick and Charlene Neal Chair in American Prosperity

YUVAL LEVIN
Senior Fellow; Director, Social, Cultural, and Constitutional Studies; Beth and Ravenel Curry Chair in Public Policy; Editor in Chief, National Affairs

KORI SCHAKE
Senior Fellow; Director, Foreign and Defense Policy Studies

MICHAEL R. STRAIN
Senior Fellow; Director, Economic Policy Studies; Arthur F. Burns Scholar in Political Economy

RESEARCH STAFF

SAMUEL J. ABRAMS
Nonresident Senior Fellow

BETH AKERS
Senior Fellow

J. JOEL ALICEA
Nonresident Fellow

JOSEPH ANTOS
Senior Fellow; Wilson H. Taylor Scholar in Health Care and Retirement Policy

LEON ARON
Senior Fellow

KIRSTEN AXELSEN
Nonresident Fellow

JOHN BAILEY
Nonresident Senior Fellow

KYLE BALZER
Jeane Kirkpatrick Fellow

CLAUDE BARFIELD
Senior Fellow

MICHAEL BARONE
Senior Fellow Emeritus

MICHAEL BECKLEY
Nonresident Senior Fellow

ERIC J. BELASCO
Nonresident Senior Fellow

ANDREW G. BIGGS
Senior Fellow

MASON M. BISHOP
Nonresident Fellow

DAN BLUMENTHAL
Senior Fellow

KARLYN BOWMAN
Distinguished Senior Fellow Emeritus

HAL BRANDS
Senior Fellow

ALEX BRILL
Senior Fellow

ARTHUR C. BROOKS
President Emeritus

RICHARD BURKHAUSER
Nonresident Senior Fellow

CLAY CALVERT
Nonresident Senior Fellow

JAMES C. CAPRETTA
Senior Fellow; Milton Friedman Chair

TIMOTHY P. CARNEY
Senior Fellow

AMITABH CHANDRA
Nonresident Fellow

LYNNE V. CHENEY
Distinguished Senior Fellow

JAMES W. COLEMAN
Nonresident Senior Fellow

ZACK COOPER
Senior Fellow

KEVIN CORINTH
Senior Fellow; Deputy Director, Center on Opportunity and Social Mobility

JAY COST
Gerald R. Ford Nonresident Senior Fellow

DANIEL A. COX
Senior Fellow

SADANAND DHUME
Senior Fellow

GISELLE DONNELLY
Senior Fellow

MICHAEL BRENDAN DOUGHERTY
Nonresident Fellow

ROSS DOUTHAT
Nonresident Fellow

COLIN DUECK
Nonresident Senior Fellow

MACKENZIE EAGLEN
Senior Fellow

NICHOLAS EBERSTADT
Henry Wendt Chair in Political Economy

MAX EDEN
Research Fellow

JEFFREY EISENACH
Nonresident Senior Fellow

ANDREW FERGUSON
Nonresident Fellow

JESÚS FERNÁNDEZ-VILLAVERDE
John H. Makin Visiting Scholar

JOHN G. FERRARI
Nonresident Senior Fellow

JOHN C. FORTIER
Senior Fellow

AARON FRIEDBERG
Nonresident Senior Fellow

JOSEPH B. FULLER
Nonresident Senior Fellow

SCOTT GANZ
Research Fellow

R. RICHARD GEDDES
Nonresident Senior Fellow

ROBERT P. GEORGE
Nonresident Senior Fellow

EDWARD L. GLAESER
Nonresident Senior Fellow

JOSEPH W. GLAUBER
Nonresident Senior Fellow

JONAH GOLDBERG
Senior Fellow; Asness Chair in Applied Liberty

BARRY K. GOODWIN
Nonresident Senior Fellow

SCOTT GOTTLIEB, MD
Senior Fellow

PHIL GRAMM
Nonresident Senior Fellow

WILLIAM C. GREENWALT
Nonresident Senior Fellow

SHEENA CHESTNUT GREITENS
Jeane Kirkpatrick Visiting Fellow

JIM HARPER
Nonresident Senior Fellow

TODD HARRISON
Senior Fellow

WILLIAM HAUN
Nonresident Fellow

FREDERICK M. HESS
Senior Fellow; Director, Education Policy Studies

CAROLE HOOVEN
Nonresident Senior Fellow

BRONWYN HOWELL
Nonresident Senior Fellow

R. GLENN HUBBARD
Nonresident Senior Fellow

HOWARD HUSOCK
Senior Fellow

BENEDIC N. IPPOLITO
Senior Fellow

MARK JAMISON
Nonresident Senior Fellow

FREDERICK W. KAGAN
Senior Fellow; Director, Critical Threats Project

STEVEN B. KAMIN
Senior Fellow

LEON R. KASS, MD
Senior Fellow Emeritus

JOSHUA T. KATZ
Senior Fellow

L. LYNNE KIESLING
Nonresident Senior Fellow

KLON KITCHEN
Nonresident Senior Fellow

KEVIN R. KOSAR
Senior Fellow

ROBERT KULICK
Visiting Fellow

PAUL H. KUPIEC
Senior Fellow

DESMOND LACHMAN
Senior Fellow

PAUL LETTOW
Senior Fellow

DANIEL LYONS
Nonresident Senior Fellow

NAT MALKUS
Senior Fellow; Deputy Director, Education Policy Studies

ORIANA SKYLAR MASTRO
Nonresident Senior Fellow

JOHN D. MAURER
Nonresident Fellow

MICHAEL MAZZA
Nonresident Fellow

ELAINE MCCUSKER
Senior Fellow

BRUCE D. MEYER
Nonresident Senior Fellow

BRIAN J. MILLER
Nonresident Fellow

CHRIS MILLER
Jeane Kirkpatrick Visiting Fellow

THOMAS P. MILLER
Senior Fellow

M. ANTHONY MILLS
Senior Fellow

TIMOTHY J. MURIS
Visiting Senior Fellow

CHARLES MURRAY
F. A. Hayek Chair Emeritus in Cultural Studies

STEPHEN D. OLINER
Senior Fellow Emeritus

NORMAN J. ORNSTEIN
Senior Fellow Emeritus

BRENT ORRELL
Senior Fellow

TOBIAS PETER
Senior Fellow; Codirector, AEI Housing Center

JAMES PETHOKOUKIS
Senior Fellow; Editor, AEIdeas Blog; DeWitt Wallace Chair

EDWARD J. PINTO
Senior Fellow; Codirector, AEI Housing Center

DANIELLE PLETKA
Distinguished Senior Fellow

KENNETH M. POLLACK
Senior Fellow

KYLE POMERLEAU
Senior Fellow

ROBERT PONDISCIO
Senior Fellow

RAMESH PONNURU
Nonresident Senior Fellow

ROB PORTMAN
Distinguished Visiting Fellow in the Practice of Public Policy

ANGELA RACHIDI
Senior Fellow; Rowe Scholar

NAOMI SCHAEFER RILEY
Senior Fellow

DALIBOR ROHAC
Senior Fellow

CHRISTINE ROSEN
Senior Fellow

JEFFREY A. ROSEN
Nonresident Fellow

MICHAEL ROSEN
Nonresident Senior Fellow

IAN ROWE
Senior Fellow

MICHAEL RUBIN
Senior Fellow

PAUL RYAN
Distinguished Visiting Fellow in the Practice of Public Policy

SALLY SATEL, MD
Senior Fellow

ERIC SAYERS
Nonresident Fellow

CHRISTOPHER J. SCALIA
Senior Fellow

DIANA SCHAUB
Nonresident Senior Fellow

ANNA SCHERBINA
Nonresident Senior Fellow

GARY J. SCHMITT
Senior Fellow

DEREK SCISSORS
Senior Fellow

NEENA SHENAI
Nonresident Fellow

DAN SLATER
Nonresident Fellow

SITA NATARAJ SLAVOV
Nonresident Senior Fellow

VINCENT H. SMITH
Nonresident Senior Fellow

CHRISTINA HOFF SOMMERS
Senior Fellow Emeritus

CHRIS STIREWALT
Senior Fellow

BENJAMIN STOREY
Senior Fellow

JENNA SILBER STOREY
Senior Fellow

RUY TEIXEIRA
Nonresident Senior Fellow

SHANE TEWS
Nonresident Senior Fellow

MARC A. THIESSEN
Senior Fellow

JOSEPH S. TRACY
Nonresident Senior Fellow

SEAN TRENDE
Nonresident Fellow

BORIS VABSON
Nonresident Fellow

TUNKU VARADARAJAN
Nonresident Fellow

STAN VEUGER
Senior Fellow

ALAN D. VIARD
Senior Fellow Emeritus

DUSTIN WALKER
Nonresident Fellow

PHILIP WALLACH
Senior Fellow

PETER J. WALLISON
Senior Fellow Emeritus

MARK J. WARSHAWSKY
Senior Fellow; Searle Fellow

MATT WEIDINGER
Senior Fellow; Rowe Scholar

ADAM J. WHITE
Senior Fellow

W. BRADFORD WILCOX
Nonresident Senior Fellow

THOMAS CHATTERTON WILLIAMS
Nonresident Fellow

SCOTT WINSHIP
Senior Fellow; Director, Center on Opportunity and Social Mobility

AUDRYE WONG
Jeane Kirkpatrick Fellow

JOHN YOO
Nonresident Senior Fellow

KATHERINE ZIMMERMAN
Fellow

BENJAMIN ZYCHER
Senior Fellow

www.ingramcontent.com/pod-product-compliance
Lightning Source LLC
Jackson TN
JSHW081328130125
77033JS00014B/451